The Theatre Student

NINE HUNDRED

AMERICAN PLAYS

The Theatre Student

NINE HUNDRED AMERICAN PLAYS

A Synopsis-History of American Theatre

by *Thomas A. Erhard*

RICHARDS ROSEN PRESS, INC.
NEW YORK, NEW YORK 10010

Published in 1978 by Richards Rosen Press, Inc.
29 East 21st Street, New York, N.Y. 10010

First Edition

Library of Congress Cataloging in Publication Data

Erhard, Thomas A   1923–
   Nine hundred American plays.

   (The Theatre student series)
   1. American drama—Stories, plots, etc.
I. Title.
PS626.E7   812'.009   77–24548
ISBN 0–8239–0406–7

Manufactured in the United States of America

For Penny,
who *cares* about the theatre

ABOUT THE AUTHOR

THOMAS A. ERHARD, professor of English at New Mexico State University, Las Cruces, teaches a number of literary period courses in drama, plus short-story and playwriting courses. His recent monograph "Lynn Riggs: Southwestern Playwright" is the most complete published work on the author whose *Green Grow the Lilacs* eventually became the musical *Oklahoma!* Erhard has also contributed entries on approximately thirty playwrights to *World Book Encyclopedia.* Working with the Winter Term in London Program coordinated by Eckerd College in St. Petersburg, Florida, Erhard takes a class to London for a full month of theatre-going every other January. At New Mexico State he also teaches an interdisciplinary course in the honors program: England as Seen Through the Drama.

Erhard has written thirty plays, almost all of them for young people. Twenty-six have been published or produced; two won national playwriting contests; and several have been longtime hits in the high-school theatre. He has also sold several dozen short stories and more than a hundred magazine articles. During the 1960's he edited eight books for the American Association for Higher Education; earlier, while working in educational journalism, he won top honors nationally from the International Council of Industrial Editors for his magazine editing.

Born in New Jersey, Erhard grew up in Hempstead, New York; served in the Army in Orangeburg, New York; and graduated from Hofstra University. His M.A. and Ph.D. (the latter in modern drama) are from the University of New Mexico in Albuquerque.

He has been at New Mexico State University

since 1960; several years ago he was named Teacher of the Year there by the Associated Women Students. Since 1961 he has directed the annual Southwest High School Creative Writing Awards Program, which publishes the best poems and stories submitted by young people in more than 500 high schools in the seven-state Desert Southwest. The program has received regional and national recognition and numerous grants from the New Mexico Arts Commission and the National Endowment for the Arts.

ACKNOWLEDGMENTS

All of this began with Willis D. Jacobs, who kindled my interest in theatre.

The compilation of this book has been helped immeasurably by the wealth of factual detail available in the *Best Plays of the Year* series, begun by Burns Mantle and carried on by numerous other editors down through Otis Guernsey; by the *Best American Plays* series edited first by John Gassner and now by Clive Barnes; and by *The New York Theatre Critics Reviews*.

Thanks, also, to Dramatists Play Service and Samuel French and to the scholarly works in American drama by Michael Anderson, Van H. Cartmell, Lehman Engel, David Ewen, Jean Gould, Jacques Guicharnaud, Phyllis Hartnoll, Harriet Kriegel, Joseph Wood Krutch, Allan Lewis, John Lovell, Jr., Bruce Mailman, Myron Matlaw, Walter J. Meserve, Richard Moody, Kristin Morrison, Lindsay Patterson, Albert Poland, Theodore J. Shank, Bernard Sobell, Gerald Weales, Garff B. Wilson, and Jack D. Zipes.

Henry Overin has lent constant encouragement; and sixteen years of Modern American Drama students, led by Tony Thomas, have added their continuing support and enthusiasm for the project.

Most important of all, however, has been the continuing professional assistance of Daniel O. Zeff, associate editor of *World Book Encyclopedia*. Zeff, widely known also as a theatre critic in the Chicago area, has not only tracked down hard-to-find factual information, but has provided important synopsis material through his reviews and has served as a continuing consultant. Without Zeff's eager support, coupled with his unstinting but healthy criticism, the work might never have grown into its present size and form. The book is, I feel, a testimony to several decades of the most meaningful kind of friendship.

INDEX OF AUTHORS

Index of Authors

Gershwin, Ira 21, 23, 25, 31–32, 40–41
Gibson, William 77, 103
Gilbert, Willie 69
Gillette, William 6–7
Gilroy, Frank 85
Giraudoux, Jean 41
Glaspell, Susan 15
Gleason, James 34
Godfrey, Thomas 3
Golden, Harry 74
Goldman, James 76, 92–93
Goldman, William 93
Goldsmith, Clifford 58, 60
Goodrich, Frances 59
Gordone, Charles 99
Gow, James 60
Gray, Clifford 33
Gredy, Jean-Pierre 96
Green, Adolph 59, 60, 64
Greenleaf, Evelyn 8
Gregory, David 56
Guare, John 93–94

Hackett, Albert 59
Haines, William Wister 67
Hamlisch, Marvin 103
Hammerstein, Oscar II 12, 21, 33, 34, 37–39, 47, 51, 69
Hanley, William 88
Hansberry, Lorraine 78–79
Harbach, Otto 12, 21, 33, 34, 38
Harnick, Sheldon 35, 78, 87, 94
Harrigan, Edward 6
Hart, Lorenz 24, 35, 36, 37, 38, 44, 47
Hart, Moss 14, 23–24, 25, 44, 68
Hart, Tony 6
Hauerbach, Otto 12
Hawthorne, Nathaniel 12, 83
Hecht, Ben 37, 44, 54
Heggen, Thomas 69
Heller, Joseph 97
Hellman, Lillian 52–53, 60
Herbert, F. Hugh 58, 60
Herbert, Victor 9, 14
Herman, Jerry 47, 74
Herne, James A. 6
Hersey, John 46
Hester, Hal 98
Heyward, Dorothy and DuBose 32, 40–41
Hickerson, Harold 27
Hirson, Roger O. 102
Holm, John Cecil 34
Hooker, Brian 12
Horovitz, Israel 90, 91, 96
Howard, Bronson 6
Howard, Sidney 14, 32–33, 69, 70
Hughes, Hatcher 26
Hughes, Langston 14, 48
Hughes, Richard 46
Huntley, Jobe 48
Husson, Albert 55
Hyman, Mac 75

Inge, William 71–72
Irving, Washington 5
Isherwood, Christopher 36, 93

Jacobs, Jim 102
Jeffers, Robinson 68
Jones Le Roi 82
Jones, Preston 105–106
Jones, Tom 69, 75, 79, 80

Kalmar, Bert 23
Kander, John 36, 70, 75, 87, 93
Kanin, Faye and Garson 67
Kaufman, George S. 14, 22–25, 31, 32, 45, 57, 69, 71, 73
Kazantzakis, Nikos 87, 93
Kelly, George 26
Kennedy, Adrienne 88
Kern, Jerome 4, 33–34, 38, 39
Kerr, Jean 67
Kerr, Walter 67
Kesey, Ken 86
Kesselring, Joseph 51, 59
Kimbrough, Emily 67
Kingsley, Sidney 50–51
Kirkland, Jack 50
Kirkwood, James 103
Kleban, Edward 103
Koch, Frederick 39
Koestler, Arthur 50
Kopit, Arthur 85
Kramm, Joseph 72
Krasna, Norman 61

Lacey, Franklin 77
Landon, Margaret 38
Lardner, Ring 23
La Touche, John 60
Laurents, Arthur 61, 63, 76
Lawrence, D. H. 64
Lawrence, Jerome 73–74
Lawson, John Howard 30–31
Lee, C. Y. 38
Lee, Gypsy Rose 76
Lee, Leslie 104
Lee, Robert E. 73–74
Leigh, Carolyn 83
Leigh, Mitch 86
Lengyel, Melchior 24, 45, 71
Lerner, Alan Jay 67–68
Levin, Ira 75
Levy, Marvin David 19
Lewis, Sinclair 33, 55
Lindsay, Howard 15, 38, 44, 51–52, 59
Link, Peter 84
Lockridge, Frances and Richard 8
Loesser, Frank 33, 35, 68–69, 71, 77
Loewe, Frederick 67–68
Logan, Joshua 38, 42, 69–70
Long, John Luther 8
Lowell, Robert 83
Luce, Clare Boothe 55–56
Ludlow, Noah Miller 4

MacArthur, Charles 37, 44, 54
MacDermot, Galt 94, 97
MacDonough, Glen 9
MacKaye, Percy 12
MacLeish, Archibald 55
McCarthy, Joseph 87

McCarthy, Justin 12
McCullers, Carson 70–71, 80
McEnroe, Robert 69
McGowan, John 32
McGrath, Leueen 24, 45, 71
McGuire, William Anthony 21, 31
McKenney, Ruth 59, 60, 64
McNally, Terrence 90, 91, 96
Maltz, Albert 48–49
Mamet, David 105
Mandel, Frank 21, 33, 38, 39
Manners, J. Hartley 44
Marasco, Robert 99
March, William 29
Marquand, John P. 24
Martin, David 48
Mason, Richard 46
Masteroff, Joe 36, 93
Maugham, Somerset 42
May, Elaine 91
Medoff, Mark 103
Melfi, Leonard 90, 91, 96
Melville, Herman 83
Meyerowitz, Jan 48
Michaels, Sidney 86
Michener, James 38, 69
Middleton, George 9
Millay, Edna St. Vincent 25
Miller, Arthur 61–62, 70
Miller, Jason 101
Milner, Ron 103
Mitchell, Langdon 10
Moffitt, John C. 55
Molière 41, 83
Molnar, Ferenc 37
Montgomery, James 87
Moody, William Vaughn 10
Moore, Edward 103
Moross, Jerome 49
Morris, Richard 77
Morton, Thomas 83
Mowatt, Anna Cora 4

Nash, N. Richard 70, 75, 79, 93
Nemerov, Howard 51
Nemiroff, Robert 78, 79
Nichols, Anne 25
Nugent, Elliott 59

Odets, Clifford 53–54, 61
O'Donnell, E. P. 59
O'Hara, John 37
O'Horgan, Tom 96, 97
O'Neill, Eugene 6, 10, 11, 15–20
Oppenheimer, George 37
Orr, Mary 64
Osborn, Paul 45–46
Overmiller, Alice 34
Owens, Rochelle 92

Pagnol, Marcel 42, 70
Parker, Dorothy 60
Pascal, Fran and John 10
Paton, Alan 29
Patrick, John 62–63
Patrick, Pat 98
Patrick, Robert 104
Peters, Paul 49
Pinero, Miguel 103

INDEX OF TITLES

Index of Titles

Index of Titles

Index of Titles

This book, containing thumbnail synopses of more than 900 plays plus brief commentary about the playwrights, is intended as a get-acquainted guidebook and rapid reference to American drama, primarily modern. Because of copyright and royalty restrictions, any truly large anthology of modern plays is almost impossible; and because the mere listing of *all* plays is the province of an entire shelf of reference books, this volume fills the intermediate need of acquainting the reader with American theatre from the 1500's to the late 1970's. Several encyclopedic single volumes contain detailed and extremely useful synopses; some of those books, however, include only a handful of major works, others include European plays, and still others are arranged alphabetically by title—all preventing the reader from following the work of any particular American writer at a glance. In this book, the reader can become acquainted, in a moment or two, with the major dramatic output of any important playwright. The reader can also see where any writer fits, chronologically, in theatre history. Further, the synopses-plus-commentary enable the reader to understand something about each playwright's niche in American theatre, along with the tone and nature of his or her body of work.

The book begins with an extremely brief sampling of the most widely known premodern plays in order to give the reader a taste of the earlier centuries of American theatre history. The major portion of the book, then, is a list of representative plays since World War I, when drama came of age in the United States. The listings are not exhaustive: in the case of major playwrights, most of their works are included; for other writers, only the plays of most importance. Some plays almost universally condemned by reviewers and later scholars are included because of their phenomenal popularity, and some extremely recent inclusions may not hold up critically in the years to come; but for the most part, the book contains the most significant, influential, and popular plays in our theatre history.

Playwrights are listed chronologically according to their first important professional productions, and all titles and authors are indexed, with musicals cross-listed under all those involved with book, music, and lyrics. With the exception of opera, all types of theatre are included.

The book stems from sixteen years of the author's teaching Modern American Drama at New Mexico State University, and this edition is the eighth compilation. Faced with great difficulty in finding a group of textbooks that would, without driving the students bankrupt, do some justice in covering some thirty to forty modern plays, I began by handing the class a two-page list of "fifty important plays" for them to become familiar with. By the second year the list had increased to more than a hundred titles; later, with the addition of authors' birth and death dates, production dates, and brief synopses, the mimeographed handout began mushrooming into a book.

This volume should prove helpful to many people: to the high-school, university, or community theatre director, who now can find all of our major titles inside one cover, without having to thumb through the various catalogues and try to assess the real worth of a play through the superlative-laden puffs; to the student interested primarily in contemporary American theatre who does not wish to plow through the endless pages written elsewhere about the mediocre premodern plays; to the

Introduction

theatre enthusiast trying to decide what to see or read next; and to anyone who desires to add rapidly to his or her knowledge about one of the nation's most fascinating and rapidly growing academic disciplines. American theatre, hello!

The Theatre Student

NINE HUNDRED

AMERICAN PLAYS

ANONYMOUS

Adam and Eve (1532). The first known Spanish "auto" or play, performed in North America, for an Indian audience, in Mexico City. Ever since, short biblical folk plays have been performed in various parts of Mexico and the United States. Some were performed in Florida as early as 1567. Actually, the first events that we can call theatre in North America were Indian dances. These religious ceremonies have had marked similarities to the origins of Greek drama and can still be seen in many parts of the American West today.

Los Pastores. This folk play, which originated in Europe, undoubtedly is the Spanish version of the medieval British *Second Shepherd's Play*. Comedy and music are added to the Christmas legend of the shepherds journeying to Bethlehem. Where the English version uses Mak the sheep stealer for comedy, the Spanish-American version features the drunken Bartolo weaving his way up the cathedral aisle before reforming when he sees the Christ Child. Lucifer plays a large part and frightens the audience with several tricks. The play has been performed in North America since the late 1500's in many versions, often with local residents playing the same parts for decades and then passing the roles down to children. One of the regularly produced versions today is in Old Mesilla, in southern New Mexico, every December. In bygone years, other Bible stories also were enacted.

Los Moros (1598). This early Spanish folk play depicting struggles between the Moors and the Christians was first performed in North America in Santa Cruz, New Mexico, some thirty miles north of Santa Fe, by members of Don Juan de Oñate's expedition. It was staged regularly in Santa Cruz until about the time of World War II. In places such as Taos, New Mexico, the play gradually was adapted to the struggles between Spanish and Indians and became known as *Los Comanches*.

CAPTAIN MARCOS FARFAN DE LOS GODOS

Comedia (1598). This play spoofed the Oñate expedition, of which Captain Farfan was a member. The play was staged near El Paso del Norte (El Paso, Texas) and thus is the first known theatre production staged by a European in what is now the United States.

WILLIAM DARBY

Ye Bare and Ye Cubb (1665). The first known play to be staged in English in what is now the United States. Produced in Accomac County, Virginia, by the author. Darby was immediately brought to trial for immorality but acquitted. Although there was considerable early theatre in Charleston, Puritan sentiment in colonies to the north made most stage productions extremely difficult in the earliest colonial period. Just one example of the subterfuges used by producers occurred in Newport, Rhode Island, in 1761 when a William Douglass staged *Othello* under the guise of "A Moral Dialogue in Five Parts."

THOMAS GODFREY (1736–63)

The Prince of Parthia (1767). This is the first play written by someone born in North America to be produced in what is now the United States. After fighting the Arabs, noble Arsaces loses his love, Evanthe, in a Romeo and Juliet—like tragedy and kills himself. The play, which is an extremely weak imitation of the English heroic drama, was performed posthumously, in Philadelphia.

MAJOR ROBERT ROGERS (1731–95)

Ponteach; or, The Savages of America (1760). The first play to treat a native American subject seriously, it was published in London in 1766 but not actually staged in North America until after the Revolution. A tragedy in which the Indian Ponteach (Pontiac) is defeated by the British but retains his pride. Rogers was the famous leader of Rogers' Rangers.

ROYALL TYLER (1757–1826)

The Contrast (1787). The first wholly successful play done by professional actors in the United States. Tyler, however, was a lawyer and a judge, not a theatre professional. The patriotic play is also known for its introduction of the stage Yankee as a character type, but overall the work is a weak echoing of Richard Brinsley Sheridan's *The School for Scandal*.

WILLIAM DUNLAP (1766–1839)

André (1798). A five-act historical tragedy in blank verse. The story of the last days of Major

John André, condemned in the Benedict Arnold plot during the Revolutionary War. Dunlap, called the Father of American Drama, began playwriting as early as 1789 with *The Father.* He became the first American professional playwright, the first American theatre historian, and worked as both a director and a theatre manager.

The Glory of Columbia; Her Yeomanry! (1803). This was a spectacle-filled patriotic play about the Battle of Yorktown, which held the stage for more than fifty years.

A Trip to Niagara, or Travellers in America (1828). A panoramic, pageantlike play commemorating the opening of the Erie Canal. Enormous murallike paintings served as backdrops depicting the most exciting scenes. One character, Leather-Stocking, is openly modeled on James Fenimore Cooper's creation.

SHOWBOATS

This was a type of theatre popular up and down the nation's great rivers, beginning in Natchez, Mississippi, in 1817 by Noah Miller Ludlow (1795–1866) and continuing until just before World War II. One of the major early leaders was William Chapman (1764–1839), whose wife and five children helped make up the company that staged fairy tales and melodramas on their own boat. Some showboats plied the Erie Canal. Perhaps the most famous leader was Captain Billy Bryant, who sailed up and down the Mississippi staging melodramas and presenting vaudeville, magic lantern shows, and Captain Billy's own lectures. He, of course, was immortalized in Edna Ferber's novel *Showboat,* later the Jerome Kern musical of the same name. Showboat productions provided the primary theatrical entertainment for a century of Americans in our great river valleys.

WILLIAM HENRY SMITH (1806–72)

The Drunkard (1843). Subtitled *The Fallen Saved,* this famous temperance play, intended seriously at first, has been staged up to the present day as comic melodrama. The first staging was by P. T. Barnum. A young man, through his drinking, brings disgrace on his wife, but he finally repents.

MINSTREL SHOWS

Another form of theatrical entertainment popular for a century was the minstrel show; the first full-scale troupe performed in 1843, although Thomas "Daddy" Rice was imitating the black men as early as 1828 along the Ohio River. The most famous troupe was led by E. P. Christy, for whom Stephen Foster wrote many of his most famous songs. The minstrel show, created by whites disguised by burnt cork for white audiences, unfortunately did a great deal toward stereotyping the black man in 19th-century America. The shows became heavily ritualized, with a white-faced interlocutor engaging in word play with two black-faced wits at the ends of the semicircular lineup of performers. The "end men" were usually called Mr. Bones and Mr. Tambo. The first portion of a minstrel show was filled with jokes and songs, the second part was a series of olio acts, and the third part was some kind of comic theatrical afterpiece.

ANNA CORA MOWATT (1819–70)

Fashion (1845). Mrs. Mowatt, a child bride, was a romantic novelist, a poet, an actress, and our first woman playwright. In the play, Governess Gertrude is discovered at the finale as a long-lost heiress—a pattern heavily used in the preceding century in British comedy. Mrs. Mowatt intended her play as a mild satire on American follies, but it is still a rather animated family album of characters. The play was much revived for many decades, including a rather famous revival by the Provincetown Players in the 20th century.

HARRIET BEECHER STOWE (1811–96)

Uncle Tom's Cabin (1852). Subtitled *Life Among the Lowly,* this book was pirated by dozens of playwrights because Mrs. Stowe had no copyright laws protecting her interests. She never complained about that, and she refused money from several of the stage versions because she considered the theatre sinful. The most famous stage version, as well as the most faithful, was done by twenty-two-year-old George L. Aiken (1830–76), whose work ran 100 nights at the Troy Museum, in Troy, New York; 25,000 people in a town of 30,000 saw it. Aiken's cousin, G. C. Howard, who paid Aiken $40 and a gold watch, took the play to

New York City, where it ran 200 nights in 1853. Dozens of companies toured the nation constantly throughout the 19th century; the estimate of total performances starts at 200,000 and goes as high as a million. In its first decade of production the play helped crystallize national sentiment about abolition. In the story, slave George Harris runs away, Eliza crosses the ice floes in the Ohio River to try to escape, Little Eva dies, Topsy reforms, and the venerable Uncle Tom dies after being beaten by Simon Legree.

GEORGE HENRY BOKER (1823–90)

Francesca da Rimini (1855). The first important poetic tragedy by an American playwright and a retelling of the Paolo and Francesca story of forbidden love in Dante's *Divine Comedy*. Revived with considerable praise as late as the 1880's.

DION BOUCICAULT (1820–90)

The Poor of New York (1857). A native of Dublin, Boucicault became an actor at age fifteen and by the time he was turning twenty had written *London Assurance,* a period comedy based on the long tradition of Restoration and 18th-century comedy. From London he moved on to Paris and in the mid-1850's came to New York. He wrote and directed more than 150 plays, in most of which he himself starred. This play is a prize example of "meller-drammer" today: men are ruined financially by a scoundrel, a young hero is almost forced to marry the scoundrel's daughter, and the crucial evidence is rescued from a burning building (on stage). Boucicault sailed continually back and forth between Europe and America, and he kept restaging this play as *The Poor of Paris* in France and *The Poor of Liverpool* in England. Revived professionally as recently as 1964, the play is sometimes called *The Streets of New York.*

The Octoroon (1859). Highly melodramatic and creaky dramaturgically by today's standards, this play was nevertheless the first attempt to treat the American black man seriously on stage. Zoe, a beautiful octoroon and daughter of a plantation owner, is bought as a slave by the villainous Jacob McCloskey; but her friends come to the rescue at the crucial moment.

Rip Van Winkle (1865). Washington Irving's story about the man who slept away a lifetime was first dramatized in 1828, but Boucicault's effective adaptation for the famous actor Joseph Jefferson was revived again and again, even into the 20th century. Boucicault is also credited with writing the first play about the American Civil War, *Belle Lamar* (1874). Critics say today that perhaps the best of all his plays were those written in Ireland: *The Colleen Bawn* (1860), *Arrah-na-Pogue* (1864), and *The Shaughraun* (1874). The latter play and *London Assurance* have been given fine revivals by the Royal Shakespeare Company in the 1960's and 1970's. Boucicault's importance to American theatre rests, however, upon several off-stage activities: he was instrumental in bringing about the first copyright law in the United States, he helped establish the road company here, and he began to do away with the wing-and-backdrop set that had been standard in world theatre for two centuries.

CHARLES M. BARRAS (1820–73)

The Black Crook (1866). This was the first American musical, and it had a stage life of more than thirty years. It was a melodramatic account of a poor young artist, Rodolphe, who conquers Count Wolfenstein and outwits the hunchbacked sorcerer, Hertzog the Black Crook, thereby winning the fair young Amina. Hertzog, who has sold his soul in Faustian fashion, is carried off to the devil. Several ballets and a number of fantastic stage effects are included.

(JOHN) AUGUSTIN DALY (1838–99)

Under the Gaslight (1867). Daly adapted this British melodrama for the New York stage. Laura Cortlandt is in love with Ray Trafford, but her foster-father, Byke, tries to prevent their love by a series of villainous deeds. This was the first play with a character tied to the railroad tracks; but contrary to popular belief today, it was the hero, *not* the heroine, who was so tied. The heroine was locked in a nearby shack. Daly created a sensation in New York by laying real tracks on the stage and bringing a real locomotive into the theatre. Daly, beginning as a drama critic at twenty-one, quickly became a producer and eventually owned several famous theatres in New York and London. He helped move the stage toward realism, and he is the first important manager who was not an actor.

DENMAN THOMPSON (1833–1911)

The Old Homestead (1876). Denman Thompson, one of the famous 19th-century actors, first wrote this as a sketch called "Joshua Whitcomb," but by 1886 he had expanded it and given it the title above. As with many others of his time, Thompson then toured in the play for virtually the rest of his life. An endearing old Yankee farmer searches for and then supports his wayward son. Highly moralistic and oversentimental, the play was later satirized by Eugene O'Neill in *Desire Under the Elms*.

EDWARD HARRIGAN (1845–1911)

The Mulligan Guard Ball (1879). One of Harrigan's many vaudeville comedies, this one is about eccentric characters in Mulligan's Alley, New York City. Dan Mulligan, leader of a bigoted group of Irish pseudo-military immigrants, puts on the ball despite complications from other ethnic groups. The one-act skit ends in a big brawl. Harrigan's work was highly popular in the 1870's and 1880's. Tony Hart was the other half of the famous Harrigan-Hart duo. Vaudeville, although never known for its scripts, was nevertheless an extremely important form of American theatre because of its long popularity from after the Civil War until the development of the talking motion picture.

BRONSON HOWARD (1842–1908)

Shenandoah (1888). Most famous of the many Civil War plays. Two West Pointers, from North and South, are in love with each other's sisters. All meet melodramatically in a farmhouse during the war. The play survived for many decades and has even been revived professionally in recent years. Howard, the first American writer to make a full-time career in playwriting, began as a journalist in Detroit and New York, had plays produced as early as 1864, was at his prime in the 1870's, and had many comedies done in both New York and London. Howard helped the cause for future writers by campaigning for copyright reforms. He also founded (1891) the American Dramatists Club, which later became the Society of American Dramatists and Composers.

JAMES A. HERNE (1839–1901)

Margaret Fleming (1890). This is probably the nation's first important realistic drama. Margaret, who has just given birth to a daughter, is in danger of losing her sight from glaucoma. When she discovers that her husband, Philip, is the father of a child born to a mill worker who dies in childbirth, Margaret takes the other child, too, even though the trauma brings on her blindness. Philip, after a suicide attempt, is reunited with Margaret and they prepare to meet their problems. The production date above is for the premiere in Lynn, Massachusetts; Herne had great difficulty in finding theatres open to him because of the daring (at the time) script. The play was highly praised by both William Dean Howells and Hamlin Garland but was some years ahead of its time.

Shore Acres (1899). Another realistic play, which several early critics commented anticipated Chekhov's realism by several years. Set in Bar Harbor, Maine, and based on summer vacation land booms there, the play about the Berry family shows Uncle Nat saving Helen's marriage. Critics were astounded because not only did the family eat a real meal on stage, but Uncle Nat was quietly alone on stage for the final five minutes. Herne, another of the many actor-managers in the 19th century, wrote many of his plays as vehicles for his actress-wife.

WILLIAM GILLETTE (1855–1937)

Secret Service (1896). A Civil War thriller and a good example of the type of play done for tears and gasps in the 19th century but staged purely as comic melodrama today. Gillette, in fact, was quite definite in his script about how it should be played seriously. Captain Thorne, who is in reality a secret service agent for the Union forces, engages in romance and intrigue while posing as a Confederate officer. Ultimately captured, he goes valiantly off to prison while Edith Varney waits loyally for him. Gillette wrote or adapted most of his plays purely as vehicles for himself. He was one of the last of the great 19th-century actors, although his career continued well into the 20th century. All told, *Secret Service* ran 1,791 performances here and there.

Sherlock Holmes (1899). Holmes saves Miss Faulkner from the infamous Moriarty gang. Gillette made the adaptation as a starring role for himself, and the play was revived in 1902, 1905, 1910, 1915, and 1929, each time with Gillette starring. The play was also done several times in London.

(WILLIAM) CLYDE FITCH (1865–1909)

Barbara Frietchie (1898). This was one of the many historical melodramas that Fitch wrote before he turned to social realism. Southerner Barbara falls for Union Captain Trumbull, and she has to face down several enemies in order to protect the wounded officer. He dies, Barbara hangs out a Union flag, she is shot by an old suitor, and the suitor's father orders his execution. Sigmund Romberg turned it into a 1927 musical entitled *My Maryland.*

The Climbers (1901). For its time, this was a strong play on social climbing and was considered quite daring. Recently widowed Mrs. Hunter has to make her way back up the social ladder by remarrying wealth, and her son-in-law, Richard Sterling, tries to make it by embezzlement. He ends up killing himself.

Captain Jinks of the Horse Marines (1901). A comedy of New York City life, in which Ethel Barrymore had her first starring role. This was Fitch's biggest year, with three hits running in New York and a fourth in London. The most prolific playwright at the beginning of the century, Fitch created successful characterizations, often began his plays with powerful social criticism, but usually provided a melodramatic happy ending to satisfy the audiences.

The Girl with the Green Eyes (1902). Jinny is so jealous of her husband, John, that she tries to kill herself, but understanding prevails at last. Another example of a play with a strong social theme and a sugary ending.

The Truth (1907). A social study of a liar, Becky, who almost loses her husband because of her faults. Many critics consider this to be Fitch's greatest play.

The City (1909). Watered-down Ibsenian realism, this play criticizes municipal corruption, with the family of a corrupt man all succumbing to various shoddy lures in a large city. Fitch, who died at forty-four, wrote 62 plays, 36 of them original. He provided a solid base for later, more important social dramatists who helped bring American drama to a high level after World War I. *The City,* his final play, was staged posthumously.

OWEN DAVIS (1874–1956)

Through the Breakers (1899). Davis, born in Maine, began writing melodramas after his graduation from Harvard, and this was the first of several hundred that he turned out during a fifteen-year period; others included such titles as *Nellie, the Beautiful Cloak Model* and *The Gambler's Daughter.*

The Family Cupboard (1913). Davis, growing as a writer and influenced by the wave of realism led by Ibsen that was sweeping Europe, broke away from his tight pattern of writing a melodrama a month in favor of this more realistic comedy. The play, although not important in itself, served as a transition in his writing career.

The Detour (1921). In his middle and late years Davis turned to stern realism and thus was historically of great importance to American theatre as one of the forerunners of serious modern drama. In this key play a strong-willed woman, Helen, tries to revolt against narrow and deadening farm life on Long Island. When she finally learns that her daughter, Kate, a would-be artist, has no creative talent, she and her daughter both must learn to make the best of everyday rural life.

Icebound (1923). A powerful, somber drama (albeit with an upbeat ending) of tensions, greed, and frustrations as a New England family fights over an inheritance. Mrs. Jordan dies, leaving her fortune to a second cousin, Jane Crosby. The family tries to wheedle money out of Jane, who keeps Ben, the wastrel son of Mrs. Jordan, almost in bondage as she holds an arson charge over his head. When she is convinced that Ben is reforming, she has the charge dropped. Ben sees that Jane is the right woman for him, with the rest of the family still greedily seeking money. A Pulitzer Prize-winner and a fine example of a regional play.

The Good Earth (1932). Excellent dramatization by Owen and his son Donald Davis of Pearl Buck's novel of life in China and how wealth finally corrupts a farmer.

Ethan Frome (1936). Another highly effective serious dramatization, again with his son Donald, of Edith Wharton's novel. Into the cold marriage between Ethan and Zenia comes a young cousin, Mattie. Ethan and Mattie fall in love and, facing separation later, decide to run their sled into a tree and kill themselves. Her spine is broken, and Ethan is left to care for her and his semi-invalid wife in an even more bitter household. Another superb regional play of New England.

Mr. and Mrs. North (1941). A mystery-comedy, based on a novel by Frances and Richard Lockridge. Pam and Gerald North lead uneventful lives until a body falls out of their closet, but Pam solves the case. The play was later made into a popular film. In his later years Owen Davis did a great deal of film-writing. More than most writers in this book, Davis spanned several large eras in American theatre.

DAVID BELASCO (1859–1931)

Madame Butterfly (1900). Based on a story by John Luther Long and subtitled *A Tragedy of Japan,* the play shows seventeen-year-old Cho-Cho-San losing her lover, American Navy Lieutenant B. F. Pinkerton, to an American wife, and then killing herself. Giacomo Puccini turned the play into an opera that has been world-famous since 1906. Belasco was another of the many 19th-century actor-manager-producers; he knew Dion Boucicault and learned from him, acted with Edwin Booth, and helped bring realism to the American stage. He was writing plays as early as 1888.

The Girl of the Golden West (1905). A mining-camp melodrama set in the Far West where Belasco grew up. A courageous heroine called "Girl" who runs a saloon tries to protect her true love, road agent Dick Johnson; but when he is captured, the miners finally let him go to try a new life with his girl. Puccini turned this, too, into an opera, which premiered at the Metropolitan in 1910 with Belasco as stage director and Enrico Caruso singing the male lead. Belasco remained active in New York theatre and wrote plays for Broadway until 1921.

(NEWTON) BOOTH TARKINGTON (1869–1946)

Beaucaire (1901). A stage adaptation of Tarkington's own short prose work "Monsieur Beaucaire," and according to some critics less effective than the original, this was a five-act costume drama that was revived in 1912, turned into a musical in 1919 in London, and revived again in modern times as a Bob Hope film. This was Tarkington's first play, written in collaboration with Evelyn Greenleaf.

Seventeen (1918). An extremely dated comedy of adolescence. Willie Baxter steals his father's dress suit, woos a girl, and ends up in many predicaments. Tarkington, in his fiction and plays, captured the genial side of life in turn-of-the-century America and reached a fairly wide audience in his time.

Clarence (1919). Clarence, last name unknown, enters the Wheeler household in a rather vague capacity, but ends up solving all the family's problems. This pleasant and well-known-in-its-time comedy of youth brought Alfred Lunt to stardom. Tarkington also wrote several plays for the well-known actor Otis Skinner.

CHAUTAUQUA

Chautauqua performances are another interesting form of early American show business. They began officially in 1903. The origin, however, was a religious institute founded in 1874 at Lake Chautauqua in upstate New York to upgrade Sunday School teaching. In 1889 the program opened to include social issues of the day, and through the 1890's entertainment began to creep in. In 1903 the touring "Chautauqua Circuit" began, with week-long stops that included evening programs on religion, temperance, and politics plus readings from the classics, short plays, and vaudeville acts. The circuit concentrated on the rural and semirural Midwest and was popular for several decades.

VICTOR HERBERT (1859–1924)

Babes in Toyland (1903). Herbert was born in Ireland, studied music in Germany, and came to the United States in 1886, where he played cello at the Metropolitan Opera House and conducted several orchestras, including the Pittsburgh Symphony. He is known now for the highly popular sentimental operettas that he composed. Glen MacDonough wrote the libretto for this production, a fantasy of childhood. Miser Barnaby is thwarted in his scheming by the children of Toyland. The show ran 192 performances and has been revived numerous times. Herbert actually was represented by his songs in New York musicals as early as 1894, but this was his first lasting triumph.

The Red Mill (1906). Book by Henry Blossom. A sentimental operetta of two American boys stranded in Holland; they play many tricks to prevent a girl's unwanted marriage. Much of Victor Herbert's music over the decades was influenced by Johann Strauss.

Naughty Marietta (1910). Book and lyrics by Rida Johnson Young. Another sentimental operetta in which Captain Dick Warrington has been sent to New Orleans to capture a pirate; he ends up winning the high-spirited young Marietta. The most memorable songs include "Ah, Sweet Mystery of Life" and "Falling in Love with Someone."

Sweethearts (1913). Book by Harry B. Smith and Fred deGresac, lyrics by Robert B. Smith. Sylvia, the princess of Zilvania, reared as a commoner, is loved by Prince Franz and discovers her true identity in time for the romantic finale. In all, Victor Herbert had a hand in thirty-three Broadway musicals and helped with a number of *Ziegfeld Follies* revues. For further work, see the Irving Berlin entry.

GEORGE M. COHAN (1878–1942)

Forty-Five Minutes from Broadway (1905). Cohan, the son of a touring vaudeville couple, spent his entire life in the world of theatre. As a child, he appeared with his parents under the billing "The Four Cohans," and he wrote some of the material for his parents when still a teenager. Cohan's first full-length play was *The Governor's Son* in 1901, but his niche became secure with the above play, which was revived successfully in 1912.

Get-Rich-Quick Wallingford (1910). A comedy in four acts from a novel by Randolph Chester, which ran 424 performances and was revived in 1917.

The Little Millionaire (1911). A musical farce produced by Cohan at the new Cohan Theatre, which he built for himself. In many of his shows, Cohan wrote, produced, directed, and starred.

Broadway Jones (1912). A happy-go-lucky young man, careless with his money, gradually gains wisdom and maturity after he inherits a big business. Cohan transformed this comedy into a musical entitled *Billie* in 1928.

Seven Keys to Baldpate (1913). A famous comic mystery melodrama at an old inn where Mr. Magee bets he can write a play in a weekend and lands in a thieves' rendezvous. Adapted from a novel by Earl Derr Biggers, later made into a film, and anthologized in a best-mystery-play collection as recently as 1973.

Hello, Broadway (1914). Cohan wrote the words and music, then played the lead in this, the first of his many revue successes. New York was the center of the universe to Cohan, and he often wrote about midtown Manhattan.

Hit-the-Trail Holliday (1915). A farce in four acts from an earlier work by George Middleton and Guy Bolton. Cohan wrote this as a vehicle for his brother-in-law, George Niblo, and it ran 336 performances. A small-town bartender, reformed, converts his townspeople to the cause of Prohibition.

William Vaughn Moody

The Cohan Revue of 1916 (1916). Cohan produced this hastily written, lightly plotted musical revue, and followed up in later years with many variations, virtually all of them box-office successes.

The Tavern (1921). A romantic vagabond charms a mixed group of people, including the state governor, in a country inn on a stormy night. This play contains much of the clap-trap of standard melodrama, including a deus-ex-machina ending.

Little Nelly Kelly (1922). In this musical, Nelly, daughter of a police captain, remains true to the leading man, who is suspected of robbery.

The Song and Dance Man (1923). One of his most popular musical revues. Over the years Cohan was virtually a folk hero of show business. Born on the Fourth of July, author of many patriotic songs, Cohan was given a medal by Congress just before World War II erupted, and a statue of him stands in mid-town Manhattan.

The Merry Malones (1927). A musical comedy that Cohan wrote, produced, directed, and starred in. Rich Joe Westcott gives up his fortune and becomes a singing soda jerk in order to woo Molly Malone, a poor girl. Joe, of course, wins Molly, and Joe's father gives her the family fortune. Cohan occasionally appeared in plays by other writers, most notably Eugene O'Neill's *Ah, Wilderness!* As a writer, Cohan turned out more than fifty plays and musicals during his lifetime.

George M! (1968). A musical based on the life of Cohan and featuring many of his all-time favorite songs, including "You're a Grand Old Flag" and "Over There." Book by Michael Stewart, John and Fran Pascal. Some lyric and music revisions were made by Mary Cohan. The nostalgic and popular musical starred Joel Grey as Cohan.

WILLIAM VAUGHN MOODY (1869–1910)
The Great Divide (1906). Moody, a professor of English at the University of Chicago and a poet, turned to the theatre in his mid-thirties, wrote several plays in verse (including the first draft of this, then titled *The Sabine Woman*), and helped lift American drama up by several large notches as he infused social realism into the traditional romantic melodrama. In this play the divide is the gulf separating a puritan Massachusetts woman and an Arizona miner at the turn of the century. Ruth Jordan marries the man who attempts to rape her, resists him because of his earlier immorality, and finally returns to New England. Stephen Ghent follows her, helps her family financially, and finally convinces her that he is totally reformed.

The Faith Healer (1910). A faith healer seeks true faith for himself. Ulrich Michaelis is staying at the Beeler farm and cures Mrs. Beeler. About to give a grand demonstration of his healing on Easter, Ulrich realizes his earthly passion for young Rhoda Williams, loses his confidence and with that his powers. When he finally realizes that his love for Rhoda is more than just physical, he goes out, unafraid, to face the angry mob. Moody died early, thus cutting short an extremely promising career in playwriting, which might well have seen him move American drama into full modernism. His two plays, although dated in many ways, do have considerable power.

LANGDON MITCHELL (1862–1935)
The New York Idea (1906). One of the best examples of social satire in early-modern American theatre. Cynthia, recently divorced from John Karslake, discovers in the nick of time before remarrying that she still loves John, that her rival has married elsewhere, and that her divorce technically was never legal. The New York "idea" is divorce, which is threatening to become a fad. Mitchell was first represented on the New York stage with a dramatization of *Vanity Fair* in 1899. He later became the first teacher of playwriting at the University of Pennsylvania. *The New York Idea* was widely anthologized and has been revived regularly over the decades.

AUGUSTUS THOMAS (1857–1934)
The Witching Hour (1907). An early effort in realism, about professional gambler Jack Brookfield, extrasensory perception, and a

10

murder case. The play still has much melo-drama, plus a moralizing ending, but it takes a big step forward toward serious modern drama. Thomas, from St. Louis, became an adapter of foreign plays, succeeding Dion Boucicault at New York's Madison Square Theatre. His own first full-length play, starring Maurice Barrymore, was *Editha's Burglar* in 1889; and around the turn of the century he wrote several plays with realistic Western settings.

EDWARD SHELDON (1886–1946)

Salvation Nell (1908). This play has aca-demic-historical importance. George Pierce Baker, an English professor at Harvard for thirty-seven years, formulated a number of theories about dramatic technique while teaching a Tudor Drama course. He also wrote several plays. When Harvard refused to permit playwriting to be offered as a regular credit course, Baker began teaching his soon-to-be-famous English 47 Workshop on the side; most of the great playwrights of the 1920's took this course. The above work by Sheldon was the first play from the work-shop to be staged professionally—and while Sheldon was still a twenty-two-year-old senior. The play was done by Minnie Maddern Fiske and was premiered at the Providence (R.I.) Opera House.

The Nigger (1909). One of the earliest stud-ies of race relations in the modern American theatre. A Southern governor discovers, in this tragedy, that his grandfather was a black slave.

The Boss (1911). Early realism of big busi-ness. Courageous Boss Regan, devoted to his standards, attracts Emily, his wife, through his strength of character, winning first pity, then sympathy, and finally love. The play is a study of modern industrial conditions, and for a time Sheldon was looked on as the great hope to bring serious drama to the stage.

Romance (1913). An Italian opera singer's romance with an idealistic young minister. This play was so popular, with successes in both New York and London and translations in many other European countries, that Shel-don was weaned away from his earlier social realism. Bit by bit, however, the background was being prepared for Eugene O'Neill to find a sympathetic climate a few years later for his serious outpouring.

RACHEL CROTHERS (1878–1958)

A Man's World (1910). Miss Crothers, from Indiana, first reached Broadway in 1906 with *The Three of Us,* a play about a Nevada min-ing camp. With this play, about the double standard, she began her career-long efforts to let the theatre-going public know about the problems of women. Miss Crothers wrote more than fifty plays, most of which she di-rected herself. For several decades she had a social comedy playing in New York almost every season. Although her plays are some-what dated today and usually have conven-tionally happy endings, she did probe impor-tant social problems.

Ourselves (1913). This social play says that educated women of good breeding are ulti-mately responsible for society's morals.

He and She (1920). A woman who is artist, wife, and mother wins a design competition over her husband, but she declines the com-mission in order to end their harmful rivalry. A study of male and female ego.

Nice People (1921). An unflinching picture of the idle rich in their mad search for pleas-ure. But young Teddy Gloucester defies her wealthy father and agrees to marry a young man who would rather work than have life handed to him.

Mary the Third (1923). A study of the atti-tudes toward marriage as seen in three genera-tions.

Expressing Willie (1924). This play shows that self-expression and freedom are not nec-essarily the same. Willie, the son of a wealthy man, gives a weekend party for a group of faddists so that they can help him to express himself. His mother and his girlfriend finally save him from making a total fool of himself.

As Husbands Go (1931). Two middle-aged

women from Dubuque, Iowa—Lucile, married, and Emmie, a widow—discover romance in Paris and learn more about marriage. Their two European men follow them to Iowa, but Lucile's novelist-suitor recognizes how good her marriage is and quietly leaves town. Husband Charles takes Lucile back without embarrassing her.

When Ladies Meet (1932). This play is about women's position in the world. A tolerant wife, Claire, and a prospective mistress, Mary, discuss an imaginary case of a philandering husband. When the imaginary suddenly turns real, Roger loses both women.

Susan and God (1937). A search for the right way to live. Susan has taken up a faddist, emotional religious cult as an escape from her alcoholic husband; but when he tries to reform she discovers in the nick of time that the right path toward God is in providing a good home for her husband and their daughter instead of gaining selfish emotional pleasure from meddling in other people's lives.

PERCY MacKAYE (1865–1956)

The Scarecrow (1911). Witchcraft in New England and a dramatization of Nathaniel Hawthorne's short story "Feathertop." A witch and a devil, Blacksmith Bess and Dickon, create an artificial being called Lord Ravensbane and breathe life into him. As Ravensbane begins to court a young woman, he comes to see himself for what he is; as he struggles to gain true humanity, he dies.

RUDOLPH FRIML (1879–1972)

The Firefly (1912). Friml grew up in Europe and came to New York at age twenty-two. This was the first of a number of his Broadway musicals; Friml helped bring the comic operetta to high stature in the early decades of the century. Music by Friml, book and lyrics by Otto Hauerbach, who continued his career with Broadway musicals under the name Otto Harbach. Nina, a street singer, disguises herself and ships out to sea as a cabin boy. She returns to marry a rich young man enamored of her firefly smile.

Rose Marie (1924). Music by Friml and Her-

bert Stothart. Book and lyrics by Otto Harbach and Oscar Hammerstein II, who made his first important theatrical contribution with this show. The operetta takes place in Canada. Rose-Marie LaFlamme has to promise to marry the villain in order to save her loved one, Jim Kenyon, accused of murdering an Indian. There's a happy ending, of course.

The Vagabond King (1925). Music by Friml. From Justin McCarthy's *If I Were King*. Book and lyrics by Brian Hooker and W. H. Post. King Louis XI makes poet François Villon ruler for one week, as a jest, after which he will be hanged. But Villon beats off a Burgundian attack, wins a noble lady, and is pardoned in the nick of time. Friml, through his many operettas, brought dozens of popular romantic ballads into American culture.

ELMER (REIZENSTEIN) RICE (1892–1967)

On Trial (1914). With Elmer Rice, serious modern American drama comes of age. Rice grew up in a tenement flat in New York City, worked as a clerk in his cousin's law office, and studied law at night school in the hope of gaining financial security. Intrigued by information in his cousin's law files, Rice wrote this courtroom drama at twenty-two, utilizing the then-new flashback technique. The play was a smash hit on Broadway. In it, a husband accused of killing his wife's supposed lover wins back his wife when the murder is judged impulsive rather than premeditated. With his royalties, Rice moved his family into a larger apartment, and for the first time in his life he had a room of his own. Rice went on to write all kinds of plays, but his lasting reputation is for standing on the side of individual freedom against the oppressors of the world. In 1916 he helped found what was to become the American Civil Liberties Union.

The Adding Machine (1923). Mr. Zero kills his employer, after twenty-five faithful years' work, when he is replaced by an adding machine. He is convicted, executed, and goes to the Elysian Fields, where he discovers that his eternal punishment is to perform on a giant adding machine. Rice got the idea for this play in a sudden flash, completed it in seventeen days, and it was staged to much acclaim by the Theatre Guild. It has a strong place in modern drama, because it is one of the first successful American plays written in expressionistic form (the distortion of outer reality to create inner truth). The play also criticized the deadening effects of the mechanized world.

Cock Robin (1928). With Philip Barry. A mystery set in a little-theatre group. Hancock Robinson is shot during a performance; we discover that the director is the murderer, avenging Hancock's treatment of a young girl.

The Subway (1929). Sophie Smith becomes the mistress of another worker in her office, fears her disgrace, and throws herself under the wheels of a New York subway train.

See Naples and Die (1929). Nanette Dodge and Charles Carroll quarrel in Paris. Nanette marries a Russian nobleman out of spite, and Charles runs off to Sorrento with another woman. When revolutionists shoot the Russian, however, the lovers can reunite. A dated, cliché- and slang-filled comedy.

Street Scene (1929). A tragically realistic picture of crowded tenement life in New York City. Willie Maurrant kills his wife and her lover and is captured like an animal. Daughter Rose sadly tells Sam Kaplan, who loves her, that she won't marry him because he needs to complete his studies and they both need to be allowed to become themselves, instead of remaining ants in the giant anthill. A Pulitzer Prize-winner and probably Rice's greatest play, this is also one of the half dozen most important social dramas in American theatre history.

Counsellor-at-Law (1931). An action-packed drama set in a background strongly reminiscent of his cousin Moe Grossman's law office, where Rice worked as a young boy. George Simon, a criminal lawyer, is saved from a tight spot by his Jewish secretary, after his gentile wife has been no help.

The Left Bank (1931). A domestic drama of two American marriages that collapse in Paris. Writer John Shelby feels that France is spiritually and culturally necessary to him; his wife, Claire, feels that expatriatism is the sterile life.

We, the People (1933). A pageantlike picture of the Depression and its tragic effects on the Davis family. There is considerable influence of the Agitprop type of theatre (see *Agitprops*). Rice, always interested in social problems and new forms of theatre, became one of the founders of the Federal Theatre during this period. He helped develop the type of theatre known as the Living Newspaper (*see* later entry), but when Congress began to interfere with the Federal Theatre, he resigned from it in fury.

Judgment Day (1934). Based on a German trial, this play depicts Nazi racism and the ultimate downfall of a Hitler-figure. Students of theatre should be aware that at a time when American politicians were calling for total isolationism from Europe, most major American playwrights were crying out for world justice to prevail.

Between Two Worlds (1934). A strongly humane social play contrasting the political systems in Russia and the United States. There is a brief encounter on a ship between an American woman and a Russian man.

American Landscape (1938). A family in Connecticut refuses to sell their land to a Nazi organization. Rice was immensely concerned about the many problems connected with the oncoming of World War II.

Flight to the West (1940). On a flight from Lisbon to Bermuda a cross section of all the warring factions is shown, against a plot background that includes the capture of a Nazi spy.

Two on an Island (1940). A comedy of a woman from New Hampshire and a man from Ohio who come to New York to try to act and to write plays; they struggle, almost give up, but finally succeed.

A New Life (1943). Edith Charles marries Captain Cleghorne, later reported lost in the Pacific in the War. The captain returns, and he and his formidable family try to bring up Edith's child in Arizona high society. Edith finally wins her husband over to her belief in the rights of the individual.

Dream Girl (1945). Georgina lives in a world of daydreams, especially about her brother-in-law, but learns to face reality as newspaperman Clark Redfield woos and wins her. A comedy with a message about the importance of facing reality, this has been a highly popular play produced widely in amateur theatre after its long professional run.

Street Scene (1947). This is a musical version of his most famous realistic play. The lyrics are by poet and playwright Langston Hughes (*see* Hughes entry for his other works), and the music was composed by Kurt Weill.

Cue for Passion (1958). This is a modern-day adaptation of the *Hamlet* plot and was one of Rice's final plays. Only his best-known plays are listed in this volume; for several decades Rice was represented on Broadway with a play a year. His concern for social justice waned slightly in some of his later plays, but to the end of his life he remained an outspoken liberal. He was no closet reformer, however, and he was responsible along with Maxwell Anderson, Robert Sherwood, Sidney Howard, S. N. Behrman, and Kurt Weill for forming the Playwrights' Company; he also was a founder of the Dramatists Guild. His autobiography, *Minority Report,* was published when he was seventy. He remains one of the top American playwrights.

IRVING BERLIN (ISRAEL BALIN) (1888–   )

Watch Your Step (1914). Born in Kirgizia, Russia, Berlin came to the United States when he was five and spent his boyhood in a poverty-stricken household. His musical talents showed early, and by the time he was sixteen he was a singing waiter in New York restaurants. He became one of the early leaders of the ragtime movement in American music, and in his mid-twenties made it to Broadway with this musical comedy.

The Century Girl (1916). With Victor Her-

bert. Produced by Florenz Ziegfeld, who also staged *The Ziegfeld Follies,* a musical revue that appeared with new material every year. Berlin helped write many of these revues. *The Follies* began in 1907 and ended in 1931.

Music Box Revue (1921). Many of the early musicals were essentially plotless, vaudeville-like productions that placed much emphasis on the chorus lines. This revue was the first of several with this title, plus the year, at the Music Box Theatre. Berlin tried in his revues to raise the quality of both the humor and the music.

The Cocoanuts (1925). Book by George S. Kaufman, music and lyrics by Berlin. This featured the Marx Brothers in one of their early romps. Groucho owns a Florida hotel at Cocoanut Beach. Harpo and Chico interrupt the plot with their zaniness.

Face the Music (1932). Book by Moss Hart, music and lyrics by Berlin. The rich Meshbeshers try to lose some of their money backing a wretched musical; but when the City of New York goes broke, the show is dirtied up in order to make a fortune for the city.

As Thousands Cheer (1933). Book by Moss Hart, music and lyrics by Berlin. Starred Marilyn Miller, Clifton Webb, and Ethel Waters. One of the hundreds of revues staged on Broadway in the 1920's and 1930's. Entertainment of this sort was extremely popular in the decades before radio, the talking film, and television gained their mass audiences.

Annie Get Your Gun (1946). Book by Herbert and Dorothy Fields, music and lyrics by Berlin. One of his most popular shows, with a Broadway run of 1,147 performances, this has also been called by some scholars of musical theatre one of the best examples of the genre. It's the story of awkward Annie Oakley, a real-life marksman, who discovers that her shooting ability is not the way to get her man. She brings up her three sisters and a brother by shooting game birds, joins a traveling show and eventually marries the marksman-leader of the troupe.

Call Me Madam (1950). Book by Howard Lindsay and Russel Crouse, music and lyrics by Berlin. Based on Washington, D.C., hostess Perle Mesta. Ethel Merman, who also starred in *Annie,* played an American ambassador to mythical Lichtenburg.

Mr. President (1962). Book by Howard Lindsay and Russel Crouse, music and lyrics by Berlin. The last few months of a President's term in office and his lonely life afterward. This was Berlin's last major musical. In addition to his shows for Broadway, he composed scores of other songs; all told, he added many dozens of great popular song hits to our culture. His greatest melodies were usually remarkably simple. "Always" and "White Christmas" are just a couple of examples of his top songs.

SUSAN GLASPELL (1882–1948)

Trifles (1916). One of the first small masterpieces in modern American theatre, this one-act play shows a Midwestern sheriff, his wife, a nearby farmer, his wife, and a young district attorney all looking for evidence in the death of farmer Wright. The men bumble about and find no evidence; the women spot all the significant trifles that showed how hatefully Wright had treated his wife. The women remain quiet, and the wife is freed. Susan Glaspell, from Iowa, was a reporter in Des Moines before coming east and joining the Provincetown Players, where she married George Cram (Jig) Cook, the founder. They set up the theatre first in their house at Provincetown, then on a wharf, and then also in a stable on MacDougal Street in Greenwich Village, New York City, for winter productions. The organization was one of the most important groups in bringing serious modern theatre to life. Another group, the Washington Square Players, which later became the Theatre Guild, also staged Miss Glaspell's *Trifles* in November, 1916.

Suppressed Desires (1917). Another one-act play, written in collaboration with Jig Cook. An early satire on psychoanalysis, it shows a wife urging her husband into therapy but giving up her beliefs when he reports that analysis shows he should leave her and run away

with her sister. Done by the Provincetown Players. Cook, who studied at Harvard and Heidelberg, tried first to establish a utopian community but then settled on the idea of a theatre troupe. From 1922 to 1929 the Provincetown Players were known as The Playwrights Theatre and staged a large number of important serious plays.

Bernice (1919). Miss Glaspell played the part of a maid in this, her first full-length play. The personality of Bernice, lying dead in the next room, still dominates her husband and friends.

The Inheritors (1921). The different views of different generations, as seen in their attitudes toward a college founded by a liberal ancestor.

The Verge (1921). A psychological study of a woman on the edge of a mental breakdown and seeking significant answers about life.

Alison's House (1930). A Pulitzer Prize-winner for 1931, this play is based on poet Emily Dickinson's life and unrequited love. Dead Alison, telling through her poems about a love for a married man, is about to go unread forever because her sister Agatha decides that the poems must be withheld from publication; but young Elsa, having had a similar experience, succeeds in gaining approval for publication. Miss Glaspell, who had remarried after Jig Cook died early, turned away from the stage after this play, lived in retirement, but continued to write fiction.

EUGENE O'NEILL (1888–1953)

Bound East for Cardiff (1916). His first short play, produced by the Provincetown Players in their Wharf Theatre, on a foggy night with foghorns blaring in the distance, tells of the death of Yank at sea, after a fall. O'Neill, author of forty-six plays and Nobel Prize-winner in literature in 1936, is considered our greatest playwright. He was the son of James O'Neill, one of the most famous 19th-century romantic actors, and grew up in the proverbial theatre trunk. Although he rebelled against his father's old-fashioned theatre, O'Neill learned from it; and when he broke new horizons in American drama, he did so from a solid base of theatrical tradition.

Eugene O'Neill

Before Breakfast (1916). A one-act Strind-bergian monologue of Mrs. Rowland nagging her husband, who is offstage shaving, about an affair he is having. He concludes his shave by slitting his own throat. This early play contains many of the seeds of O'Neill's own mixed feelings about marriage and about his parents. O'Neill, involved in a lifelong love-hate relationship with his parents, dropped out of Princeton, drifted along the New York waterfront, became an able-bodied seaman, turned alcoholic, then was hospitalized for consumption. When he recovered his health, he turned to playwriting and became associated with the Provincetown Players who brought him to world fame.

Ile (1917). Done by the Provincetown Players in New York City. An early one-act play anticipating *Long Day's Journey into Night*. Captain Keeney, on a voyage for whale oil, does not listen to his wife, who is on board, when she pleads with him to return home. Keeney's insistence that it is his male role to get the oil drives his wife insane.

In the Zone (1917). Another early one-act play, part of what has been called the "S.S. Glencairn Series," the ideas for which came from his experiences on board ship or along the waterfront dives. Several crew members think Smitty is a spy because of a box he is hiding; he is mortified when confronted with it, because it contains letters from the woman he loves but who has broken up with him because of his drinking. When O'Neill found his calling as a playwright, he wrote with enormous energy and was able to turn his back on liquor, something his older brother Jamie could never accomplish.

The Long Voyage Home (1917). A deterministic one-act play about a Swedish sailor, Olson, shanghaied in an English waterfront bar after his unsuccessful attempt to stay sober and return home at last to the family he loves. The play is overstated but nonetheless powerful in its look at how man usually fails in his quest for his dreams, with women and liquor as the major enemies. O'Neill is usually accused of overstatement even in his greatest plays, but he always plays better than

he reads; he had an unerring feel for dramatic scenes that work on stage.

The Moon of the Caribbees (1918). An atmospheric one-act play filled with a sense of defeat and fate, and a good example of early poetic naturalism in the theatre. The Glencairn Series featured the same characters in play after play, including Smitty, Driscoll, Ivan, Cocky, and others. Many of the motifs seen in his late and great plays can be found in miniature in the early one-acts.

The Dreamy Kid (1919). Abe, a black gangster in New York, comes to visit his dying grandmother and refuses his girlfriend's urging to flee as police close in to avenge his murder of a white man. Dreamy vows to die shooting. This play antedates *The Emperor Jones* and the part of Joe Mott in *The Iceman Cometh;* O'Neill was one of the first playwrights to try to depict the black man seriously.

Beyond the Horizon (1920). A realistic tragedy of New England rural frustration and defeat. Robert Mayo wants to travel on the seas but is crushed under the joyless toil on his parents' farm after he marries the woman he thought loved his brother. The brother, who loves the soil, goes to sea to escape the triangular situation; and he, too, is defeated in life. The play foreshadows O'Neill's many future works about his mother and father; his father loved to take shows on the road, and his mother always wanted a permanent home. This was O'Neill's first major three-act play, and it won his first Pulitzer Prize for drama. By this time, O'Neill had already written 18 plays, 11 of which had been produced, mostly by the Provincetown Players. With this play, O'Neill became a national figure in the theatre.

The Emperor Jones (1920). Expressionism at its best in the theatre. Brutus Jones, a black former Pullman-car porter and an escapee from a chain gang, takes over an island of uneducated natives in the Caribbean and rules them blusteringly. When he realizes that they have all fled to the forest, he starts an escape to the seacoast, where he will leave with a small fortune. Losing his way in the woods, however, he fires his revolver at creatures of his frightened imagination, which also represent the various stages in the history of his race. He is finally killed. An eight-scene, non-intermission, long one-act play that is as excellently constructed as any American drama. It is also an effective study of superstition.

Diff'rent (1920). Emma Crosby learns just before her intended marriage to Captain Caleb Williams that he has had a mistress one night in the South Sea Islands. Emma refuses to marry Caleb. For thirty years they struggle on in life; but when she finally succumbs to her sexual feelings for a much younger man who falsely promises marriage, Caleb hangs himself and Emma then heads toward her barn to kill herself. Emma had always wanted Caleb and herself to be different from other people, but actually she was trying to deny mankind's physical nature. The early events in the play anticipate the Blessed Isles section in *Mourning Becomes Electra*.

Anna Christie (1921). Waterfront realism that won a second Pulitzer Prize for O'Neill. Anna, a prostitute, comes East and joins her father, Chris, for the first time in years. She falls in love with Matt, a young Irishman working on the barge; but Chris and Matt struggle over Anna, and she tells them of her past. After a period of despair for both men, they vow to change their ways; Anna promises to keep a home waiting for them when they return from the sea. Overstated.

The Hairy Ape (1922). Yank, a rough and tough coal stoker on an ocean liner, is called an ape by delicate-featured Mildred, who goes slumming to see what life below decks is like. Yank, enraged, tries to understand himself and find out where he belongs in life. On shore, defeated, he goes to the zoo and is crushed by a large ape. This play is rich thematically and also uses expressionism throughout, but it is perhaps less a masterpiece than *The Emperor Jones*.

All God's Chillun Got Wings (1924). A tragedy of interracial marriage, in New York City, near the turn of the century, between the black Jim Harris and the white Ella Downey. As Ella's prejudice grows, she prevents Jim

from passing his bar exams, which have been a tremendous goal for him. Ella, insane, reverts to memories of their childhood when he protected her; Jim, his dreams gone, will take care of her as best he can. A powerful love-hate play, fascinating because of its use of the same first names as his parents. Critics did not realize, for the most part, until after *Long Day's Journey into Night* that O'Neill was even here writing about his parents and disguising slightly his mother's drug addiction. (The addiction had been caused by difficult childbirths and a breast cancer operation.) *All God's Chillun Got Wings* was several decades ahead of its time in depicting racial tensions.

Welded (1924). Eleanor Owen and Michael Cape, actress and playwright, wife and husband, undergo marital tensions because of jealousy; but when they bitterly seek outlets with others, they find themselves psychologically welded to each other. Not as effective as most of the other plays of this period.

Desire Under the Elms (1924). A powerful tragedy of stony-hard New England farm life which, underneath, is the Greek Phaedra-Hippolytus myth. Old Ephraim Cabot brings home a new wife, Abbie; and two of his sons run off to seek gold in California when they believe that they will never inherit anything. Abbie, seeking a home and security, is drawn physically to Ephraim's son Eben and has a child by him, which old Ephraim thinks is his own. Ephraim motivates Eben to repudiate Abbie, and she kills the baby to prove her love for Eben. The sheriff comes to arrest Eben and Abbie, and old Ephraim goes off to do his farm chores, alone again, and saying resolutely, "God's hard and lonesome." This is one of O'Neill's best plays, and is probably the greatest example of New England folk drama.

The Great God Brown (1926). One of the first modern plays to make use of masks, this is the story of two characters who fuse into one in the split personalities of Dionysus and St. Anthony. Billy Brown, always jealous of the artistic Dion Anthony, eventually tries to become Dion. This is accomplished by

Brown's putting on Dion's mask after Dion dies. Brown is even able to continue Dion's marriage to Margaret, the woman he also loved, through the mask disguise. One of the major themes, obviously, is that people never look at other people closely, and the person who wears a figurative mask can almost always hide from the world. The play also shows O'Neill's own feelings in a speech by Cybel, a prostitute, who speaks of "the intolerable chalice of life." In play after play through the 1920's, O'Neill experimented with different forms of theatre. He did more than anyone else to widen the horizons of modern American drama.

Lazarus Laughed (1928). A play of religious groping, set against a background of masked chorus members representing the seven ages of man. Jesus brings Lazarus back to life, and Lazarus reports that there is no death, nothing but God's laughter. Tiberius kills many of Lazarus' followers and sees that they die laughing. Caligula arrives to find Tiberius burning Lazarus at the stake, strangles Tiberius and lets Lazarus die, then realizes that he has "killed laughter." Another highly innovative play, but it has rarely been produced.

Marco Millions (1928). Social satire on Babbittlike materialism as depicted in the story of the dense, crass, commercial Marco Polo who cannot recognize things of the spirit even when they are under his nose. Marco travels to the court of the great Khan, where Princess Kukachin falls in love with him. Marco becomes wealthy and returns to marry his childhood sweetheart in Italy; he never is aware that Kukachin has died of love for him. O'Neill underscores the materialistic indifference of the average American businessman by having the play end with the actor playing Marco Polo seated in the audience, looking a bit puzzled as he comes up the aisle, shrugging off all concerns about the play as he reaches the lobby, and finally, in his 13th-century costume, yawningly hailing a taxicab and disappearing into the New York night. Produced by the Theatre Guild, it starred Alfred Lunt.

Strange Interlude (1928). A psychological drama of a woman, Nina, who has loved dead flyer Gordon romantically, her father paternally, her husband Sam dutifully, her doctor Ned sexually, and her older writer-friend Charlie platonically; to be fulfilled, she must have the love of all of them. Afraid because of Sam's mother's warnings about insanity in the family, Nina has Ned father her child instead. Taking place over half a lifetime, the play ends with Sam dying and Nina resting quietly in the arms of "Good Old Uncle Charlie" who is, in part, a death symbol. The play has nine acts and was first performed with a dinner break. The play also uses interior monologue on stage, as the characters give voice to their thoughts; the work is very much like a novel. It was revived brilliantly by the Actors Studio in 1963, which cut heavily, reducing some of O'Neill's overstatement and fitting the play into one evening's sitting.

Dynamo (1929). Rivalries between a religious family and an atheistic family that lives next door. Reuben, son of the minister, comes to look on electricity as the only God. When he is tempted by Ada, daughter of the atheist, he kills her and then throws himself in the dynamo and commits suicide. Now considered one of O'Neill's lesser plays.

Mourning Becomes Electra (1931). This play, actually a trilogy of three plays, is in thirteen acts and was also performed all afternoon and all evening, with a dinner break. One of O'Neill's most ambitious works, it is a modern retelling of Aeschylus' *Oresteian Trilogy,* plus an Oedipus-complex treatment, set after the Civil War in the United States. General Mannon returns from the war and is killed by his wife, Christine; they have never been able to understand each other. Their daughter, Lavinia, suspects her mother and waits for her brother, Orin, who has been wounded, to return from the war. When Christine goes to her lover, Captain Adam Brant, on his ship, Lavinia and Orin kill Brant. Christine and Orin are both eventually driven to suicide by their guilt feelings. Lavinia, who had momentarily overcome her family's long years of puritanism while on a voyage to the South Sea Islands with her brother, loses her suitor, Peter Niles, when he begins to learn more about the family's horrors. Lavinia ends up locking herself into the Mannon family mansion, to live out the rest of her haunted days in total isolation. Marvin David Levy did a powerful operatic version, which was staged at the Metropolitan Opera in 1967.

Ah, Wilderness! (1933). Sixteen-year-old Richard Miller is accused of writing dirty poetry, gets drunk, and is beaten up—but begins to mature. This is O'Neill's only nostalgic comedy and is a mellow look at the brighter side of life that O'Neill saw around him during his boyhood summers at the family home in New London, Connecticut. Several critics have said that this play and *Long Day's Journey into Night* probably give the total picture of O'Neill's life in New London.

Days Without End (1934). A search for Christian meaning in life. John Loving, embittered with life, turns against religion. The main character is played by two actors, John representing the better side, Loving the worse. Not one of O'Neill's great plays but interesting because of the theatrical experimentation.

(From this point in the O'Neill listings, the dates represent writing, not production, of the plays.)

More Stately Mansions (1938–41). A four-and-a-half-hour play produced posthumously in Stockholm in 1962, published in the United States in 1964, and first produced here in 1967. Mother Deborah and wife Sarah struggle for Simon Harcourt, who starts out with a touch of the poet in him and ends as a selfish business tycoon. This was the fourth play in O'Neill's proposed eleven-play cycle, *A Tale of Possessors Self-Dispossessed.* The cycle was never completed because O'Neill became more and more afflicted by a paralyzing disease that made writing extremely painful and difficult. From the mid-1930's on, O'Neill's third wife, Carlotta Monterrey, kept him in virtual seclusion. At the time, many theatre critics felt that Carlotta was selfishly monopolizing him; few realized that she was serving as nurse and guardian and kept interruptions away so that O'Neill could labor

at his writing. O'Neill, in a fit of despair, burned several manuscripts in the great cycle; he thought he had burned this along with plays one and two, *Greed of the Meek* and *And Give Me Death,* but a copy had been given to the Yale University Library by mistake and thus survived.

The Iceman Cometh (1939). O'Neill interrupted his proposed great cycle of plays to exorcise his old family ghosts with a series of domestic dramas that were to become his masterpieces. All were heavily autobiographical. Set in Harry Hope's saloon in lower New York City in 1912, the play reproduces many of the people and the locale of Jimmy the Priest's saloon, in which O'Neill lived as a young man before he began his writing career. A group of derelicts wait for fast-talking, fun-loving salesman Hickey (19th-century slang for a corpse) to come to help celebrate Hope's birthday party. When Hickey arrives, instead of booze and fun, there is discomfort and great tension, because Hickey tries to sell the group on giving up their pipe dreams of doing something with their lives. Late in the play, when they discover that Hickey has murdered his wife because she has made him feel guilty all his life, the derelicts insist to police officers that Hickey was crazy. Once again able to rationalize everything away, the derelicts can get happily drunk once more. A powerful, long four-act drama of man's need for illusions if he is to survive, and one of the top dozen American plays. O'Neill held back production because he felt that the oncoming of World War II was not the best time for a play as heavy as this one; when it was finally done in 1946, reactions were mixed. Revived under José Quintero's brilliant direction at the Circle in the Square off-Broadway in 1956, the play found an audience and has been considered a classic ever since. A superb film version was made in 1973.

Long Day's Journey into Night (1939–41). O'Neill left orders that this autobiographical play was not to be produced until twenty-five years after his death; but his widow, Carlotta, realized that O'Neill's family were all dead, and production was arranged in 1956 with an all-star cast including Frederic March, Florence Eldridge, Jason Robards, and Bradford Dillman. The play won a Pulitzer Prize and has been unanimously acclaimed as O'Neill's masterpiece and possibly the best domestic drama ever written. In four acts, the long play begins in the morning and goes on beyond midnight at the family home in New London. O'Neill exorcises all his love-hates, showing his father's vanity, selfishness, and liquor problem; his mother's morphine addiction and her subtle control of the family by means of guilt; his brother's growing alcoholism, decadence, and self-loathing; and his own torments and fears highlighted by extreme tensions over his oncoming tuberculosis. The greatness of the play lies in O'Neill's ability to draw shades of gray, showing good and bad in each of the characters. Each character is provided with rich motivations for his or her past actions. The play has been staged all over the world, with a brilliant production at the National Theatre of Great Britain with Sir Laurence Olivier in 1972–73.

A Touch of the Poet (1935–42). Produced posthumously in 1958, this was play three in the proposed great cycle. An Irish immigrant, Con Melody, who runs a saloon in the United States, continually puts on airs and sneers at his humble wife, Nora. Daughter Sara is having a love affair with young aristocrat Simon Harcourt. When Con, in his old military uniform, goes to the Harcourts' house and is beaten up, he goes to the barn and fires a shot. Instead of killing himself, he has killed his mare, the symbol to him of high-class pretensions. Strongly related thematically to *The Iceman Cometh* as a study of man and his illusions, this is one of O'Neill's better plays.

Hughie (1941–44). A one-act play, produced posthumously in 1957, this was the first in a projected series of short plays to be called *By Way of Obit*. Erie Smith, a tinhorn loser in life, is disconsolate because his rundown hotel's night clerk, Hughie, who listened avidly to his lies about his gambling triumphs, is dead. He finally gets the new clerk to play the same role, so that they both can have their pipe dreams about being big-shot New York sports instead of nobodies in the giant anthill of a city. Barbara Gelb says that

O'Neill was writing about his brother, Jamie, and that this is really one of O'Neill's series of family plays. The two best studies of O'Neill are by Arthur and Barbara Gelb, and by Louis Sheaffer.

A Moon for the Misbegotten (1943). His last play, not produced until 1947 and then quickly withdrawn by O'Neill before it reached New York. It finally reached Broadway in the late 1950's but did not take its place as one of O'Neill's masterpieces until given a spectacular Broadway revival in 1973–74, becoming the hit of the entire season. Another extremely rich play, highly biographical, about O'Neill's dissolute brother, Jamie, and the hurts in his life. We see Jamie's love for his mother, his guilt at backsliding into alcoholism again, and his great self-hatred, all woven into a night spent with overweight Josie Hogan. O'Neill's shaking paralysis prevented him from completing anything after this play, even though his mind remained clear until his death. In his entire body of work, which was extremely ambitious, he experimented constantly and made great demands on actors and audiences; ultimately, however, the major part of his reputation stems from the handful of plays written with great compassion, late in his career, about his family.

JESSE LYNCH WILLIAMS (1871–1929)

Why Marry? (1917). Historically important because it is the first winner of the Pulitzer Prize for drama. It is a study of several types of marriage as seen within a family and centering around Helen, who can't decide whether to marry or just live with her man. She is tricked into marriage at the end, thus sugarcoating what might have been an extremely powerful play.

Why Not? (1922). A sequel, much less successful than the earlier play. It is interesting to look at other plays written in the period after World War I and see how many of them tried to be serious but turned to conventional endings; this trend makes the uncompromising seriousness of Eugene O'Neill all the more impressive.

SIGMUND ROMBERG (1887–1951)

Maytime (1917). Romberg, a Hungarian, studied for an engineering career but also studied music in Vienna. When he came to the United States at age twenty-two, he became a staff composer for the Winter Garden Theatre on Broadway, one of the top vaudeville houses. His first Broadway show was *The Midnight Girl* in 1913, but with *Maytime* and its hit song, "Sweethearts," Romberg began a long career of writing music for immensely popular operettas and films. He was influenced considerably by the music of Strauss. This show, a sentimental operetta in four acts, was produced by the Shuberts and played in five New York theatres for a total of 492 performances. The book and lyrics were by Rida Johnson Young. It is the story of two young lovers, thwarted by their parents, who remember each other throughout life.

Blossom Time (1921). Music by Romberg, book and lyrics by Dorothy Donnelly. This loosely retells the life of composer Franz Schubert and how he lost his love to another man.

The Student Prince (1924). Music by Romberg, book and lyrics by Dorothy Donnelly. A sentimental operetta about young lovers in old Heidelberg. Karl Franz melodiously loves Kathie, the waitress in a tavern; but he must leave, become a king, and marry a princess.

The Desert Song (1926). Music by Romberg, book and lyrics by Oscar Hammerstein II, Otto Harbach, and Frank Mandel. Pierre Birabeau, defending the Riff tribe in North Africa from the cruelties of his own commanding officer, has to contend with and win over his own father; he also kidnaps and wins Margot Bonvalet. Pierre is disguised as the Red Shadow in his intrigues. Top songs include "One Alone" and "Desert Song."

Rosalie (1928). Music by George Gershwin and Romberg, book by William Anthony McGuire and Guy Bolton, lyrics by P. G. Wodehouse and Ira Gershwin. Produced by Florenz Ziegfeld. Rosalie, princess of Romanza, has a romance with Lt. Richard Fay of West Point. This show is a good example of how many a hit musical in New York has been written by virtually a committee.

The New Moon (1928). Music by Romberg, book and lyrics by Frank Mandel, Laurence Schwab, and Oscar Hammerstein II. Robert, a bondman in New Orleans in 1788, loves the daughter of his owner. On a ship headed back to Paris to be tried on an old charge, Robert leads a revolt of bondmen who form their own republic. He finally wins Marianne. Romberg, in all, was involved in well over fifty Broadway shows. He spent his later years writing musical scores for numerous motion pictures in Hollywood.

WINCHELL SMITH (1876–1933) and FRANK BACON (1864–1922)

Lightnin' (1918). A combination of contrived melodramatic intrigue, heavily sentimental comedy, and local color. Lightnin' Bill Jones is a homespun innkeeper on the Nevada-California line. Young John Marvin rescues the inn from land-company crooks and gets the girl. Old Lightnin' is the show-stealer. This is an example of an extremely poor play that nevertheless ran for several years on Broadway and is among the top all-time box-office hits. The authors were also represented on Broadway with several other comedies in the era around World War I.

MARK REED (1890–   )

She Would and She Did (1919). The first of Reed's many light comedies that appeared on Broadway over a period of three decades. Hot-tempered Frances Nesmith has dug holes in a green at her country club and must use all her tricks and wiles to get back in good graces.

Petticoat Fever (1933). A light comedy about Dascome Dinsmore, a wireless operator in Labrador, who falls for Ethel Campion when she and her stuffy fiancé, Sir James Fenton, crash their plane into a snowdrift. When Dinsmore's equally stuffy fiancée, Clara Wilson, arrives with a sea captain, Dinsmore's machinations win Ethel and get Clara married to Sir James through a trick.

Yes, My Darling Daughter (1937). Ellen spends a weekend with her boyfriend. Her father, violently angry, insists that they marry. Ellen finally agrees when she admits to herself that she really loves the young man. It is quite a good comedy, primarily because we see two generations of women reacting similarly. Ellen's mother had once been a radical free-thinker but now has turned conservative, and she sees her former self in her daughter.

ZONA GALE (1874–1938)

Miss Lulu Bett (1920). A Pulitzer Prize-winner for 1921 and one of the poorer choices ever made by the committee. A typical small-town unmarried woman, with little hope for a future, blossoms when a man enters her life. The trials and tribulations connected with the possibility of bigamy are finally resolved.

Mister Pitt (1925). Mr. Pitt's lack of self-confidence loses him a wife and later his son; but at last a few good qualities begin to show in him.

GEORGE S. KAUFMAN (1889–1961)

Dulcy (1921). Kaufman is known as the American stage's greatest collaborator; he wrote or helped write 45 productions in 37 years. In addition, he directed another 40 shows on Broadway. Early in his career he was drama editor for the New York *Tribune* and then the New York *Times*. His name is associated with some of the greatest, most enduring comedies in our theatre. Kaufman's first show was in 1918, but with *Dulcy* he made it big as a writer and began his collaboration with Marc Connelly. This play was based on a Franklin P. Adams character and satirizes feminine ineptitude; it also brought Lynn Fontanne to stardom.

To the Ladies (1922). With Marc Connelly. The problems of a young married couple, with the wife, Mrs. Leonard Beebe, saving the day for her husband's business by making a clever speech after he had failed in his attempt. This was written as a starring vehicle for the young actress Helen Hayes.

Merton of the Movies (1922). With Marc Connelly and taken from the *Saturday Eve-ning Post* short story of the same name by Harry Leon Wilson. A spoof on filmmakers in which country yokel Merton thinks he is a romantic hero. In all, Kaufman and Connelly collaborated on eight plays. In addition to his other creative activities, Kaufman also served as a play-doctor to scores of scripts by other writers. (A play-doctor is a writer who does late revisions, without credit or by-line, on plays that producers feel may fail.)

The Deep-Tangled Wildwood (1923). With Marc Connelly. James Leland, disappointed in the failure of his newest play, goes home to find the simple life in order to revitalize himself. He doesn't find the simple life but does find a bride. Plays about show business have long been popular fare in all countries and in all time periods; American theatre is no exception.

Beggar on Horseback (1924). With Marc Connelly. A satire on big business and its threat to individuality and creativity in a young composer. Neil McRae loves Cynthia but contemplates marrying rich Gladys in order to have the money to study music. In a dream sequence that comprises most of the play, Neil marries Gladys; and using expressionistic stage devices, Kaufman and Connelly show the deadening effect of a mercenary life on Neil, who kills his wife's family and is sentenced to work forever in a candy factory. When Neil wakes up, he marries the poor girl, Cynthia, instead. Despite the happy ending, this play, with its use of expressionism and serious theme, was one of the more significant social documents on stage in the 1920's.

The Cocoanuts (1925). Music and lyrics by Irving Berlin. A romp for the Marx Brothers, who were every bit as zany in real life as they were on stage and in films. Groucho runs a Florida hotel at Cocoanut Beach; Harpo and Chico complicate things with their slapstick actions. Groucho's later mannerisms of walking and talking, which made him famous, were actually created by Kaufman. Kaufman was a close friend of the Marx Brothers, particularly of Harpo, who was part of the regular card games among a group of writers and wits in New York City, and did much creative work for them. During the depths of the Depression, for example, Kaufman was given $100,000 to write the film script for their *A Night at the Opera.*

The Butter and Egg Man (1925). Kaufman's only Broadway play that he wrote entirely by himself. Kaufman said often that in a good collaboration both writers would stimulate each other to peaks unattainable alone. Kaufman long distrusted his own inventiveness and felt more secure working with a partner; in the final analysis by critics, however, Kaufman was one of the most inventive and witty people in our theatre. In this play a country boy from Ohio is gulled into backing a Broadway flop; unbelievably, it becomes a hit, and he sells it back at a huge profit and wins his sweetheart.

The Royal Family (1927). With Edna Ferber, who did six plays with Kaufman. Probably based on the Barrymores, the play is about the Cavendish family, all famous theatrical personalities, and how they pull together in the face of obstacles inside and outside the family. Fanny Cavendish is the grandmother, desiring to return to acting through a road show; daughter Julie, at the height of her career, thinks she may marry her longtime businessman admirer; and granddaughter Gwen does marry and have a baby. But at the end Julie and Gwen return to their careers, and the play actually ends with the grandmother's quiet death. This is a rich comedy about living a meaningful life. Revived brilliantly on Broadway under Ellis Rabb's direction in 1975.

Animal Crackers (1928). A musical comedy with Morrie Ryskind; music and lyrics by Bert Kalmar and Harry Ruby. Another romp made famous by the Marx Brothers, who pose as celebrities. While visiting the socially elite hostess, Mrs. Rittenhouse, on her Long Island estate, they rob all the guests.

June Moon (1929). With Ring Lardner (1885–1933), a famous major-league baseball writer and American humorist. Kaufman

also adapted several of Lardner's most famous short stories for stage use. In this play, Freddy, a naive young songwriter from upstate New York, thinks that a sophisticated woman is more his style than his hometown sweetheart; after a series of mistakes, Freddy returns to his true love. The play is a loving satire on the popular music business.

Once in a Lifetime (1930). With Moss Hart. This began the long and rich Kaufman and Hart collaboration. See Hart's autobiography, *Act One,* for a fascinating and full description of the creation of this play. Hart had hero-worshiped Kaufman for years, wrote this play as much like a Kaufman script as he could, and had the good fortune to meet Kaufman and have him help with the final drafts. All told, they did eight plays together, and Kaufman considered Hart his best co-worker. This play is a spoof of the stupidities in Hollywood as it entered the talking-picture era. Three vaudeville performers in New York head to Hollywood; one of them insults the big producer, who is so impressed that he makes the ex-vaudevillian general manager despite his foolishness.

Of Thee I Sing (1931). With Morrie Ryskind. Music by George Gershwin, lyrics by Ira Gershwin. A musical satire on how to win a presidential election. Even though primarily a romp, it was nevertheless one of the first American musicals with any real thematic content, and it became the first musical to win the Pulitzer Prize for drama.

Dinner at Eight (1932). With Edna Ferber (1887–1968). A comedy with serious overtones, as a society hostess frets about her dinner party and is oblivious to the tortured and tangled private lives of her guests.

Merrily We Roll Along (1934). With Moss Hart. A serious play. Wealthy playwright Richard Niles, with a brand-new hit, sees his emotional life crumbling at a disastrous party after opening night as he turns forty. The play moves steadily backward in time, ending with his idealistic valedictorian's speech at college, and we see how he becomes a complete moral sellout. A powerful play.

Stage Door (1936). With Edna Ferber. Life in a crowded women's theatrical boarding-house in New York. Terry Randall struggles to become a success in legitimate theatre. The play shows both the idealism and the excitement of theatre as well as the shoddy practices all too common in the world of show business.

You Can't Take It With You (1936). With Moss Hart. The carefree Sycamore family, headed by Grandpa Vanderhof, combat the materialism of the Great Depression with their own eccentric love of life. Suitor Tony Kirby finally wins Alice Sycamore, and his wealthy parents come to understand a way of life that is not all pressure for money. This delightful comedy about self-fulfillment won a Pulitzer Prize and has been revived several times on Broadway. It is still done constantly in amateur theatre and, despite its seeming lightness, remains one of the best theatrical statements about individuality.

I'd Rather Be Right (1937). With Moss Hart. Music by Richard Rodgers, lyrics by Lorenz Hart. A musical satire on the Roosevelt administration, with Phil Barker unable to marry Mary Jones because of his small salary. Phil dreams of meeting Franklin D. Roosevelt, who decides that the federal budget should be balanced.

The American Way (1939). With Moss Hart. The patriotic, historical saga of Martin Gunther, a German immigrant to Mapleton, Ohio, in 1896, who builds a furniture business, loses a son in World War I, loses his factory and fortune through a magnanimous deed in the Depression, and is finally killed by a young Fascist group that his grandson is about to join. The grandson repents and turns patriot at the funeral. A serious play, but a bit too overstated and colored by the hysteria just before World War II. It is interesting to note that even though Kaufman and Hart wrote several of our greatest comedies, they also did quite a bit of collaboration on serious subjects.

The Man Who Came to Dinner (1939). With Moss Hart. Based on the talented but egotistical literary critic Alexander Woollcott, who was a close friend of Kaufman. Sheridan Whiteside breaks a leg on a lecture tour and proceeds to create havoc in a middle-class household in which he is bedded. After all the confusions and crises are solved, Whiteside prepares to leave, falls, and breaks his leg again. A big hit, and one of the most frequently produced plays in amateur theatre ever since.

George Washington Slept Here (1940). With Moss Hart. The farcical and trying problems that Newton and Annabelle Fuller have in acquiring a peaceful house in the country, in Bucks County, Pennsylvania. Kaufman owned a home there for a time.

The Land Is Bright (1941). With Edna Ferber. A drama that shows the Kincaid family amassing a fortune; but, sobered by events leading up to World War II, the third generation of the family begins to show some signs of social and moral reform. Many plays written during the Depression and in the years approaching World War II were highly idealistic.

The Late George Apley (1944). With John P. Marquand, and adapted from his novel of the same name. A comedy of manners, in which a Boston family at the turn of the century resists the changing ways all around them.

The Solid Gold Cadillac (1953). With Howard Teichman. Teichman, a professor at Columbia University, wrote the definitive biography *George S. Kaufman, an Intimate Portrait* (1972), which tells about Kaufman's collaborations, his play-doctoring that few people knew about, his directing, and all his other work in the Broadway theatre. The book is also filled with fascinating glimpses into his private life and anecdotes about his many friends in show business. *Cadillac* is a comedy of big business, in which a lady overturns the board of directors. Throughout his writing career Kaufman often had the underdog triumph.

Silk Stockings (1955). With Abe Burrows and Kaufman's young second wife, British actress-writer Leueen McGrath. Music by Cole Porter. Based on Melchior Lengyel's film, *Ninotchka*. A Russian pianist, in Paris, won't return home; neither will the secret agents sent after him. This was the last of the forty-five full-length shows Kaufman worked on in his thirty-seven-year Broadway career. He did three collaborations with Leueen McGrath; his first wife, Bea, a well-known New York fiction editor, died in 1945.

MARC CONNELLY (1890–   )
(Plays other than with George S. Kaufman)

The Wisdom Tooth (1926). A simple, dated comedy of a clerk, Bemis, who loses his girl because he has no originality. A supernatural visit to the past jolts him, he sasses his boss and is fired, but wins back his girl when he finally gains some individuality. This is one of the few plays that Connelly wrote by himself that achieved success.

The Green Pastures (1930). A folklike religious play that tells the story of Christianity from the point of view of a genial group of black people and is based on Roark Bradford's *Ole Man Adam and His Chillun*. This one play made secure Connelly's niche in American theatre. Connelly, born in Pennsylvania, began as a journalist, came to New York, and began writing lyrics for songs. He reached his peak as a creative writer with his collaborations with George S. Kaufman (*see* preceding entry), wrote a number of lesser collaborations with other writers, and ended up a professor of playwriting at Yale University after World War II.

MOSS HART (1904–61)
(Plays other than with George S. Kaufman)

Lady in the Dark (1941). Music by Kurt Weill, lyrics by Ira Gershwin, book by Hart. Liza Elliott, editor of a fashion magazine, feels lost, seeks help from a psychoanalyst, acts out her dreams in fantasy scenes set to music, and finally comes out of her dark world to face life unafraid. This was soon made into a popular film. As with Marc Connelly (above), Moss Hart did most of his greatest work in collaboration with George S. Kaufman.

Winged Victory (1943). A play about the United States Army Air Corps, this used soldiers as actors during World War II. Highly popular because of its patriotism, but ephemeral. Hart, a New Yorker, grew up in extremely modest financial circumstances and worked in the office of a producer. He turned to writing but did not make it big until he began collaborating with Kaufman. For fascinating background on this collaboration, see Hart's autobiography, *Act One*.

Light Up the Sky (1948). This play shows the building tensions in connection with a theatrical production opening out of town in Boston. It is a satire on theatre people, including several recognizable individuals and types at that time, but it also provides a good behind-the-scenes look at the powerful pressures in the world of show business. Hart wrote several other plays by himself, did some films, and had considerable success as a Broadway director, including the great musical hit *My Fair Lady*.

EDNA ST. VINCENT MILLAY (1892–1950)

Aria Da Capo (1921). One-act ironic and satirical fantasy in poetry in which life is depicted as primarily a harlequinade and the human race always greedy enough to kill. Pierrot and Columbine chatter pointlessly while some shepherds are killed; they push the bodies underneath a table and chatter on. This play was extremely popular with amateur companies for decades, after its premiere by the Provincetown Players. Although Miss Millay wrote several other plays, her reputation is tied to her poetry of the 1920's.

ANNE NICHOLS (1896–1966)

Abie's Irish Rose (1922). Despite one of the longest New York runs, with 2,327 performances, this is an extremely trite play about a Jewish boy's comical problems of foisting off his Irish bride as a Jewish girl. The play succeeded because of the imitation Romeo-Juliet motif that pitted Jews against Catholics in New York City, and because the management flooded the city with low-priced tickets to maintain an audience. Miss Nichols, once a chorus girl, wrote several other plays, but this was the only one to attain any popularity. It remains an outstanding example of how, at times, an extremely poor play can nevertheless become highly popular for a time.

GEORGE KELLY (1887–1974)

The Torch Bearers (1922). A delightful satire on amateur theatricals and the many types of affectations seen in the theatre. Mrs. Pampinelli, the director, encourages the talentless Mrs. Paula Ritter, who makes her one and only stage appearance in the extremely farcical second act. Act III is contrived to make the play fit the three-act Broadway formula of the time.

Poor Aubrey (1924). The one-act play that served as the basis for the following play in this listing. Kelly, a Philadelphian, began as a child actor and later wrote many popular sketches for vaudeville, including this one.

The Show Off (1924). A satirical picture of egotism and high-pressure salesmanship in the Babbitt vein. Aubrey Piper is the blindly egocentric character. Long considered one of Kelly's better plays, this was revived in 1968 by the APA-Phoenix Repertory Theatre, with Helen Hayes; the production emphasized the play's theme of the emptiness of many middle-class lives.

Craig's Wife (1925). Pulitzer Prize-winning character study of a middle-class woman, Harriet Craig, who substitutes homemaking for love. Craig finally leaves her, alone in her sterile house. Kelly's most famous play, although it is somewhat dated now. When Kelly was at his best, he created strong central characters and believable realism.

Daisy Mayme (1926). A long, talky comedy, popular in its day but dated now, of a match between a forty-three-year-old man who has been taking care of his mother, now dead, and forty-year-old Daisy, over the objections of the man's selfish sister.

Behold, the Bridegroom (1927). A sophisticated comedy-drama about rich, twenty-seven-year-old Tony Lyle, who has had everything in life except maturity and honest love. When she meets a man who she teasingly says looks like a bridegroom and who does not instantly fall for her, she finally sees herself for what she is. A former lover kills himself, and Tony falls ill; but at the end, there is much hope for her. Kelly broke no new barriers in his playwriting; even in his serious plays he did not really jolt his audiences.

Maggie the Magnificent (1929). A character study of a mother and daughter who can't get along but finally, in mature years, begin to grope toward understanding. George Kelly continued to write and direct a number of his own plays, with lessening critical success. His decade was primarily that of the 1920's; much of his writing after that time was for Hollywood. The Kelly family soon became much more widely known for George's niece, Grace, movie star and Princess of Monaco.

The Fatal Weakness (1946). One of his last Broadway productions. A sentimental, middle-aged wife who loves to go to weddings sits by in masochistic silence as her husband leaves her, and then actually attends his wedding. This is a brittle drawing-room play, dated even when it first appeared. More than many of the highly popular playwrights of the 1920's, Kelly has dated strikingly with the passage of time.

LULA VOLLMER (1898–1955)

Sun-Up (1923). The widow Cagle feuds with the law that killed her husband and took her son off to France to fight in World War I. This was one of the first important regional plays and shows Southern mountain folk motifs. Miss Vollmer, who grew up in North Carolina, was later a clerk in a New York theatre. She wrote several other plays, but this was her most important work.

HATCHER HUGHES (1883–1945)

Hell-Bent for Heaven (1923). A Pulitzer Prize-winning play of folk patterns in the Blue Ridge Mountains. An evangelical hypocrite, Rufe Pryor, tries to eliminate a rival by stirring up an old feud. Hughes, who grew up in the Southern mountains, wrote several other regional plays. He began his career by collaborating with Elmer Rice, and he spent several decades as a professor of drama at Columbia University.

26

MAXWELL ANDERSON (1888–1959)

White Desert (1923). This is a tragedy of loneliness of life on a homestead in North Dakota in the winter. Michael Kane is jealous of his nearest neighbor, Peterson; Michael ends up shooting his wife, Mary. Anderson began his career as America's foremost verse-dramatist here. A Pennsylvania native, he was graduated from the University of North Dakota, was dismissed as a faculty member at Whittier College in California because of his pacifist views, suffered a similar fate at the San Francisco *Bulletin,* and eventually became a journalist in New York City.

What Price Glory? (1924). With Laurence Stallings (1894–1968). Stallings, a World War I veteran who had been severely wounded, was a colleague of Anderson's on the New York *World*. Stallings wrote film scripts in Hollywood for almost thirty years after the success of this play. In the play, the most famous of all World War I dramas in the American theatre, Captain Flagg and Sergeant Quirt battle over a French girl; but when the call of duty comes, they forget their feud and return to the front lines. The second act, which is set in the trenches on the Western Front in France, is an extremely powerful antiwar document.

Saturday's Children (1927). A social comedy about Bobby and Rims, two very young people who marry, and the emotional and economic problems that they face. Love finally conquers money. Anderson soon became one of the nation's most prolific playwrights; and although almost all his plays are entertaining, he was always concerned with social problems.

Gods of the Lightning (1928). Written with musician Harold Hickerson, this was one of several dramatic interpretations of the Sacco and Vanzetti trial of the mid-1920's. Law-court justice is depicted as brutal, corrupt, and highly influenceable by mass hysteria as Macready and Capraro, leaders in a mill-town strike, are wrongly convicted and executed for the murder of a payroll messenger. In real life, Sacco and Vanzetti were two admitted anarchists who were arrested, convicted, and executed for a similar crime that they probably did not commit. Anderson used the same theme later in *Winterset*.

Elizabeth the Queen (1930). This was the first of a number of major historical dramas in verse. In it we see the conflict in Queen Elizabeth I between her love for Essex and her desire to rule alone. She expects Essex to plead for mercy when she arrests him, but he does not and is executed. The production starred Alfred Lunt and Lynn Fontanne. This play has stood up as one of Anderson's most outstanding efforts.

Night Over Taos (1932). A historical verse drama about the stubborn last stand of Pablo Montoya, a large landowner in 1847, as the old Spanish feudal regime in the American Southwest knuckles under to both the United States soldiers and Pablo's forward-looking son.

Both Your Houses (1933). A Pulitzer Prize-winning play. A biting political satire that shows young Alan McLean, recently elected to Congress from Nevada, discovering that a powerful lobby has been responsible for his victory. McLean opposes a huge pork-barrel bill and finally tries to make it appear totally ludicrous by loading the bill with many ridiculous expenditures. To his horror, the bill passes, and he realizes that political gamesmanship, not statesmanship, runs the country.

Mary of Scotland (1933). Another famous historical verse drama that depicts, fairly accurately, the major events in Mary Stuart's life: her marriage to the weak Lord Darnley, her marriage to Lord Bothwell, John Knox's interference in her life, her imprisonment in England. Anderson adds a nonhistorical confrontation between Mary and Queen Elizabeth, in which Mary smugly rebukes Elizabeth and tells her that she, at least, has known love. The play was made into an excellent film, starring Glenda Jackson, in the early 1970's.

Valley Forge (1934). An anguished picture of the hunger and suffering of George Washington and his forces in the dark winter of

1777–78. Washington, having learned that Congress wants to make peace with the English general Howe for business' sake, meets in a barn with Howe and is about to surrender. But when he learns from a woman he loved long ago that the French have agreed to help and then learns from his ragtag men that they have captured the British corn supply, Washington realizes he has support from his men, even if not from Congress, and he will fight on. The play glorifies the little man and the cause of freedom and criticizes the businessmen of the time who are bureaucrats in Congress. This work fits into the pattern of the plays of the 1930's in saying that men must lift themselves up and struggle for their ideals.

Winterset (1935). A poetic tragedy of evil and injustice in modern life, which won the New York Drama Critics Circle Award and has long been considered Anderson's greatest play. Mio seeks to clear the name of his father who has been executed for a crime he did not commit. He discovers that the judge who presided over the trial is going insane from pent-up guilt, and he also discovers a witness who knows the truth; but Mio is finally killed by a gang leader's gunmen before he can secure justice. This play was also patterned after the events in the historical Sacco and Vanzetti case (*see* the entry for *Gods of the Lightning*).

The Wingless Victory (1936). This verse tragedy shows the hypocrisy and intolerance of the Puritans in early Salem. Sea captain Nathaniel McQueston has married Oparre, a princess from the South Sea islands. When his family and colleagues in New England oppose her presence in their community, McQueston's love turns sour and Oparre kills herself and their children.

High Tor (1937). A poetic fantasy of man's rebellion against the machine age. Van Dorn is pressured to sell the mountain, High Tor, that he owns in the Hudson Valley of New York. On a stormy night he meets a long-dead crew of Dutch sailors and a young Dutch girl whom he falls for; but when the clear light of morning comes, Van Dorn sells the mountain and plans to move west. The play

won the New York Drama Critics Circle Award.

Knickerbocker Holiday (1938). Music by Kurt Weill, book and lyrics by Anderson. Set in New Amsterdam (New York) in the 1600's, with Washington Irving acting as master of ceremonies, the play shows little man Brom Broeck in conflict with governor Peter Stuyvesant. Anderson's theme is that less government is preferable to more, and the play actually is a satire on President Franklin D. Roosevelt and his New Deal policies.

Key Largo (1939). A verse drama set on the Florida keys. King McCloud, who has not chosen to die with his comrades fighting against Franco in the Spanish Civil War, is tormented by guilt when he returns to Florida. When gangsters, however, threaten to destroy a family, McCloud kills them even though he knows that he himself will be killed. He finally realizes that it can be noble to die for a worthy cause. This is one of many American plays in the late 1930's based on the premise that the little people should stand up and fight the bullies of the world. At a time when mass and political feeling in the United States was still isolationist, many playwrights were urging the thinking people to take a stand on the side of freedom.

Candle in the Wind (1941). An American actress forfeits her life in order that her French lover can escape from a Nazi prison camp in occupied France early in World War II. Anderson again says strongly that man must stand up to the beasts in the world.

The Eve of St. Mark (1942). Young Quizz West is on a Pacific island about to be attacked by the Japanese during World War II. He and his fellow soldiers vote to stay and face almost certain death, because life must have meaning for them. Many highly patriotic plays were produced during the war, but, as with most of Anderson's efforts, the results here rose up above mere theatre-of-the-moment.

Joan of Lorraine (1946). The Joan of Arc

story set in a modern American theatre. Actress Mary Gray protests to the director that the character of Joan is selling out to the forces of evil, and the director counters by pointing out that even their acting troupe has to work together with various evil groups in order to get the play produced. The actress finally gains some idealism as the words of Joan of Arc sink in. Anderson makes a serious point about the necessity of occasional compromise in the world, but the play's seriousness is leavened with considerable comedy, before the final burning of Joan.

Anne of the Thousand Days (1948). A powerful and extremely effective poetic drama about the courtship and marriage of Anne Boleyn to Henry VIII. The play ends with the trumped-up trial of Anne and her beheading in the Tower of London. Written in a memory-play style and providing rich characterizations, the drama was made into a superb film in 1969. Anne and Henry have their brief moments of love, but Henry's overriding desire for a male heir brings about Anne's tragedy.

Lost in the Stars (1949). Music by Kurt Weill (1900–50). A musical dramatization of Alan Paton's novel about race relations in South Africa, *Cry, the Beloved Country*. The Reverend Stephen Kumalo goes to Johannesburg to find his son and discovers that Absalom has shot a white man. Absalom is sentenced to be hanged. The Reverend Kumalo despairs about a God that permits this, but the white man's father comes to Kumalo to try to help plan for a future that will include integration. Revived on Broadway in 1972 and put on the screen soon after by the American Film Theatre series.

Barefoot in Athens (1951). The martyrdom of Socrates in ancient Athens, this is an extremely powerful play about freedom of thought. Even toward the end of his career, Maxwell Anderson was concerned with the basic human freedoms and with man's need to stand up and be counted on issues of importance to him.

Bad Seed (1954). Adapted from William

March's novel *The Bad Seed,* this play is an exciting account of a small girl who cold-bloodedly murders several people. This was Anderson's last Broadway success; he wrote several other plays that failed. His reputation, however, appears secure as one of the nation's top dozen serious dramatists. Although this final hit was pure thriller, most of Anderson's plays were rich thematically, always on the side of individuality, justice, and freedom.

PHILIP BARRY (1896–1949)

You and I (1923). Artistic ambitions and practical realities come into conflict. Barry's always-polished dialogue emerges here, as does his continuing theme of fulfillment in marriage. Barry was graduated from Yale and worked at the American Embassy in London at the very end of World War I. From there he went to Professor George Pierce Baker's famous playwriting class at Harvard and wrote this play, first titled *The Thing He Wanted to Do,* then titled *The Jilts.* The play was produced on Broadway while Barry was in Baker's course for a second year and established him as one of the nation's leading writers of the comedy of manners.

In a Garden (1925). A sophisticated depiction of a wife who has had life too neatly arranged for her by her onetime lover and her playwright-husband who has been dissecting her as a character.

Paris Bound (1927). A polished comedy about marital infidelity, an impending divorce between Jim and Mary Hutton, and a resolution affirming that the spiritual bond is more important than the physical in marriage. Barry, who gravitated to people of good birth and substantial means, became America's chronicler of the upper classes.

Holiday (1928). Another polished comedy and one of Barry's most famous; certainly this has been the most frequently revived of his plays. It concerns the rebellion of Linda, an upper-class girl, against her family's stuffy materialism. Johnny is engaged to her more conventional-minded sister, but Johnny and Linda end up together. We see Barry's concern, even in his light comedies, that people should be suited to each other. Barry's typical comedies of manners often centered around fancy homes meticulously furnished and almost-ceremonial meals. Barry was as fastidious a person as most of his characters.

Hotel Universe (1930). After a series of lighter plays, Barry wrote this philosophical, psychological, serious study of warped and self-defeated lives that acquire meaning and understanding during a long night of mystical experiences on the terrace of a Riviera villa. Barry wrote the drama without an intermission and made use of the technique of psychodrama to bare the characters' inner feelings; critics and the public were negative to the play. Throughout the rest of his career Barry succeeded with his polished comedies but tried on several occasions to write meaningful dramas primarily about religion and self-fulfillment.

Tomorrow and Tomorrow (1931). A popular comedy, this play is also a profound study of a wife's needs. Eva Redman, happily married but childless, bears a son by a psychologist who has come to visit. Years later he tries to win her, but she stays with her husband where her life has more meaning.

The Animal Kingdom (1932). Again, in this play, the emphasis is on the spiritual bond of true communication and honesty in marriage. Tom Collier leaves his mistress, marries, begins to lose his idealism and creativity, and ultimately returns to the mistress who is more truly his wife. Barry's message is at times down-played to the witty and polished comedy.

Here Come the Clowns (1938). This dramatization of a novel that Barry wrote puzzled public and critics because it was so different from his comedies. A symbolic drama, it was set in a café next to the Globe Theatre, and we see an assorted crew of vaudeville performers who begin to gain understandings about themselves through a series of psychodrama-like scenes. Dan Clancy, seeking God, thinks he finds him in the mysterious owner of the theatre, but finally realizes that God exists in mankind's free will.

The Philadelphia Story (1939). A polished high comedy of the socially elite, this popular success shows Tracy Lord about to marry a stuffed shirt. Tracy has a brief fling with a journalist sent to the family estate to cover the wedding, but she returns to her good-guy first husband, Dexter. The play starred Katharine Hepburn in a Theatre Guild production and was later made into an equally successful motion picture. Most critics consider this Barry's finest comedy of manners, and it has often been revived.

Without Love (1942). Jamie Coe Rowan, a widow, and Pat Jamieson, needing a house in Washington, D.C., agree to marry in order to hold down gossip as they plan to share her house in the overcrowded city. They do not plan to consummate the marriage, but love wins out.

Second Threshold (1951). Josiah Bolton, after a long career as a lawyer in public service, has lost his will to live; but his daughter Miranda saves him by threatening to kill herself if he kills himself. Bolton rediscovers love and meaning in life. Miranda breaks her engagement with a stuffy man and falls for a good young doctor; this portion of the play shows Barry's old skills in polished comedy. Barry had tinkered with this play for years; the motif of a close father-daughter relationship had haunted him for decades after his only daughter died as an infant. Barry's friend Robert Emmett Sherwood did the final revisions and polishings on this posthumous play. Although Barry said something thematically in his comedies and attempted several extremely serious plays, his reputation now seems secure as one of our top stylists in the comedy of manners.

JOHN HOWARD LAWSON (1894–   )

Roger Bloomer (1923). Lawson's first New York success after serving in Europe with the Volunteer Ambulance Corps during World War I and living for a time with the so-called Lost Generation Americans in Paris. This was the first successful expressionistic play on the American stage and is a psychological character study of a rebellious young man whose parents want him to be a conventional success. His girlfriend kills herself and he struggles, through a dream sequence, to understand the obsessions within him. From the beginnings of his playwriting career, Lawson indicted the American way of life.

Processional (1925). This expressionistic look at prejudices in modern life has been called Lawson's greatest play. Class war is dramatized through a coal strike in West Virginia, and Lawson gives the story of the angry workman Jim an almost upbeat ending in order to show his belief in the future of the proletariat. Most of Lawson's plays are angry protest documents, and he is one of the few writers who openly espoused Communism.

Loud Speaker (1927). This play also shows the problem of injustice in modern America. A politician running for the governorship of New York gets drunk, tells the voters in a radio speech to go to hell, but is elected. Lawson, always active on behalf of various causes, helped found several proletarian workers' theatre groups in New York City in the late 1920's, even before the Depression turned everyone's eyes toward protest theatre.

The International (1928). Another experimental mixture of Freud and Marx, with the strident themes overriding characterization. Lawson anticipated the Total Theatre movement of the 1960's by forty years. His plays, although stageworthy, are almost never done today because the themes are too shrill.

Success Story (1932). This was a Group Theatre success that was an exposé of corruption in the advertising world. Sol Ginsberg rises to success only to end up shot by the girl who loved him. For a while the Group Theatre looked on Lawson with strong favor because of his socially oriented work, but gradually he became even too leftist for them. Ironically, at the same time the Communist Party chided Lawson for not being leftist enough.

Marching Song (1937). An extremely leftist play, staged by the Theatre Union. Peter Russell, a blacklisted auto worker on strike, is evicted by a bank from his home and then takes up residence in an abandoned factory. Lawson published a book, *Theory and Technique of Playwriting,* in 1936, which remained in print for several decades and still contains many useful suggestions. He wrote several more plays that were less expressionistic and then became a successful Hollywood scriptwriter. Brought before the House Un-American Activities Committee in the McCarthy era, Lawson was imprisoned in 1950–51 for refusing to testify. Although put on the Hollywood blacklist, he wrote many films anonymously. Of all American writers Lawson remained the most openly leftist throughout his career.

GEORGE GERSHWIN (1898–1937)

Lady, Be Good (1924). Lyrics by his brother, Ira Gershwin. Book by Guy Bolton and Fred Thompson. Music by Gershwin. His first smash-hit musical comedy. The upper-crust Trevor family is dispossessed but regains its fortune at the finale. Gershwin's music was first heard on stage in the production *La La Lucille* in 1919.

Funny Face (1927). Music by Gershwin, lyrics by Ira Gershwin, book by Fred Thompson and Paul G. Schmidt. The heroine tries to get some hidden pearls from her guardian, while burglars have the same thing in mind. A musical, dancing romp starring Fred and Adele Astaire.

Rosalie (1928). Music by Gershwin and Sigmund Romberg, book by William Anthony McGuire and Guy Bolton, lyrics by P. G. Wodehouse and Ira Gershwin. Produced by Florenz Ziegfeld. Rosalie, the princess of Romanza, has a romance with Lieutenant Richard Fay of West Point.

Strike Up the Band (1930). Music by Gershwin, lyrics by Ira Gershwin, book by Morrie Ryskind and George S. Kaufman. An American chocolate tycoon, angered at Swiss competition, dreams he is general of an American Army in Switzerland, with much comic confusion.

Girl Crazy (1930). Music by Gershwin, lyrics by Ira Gershwin, book by Guy Bolton and

John McGowan. Danny's millionaire father sends him to Arizona in a taxi, for his health, where he starts a dude ranch and imports a Broadway chorus line. The show introduced Ethel Merman to Broadway audiences.

Of Thee I Sing (1931). Music by Gershwin, lyrics by Ira Gershwin, book by George S. Kaufman and Morrie Ryskind. A musical satire on how to win a Presidential election. Primarily a romp, it was nevertheless one of the first American musicals with any real thematic content; and it became the first musical to win the Pulitzer Prize for drama.

Porgy and Bess (1935). From Dubose and Dorothy Heyward's play *Porgy*. Music by Gershwin, lyrics by Ira Gershwin. Crippled Porgy kills the bully Crown, but Bess runs away. This was the pinnacle for the Gershwin brothers in their long history of writing Broadway musicals and popular songs. Many critics call it more an opera than a musical, and it has remained immensely popular, with a spectacular New York revival as recent as 1976. The Gershwins have contributed scores of undying melodies to American life.

SIDNEY HOWARD (1891–1939)

They Knew What They Wanted (1924). A good example of early realism, this play is set in the vineyards of California and combines powerful sexual jealousy with a comic view of life. Elderly Tony gets a wife, although her child is not his; Amy gets a husband, a child, and a home; and Joe the hired hand gets his freedom. Good sense prevails over old-style Sicilian justice. Sidney Howard, a Californian, was graduated from Berkeley, studied playwriting under George Pierce Baker at Harvard in 1915–16, was an ambulance driver overseas, and returned to the world of journalism. He had an earlier play, *Swords,* produced, but this was his first hit—and it had been turned down by sixteen producers before the Theatre Guild took it. It won the first Pulitzer Prize for any Theatre Guild production.

Lucky Sam McCarver (1925). A serious character study of a nightclub owner who falls for a society woman. They marry but cannot accept each other's worlds; after various troubles connected with a murder, Carlotta dies. After a number of early historical dramas, Howard made his name in the 1920's with a series of realistic plays.

Ned McCobb's Daughter (1926). A realistic character study of staunch, thirty-year-old Carrie, who lives in Maine and who survives her father's death, her husband's thefts and cheatings on her, and her brother-in-law's threats when she stands up to his bootlegging.

The Silver Cord (1926). A powerful Freudian drama of excessive mother love. Mrs. Phelps, long a widow, attempts to break up her son David's new marriage to scientist Christina, who threatens to leave David. Son Robert's fiancée, Hester, leaves Robert kneeling at his mother's side, where he will remain forever. David breaks away from his mother's pull at the last second. This play, although considerably overstated by today's standards, has long been considered Howard's most important achievement in realistic drama.

Half Gods (1929). A serious character study of Hope and Stephen, married eight years, and their struggles toward domestic tranquility.

The Late Christopher Bean (1932). An adaptation of the French play *Prenez garde à la peinture* by René Fauchois. Based in part on the life of painter Vincent Van Gogh, this play shows a doctor's family consumed with greed when they discover that some old paintings done by a now-dead patient, Christopher Bean, are worth a fortune. Their greed is thwarted, however, when their maid Amy turns out to be Bean's widow. Howard did a number of successful adaptations during his career.

Alien Corn (1933). Elsa Brandt, a piano teacher, is an artist in an unsympathetic, narrow-minded Western college town.

Yellow Jack (1934). An adaptation of a section of Paul de Kruif's book *Microbe Hunters,* which told about Walter Reed's work in the tropics. Dr. Finley and four brave soldiers prove the mosquito-transmitting theory about yellow fever by inoculating themselves with the new serum.

Dodsworth (1934). An adaptation of the 1929 novel of the same name by Sinclair Lewis, this is a satire on American business and a fine character study of a retired automotive manufacturer. Sam Dodsworth travels to Europe where his wife dallies with a young German; Sam finds more happiness with Mrs. Cartwright.

The Ghost of Yankee Doodle (1937). Howard was one of many American playwrights seriously concerned about the approaching World War. In this drama Sara Garrison, widow of a World War I aviator, refuses publisher James Clevenger because his newspapers are urging the United States to join the new war. Through most of his career, Howard was strongly interested in social realism. His plays did not break any new ground structurally, but his characterizations were almost always solid. Howard's career was cut short when a tractor on his farm rolled over and killed him.

The Most Happy Fella' (1956). Music, book, and lyrics by Frank Loesser. This musical, which won the New York Drama Critics Circle Award, was adapted from Sidney Howard's first big hit, *They Knew What They Wanted.*

GARLAND ANDERSON (1885–1939)

Appearances (1925). Although this play ran for only twenty-three performances in New York, it was noteworthy because it was the first full-length play written by a black man to be produced on Broadway. Anderson wrote it while working as a switchboard operator in a San Francisco hotel, and Al Jolson staked him to a year in New York City in order for Anderson to find a producer. It is a message play about how an inspired man can succeed in life. The play was later produced successfully in London, where Anderson moved and ran a restaurant. The first one-act play by a black writer on Broadway was *The Chip Woman's Fortune,* by Willis Richardson, done by the Ethiopian Art Theatre on May 7, 1923,

as a curtain-raiser to Oscar Wilde's *Salomé.* Richardson's play was a folk drama about Silas, who fails to pay installments on his victrola, and Aunt Nancy who digs up her money from the backyard. The play ends with everyone dancing to a jazz record. The first black theatre in the New York area was the African Grove Company, in Greenwich Village in 1821, but it was soon closed down by the city. The first black playwright in the nation was William Wells Brown, who wrote *The Escape, or, a Leap to Freedom* in 1858.

VINCENT YOUMANS (1899–1946)

No! No! Nanette! (1925). Music by Youmans, lyrics by Irving Caesar and Otto Harbach, book by Harbach and Frank Mandel. Billy Early, a publisher of Bibles, has a weakness for pretty girls, but his wife discovers him. The hit songs include "I Want to Be Happy" and "Tea for Two." The show was revived with spectacular success in 1971 for a two-year run and a triumphant national tour at the time when the nation was in a nostalgia craze. Ruby Keeler played in the revival; she had been one of the top stars in musical comedy in the 1920's and 1930's.

Hit the Deck (1927). Music by Youmans, lyrics by Leo Robin and Clifford Gray, book by Herbert Fields, and adapted from the play *Shore Leave.* Coffeeshop waitress LouLou falls for Bilge, a sailor; when LouLou inherits a fortune, Bilge doesn't want to live on her money, so she wills it to their first child. Youmans wrote the music for a large number of other hit Broadway shows, then went on to a long Hollywood career.

JEROME KERN (1885–1945)

Sunny (1925). Music by Kern, lyrics by Oscar Hammerstein II, book by Otto Harbach. A tuneful musical in which an English girl circus rider stows away on a ship to follow an American she met in Paris. She becomes a successful singer and dancer. Among the hit songs in the show is "Who Stole My Heart Away?" Kern, a great songwriter in the days of New York's Tin Pan Alley, was involved in dozens of Broadway shows dating as early as 1912, when he wrote the score for *The Red Petticoat*. A native New Yorker, Kern wrote music for shows in his public school, studied music, then became a song plugger before making it to Broadway. One of his earliest shows, *Very Good, Eddie,* from 1915, was revived for a long run in New York in 1975 and in London in 1976.

Show Boat (1927). Music by Kern, book and lyrics by Oscar Hammerstein II, from the novel by Edna Ferber (1887–1968). This was the first almost-serious musical on the American stage, and it is a landmark in the genre. Verging toward opera, this musical tells of Cap'n Andy and his wife, on the Cotton Blossom Showboat, and their troubles in bringing up their daughter Magnolia, who marries actor Gaylord Ravenal. All ends well after strong threats of disaster. The play has one of the most memorable scores in American theatre, including such longtime popular favorites as "Ole Man River," "Only Make Believe," and many others.

The Cat and the Fiddle (1931). Music by Kern, book and lyrics by Otto Harbach. Two American music students in Brussels tangle over the composition of an opera, but love wins out. Among the hit songs were "She Didn't Say Yes, She Didn't Say No," and "The Night Was Made for Love."

Music in the Air (1932). Music by Kern, book and lyrics by Oscar Hammerstein II. Three people from the little village of Edendorf go to Munich to get a song, "I've Told Every Little Star," published; before all the complications are unraveled, they are happy to return to the simple village.

Roberta (1933). Music by Kern, book by Otto Harbach, from a novel by Alice Overmiller. Athletic John Kent inherits his aunt's Parisian modiste shop and marries the shop's assistant, Stephanie, who is really a Russian princess. The plots of the American musicals of the 1920's and 1930's were almost always trite, but the music of that era has survived strongly. Top songs in this particular show include "Lovely to Look At" and the ever-popular "Smoke Gets in Your Eyes." Jerome Kern also wrote the scores for numerous motion pictures.

DAN TOTHEROH (1894–1977)

Wild Birds (1925). A bit dated today, a bit black and white, a bit melodramatic, but a powerful example of the regional folk play. Cruel farm owner John Slag kills his young hired man and drives his young hired girl to suicide after their love is discovered. The stern quality of Western prairie life is shown. The play won a contest at the University of California before its New York production. Totheroh later wrote a number of other regional plays about California life, wrote film scripts, and eventually became a drama professor at the University of California.

GEORGE ABBOTT (1887–   )

The Fall Guy (1925). Written with James Gleason. A comedy about a young husband, a sucker to some crooks, who finally catches them for the cops. Abbott studied under George Pierce Baker at Harvard University; since then he has been an actor, director, playwright, producer, and most of all, a collaborator and play-doctor for more than half a century after his first stage appearance in 1913.

Broadway (1926). With Philip Dunning. This is a comedy-melodrama set in a speakeasy, with a romance between two hoofers against a background of gangster warfare. This was one of his big early hits and is typical of his best work in its fast-paced comedy of urban life.

Coquette (1927). With Ann Bridgers, a young actress from the South who suggested the plot to Abbott. This is a serious drama of a Southern belle who shoots herself, after her father has shot her lover, in order to save her father embarrassment over her pregnancy at his trial for murder.

Three Men on a Horse (1935). With John Cecil Holm. A slapstick comedy about a little man, Erwin Trowbridge, who writes meek greeting-card verse and who becomes involved with gamblers and gangsters when they think he has the power to pick winners in horse races. The play has been done often in amateur theatre and was revived for a second long New York run in 1969–70.

On Your Toes (1936). Music by Richard Rodgers, lyrics by Lorenz Hart, book by Rodgers, Hart, and Abbott. This was the first musical to make use of serious, artistic dance in the American theatre; and famed ballet creator George Balanchine did the choreography, most notably the "Slaughter on Tenth Avenue" ballet. Phil Dolan, son of two vaudeville hoofers, spurns his girl, Frankie, and yearns for a ballet career and the hand of Russian ballerina Vera. Phil saves the Russian company when a friend of his brings in the "Slaughter" ballet, and Phil finally returns to Frankie.

The Boys from Syracuse (1938). Music by Richard Rodgers, lyrics by Lorenz Hart, book by Abbott. This romp was based upon Shakespeare's *The Comedy of Errors,* which in turn was based upon Plautus' Roman comedy *The Twin Menaechmi.* It is a farce about mistaken identities using many of the oldest devices in the history of comedy. A great many of the aspects of farce are almost two thousand years old.

Where's Charley? (1948). Music and lyrics by Frank Loesser, book by Abbott, from the old British farce by Brandon Thomas, *Charlie's Aunt.* Another romping musical farce with some college boys disguising a man as a visiting aunt in order to be able to invite some girls to their party. From the time the play was first produced in 1892 until the present, the play and the musical have been revived and staged virtually everywhere.

The Pajama Game (1954). Music and lyrics by Richard Adler and Jerry Ross, book by Abbott, from the novel *Seven and a Half Cents* by Richard Bissell. A romance in a labor-torn pajama factory. One of the fascinating anecdotes about the Broadway run sounds like a typical George Abbott plot: when one of the leads became ill, understudy Shirley Maclaine went on, succeeded brilliantly, and headed toward stardom.

Damn Yankees (1955). Music and lyrics by Richard Adler and Jerry Ross, book by Abbott, from the novel *The Year the Yankees Lost the Pennant* by Douglass Wallop. A Faust-like story in which supernatural assistance enables the lowly Washington Senators baseball team to beat the high-and-mighty New York Yankees.

Fiorello! (1959). Music by Jerry Bock, lyrics by Sheldon Harnick, book by Abbott and Jerome Weidman. A musical biography of Fiorello H. La Guardia, the famous mayor of New York City from 1934 to 1945. The prologue shows La Guardia reading the comics over the radio to children during a newspaper strike; the show then flashes back to his early career as a lawyer interested in the plight of the poor, his election as the first Republican in Congress from New York's 14th district, his loss in the mayoralty race against Jimmy Walker, and finally his victory and personal ups and downs. The show won a Pulitzer Prize, the New York Drama Critics Circle Award, and the Tony Award and ran for 795 performances.

Tenderloin (1961). Music by Jerry Bock, lyrics by Sheldon Harnick, book by Abbott and Jerome Weidman, based on a novel by Samuel Hopkins Adams. A musical about a clergyman crusading against sin in New York City around the turn of the century. George Abbott's interesting autobiography, *Mister Abbott,* was published in 1963. He remained active in theatre well into his eighties, being perhaps the oldest participant in 20th-century show business.

JOHN VAN DRUTEN (1901–57)
Young Woodley (1925). The story of an adolescent schoolboy and an English schoolmaster's wife, this play was denied a license in Great Britain and was first staged in New York. The play anticipates Robert Anderson's *Tea and Sympathy* and is not at all shocking today. Van Druten, born in England and a law student in London, came to the United States to stay in the 1930's and became a citizen in 1944. Most of his writing career was spent in New York City.

There's Always Juliet (1932). Leonora, an English girl, and Dwight, a young American, meet at a party in England two days before his scheduled return to the United States. The rapid courtship appears hopeless, but a sudden change of plans allows them to meet again and to become engaged. Van Druten earned a solid reputation as a writer of polished comedies.

The Distaff Side (1934). British widow Evie quietly steers her daughter Alex to the right man, cares for her crotchety old mother, doesn't interfere as sister Liz makes a sensible choice of a man, and turns down a proposal for her own hand. This play contains several excellent characterizations in differing feminine attitudes toward fulfillment in life.

Old Acquaintance (1940). The plot shows the stresses on the lifelong friendship between unmarried, forty-two-year-old serious novelist Kit Markham, and popular novelist Millie Drake. Kit loses her thirty-year-old lover to Millie's daughter. The theme is that old friendship is important and necessary, even in widely different types of people. The play contains fine characterizations, is highly polished, and has not dated much over the decades.

The Damask Cheek (1942). Coauthored with Lloyd Morris. Rhoda, a plain, demure English girl of thirty, visits her snobbish aunt in New York City and wins her cousin Jimmy away from his actress-fiancée when Rhoda humanizes herself in the nick of time for a happy ending.

The Voice of the Turtle (1943). A three-character comedy of love in wartime. Sally wins Olive's soldier-lover away from her. Considered daring at the time because of its sophisticated approach to sex, the play is now a very tame and conventionally pleasant comedy.

I Remember Mama (1944). A nostalgic dramatization of Kathryn Forbes' novel *Mama's Bank Account*. A Norwegian immigrant family goes through assorted tribulations as Mama looks after her children. Extremely popular play.

The Druid Circle (1947). One of Van Druten's few serious plays, this shows the dull, narrow life of a headmaster at a run-down college on the Welsh border in the 1920's. The headmaster, filled with complexes, dislikes young people and almost ruins a love between two students. Earlier in his life, Van Druten taught law for a time at a college in Wales.

Bell, Book, and Candle (1950). An extremely popular polished comedy, this is the story of Gillian Holroyd, a lovely young witch who falls in love with Shep, a young publisher living in her apartment building. By falling in love, Gillian loses her supernatural powers but wins her man and her humanity. This motif of a witch treated comically has been used on television in subsequent decades, after Van Druten's original idea.

I Am a Camera (1951). Based upon British author Christopher Isherwood's *Goodbye to Berlin* (1939) short stories, this is one of Van Druten's few serious plays, and it is an excellent dramatization of the hedonistic life in Germany just as the Nazis began coming to power. Young Isherwood falls for Sally Bowles, but they go their separate ways, with Isherwood later to understand the meaning of all that has happened to him. Later transformed into a superb musical (*see* next entry).

Cabaret (1966). Music by John Kander, lyrics by Fred Ebb, book by Joe Masteroff, from Van Druten's play, above. The authors of the musical sandwiched Van Druten's story of Sally Bowles into a series of decadent nightclub scenes that heightened the several themes of refusing to care about people and fiddling life away while Rome burns. The catchy score was enriched still more by the masterful acting of Joel Grey as the master of ceremonies. It won the New York Drama Critics Circle Award for best musical, 1966–67, and was later made into a film.

RICHARD RODGERS (1902–)

The Girl Friend (1926). Music by Rodgers, lyrics by Lorenz Hart, book by Herbert Fields. This was just one of a long series of musical collaborations with Hart, who died in 1945. Their first show together was *Poor Little Ritz Girl* in 1920, and the first show Rodgers worked on was *One Minute, Please* in 1917. For well over a decade Rodgers and Hart formed one of the greatest teams in the history of musical theatre. In this particular play, Mollie, the daughter of a six-day bicycle racer, helps train young Leonard; gamblers try to interfere with a big race, but Leonard wins and remains true to Mollie.

A Connecticut Yankee (1927). Music by Rodgers, lyrics by Lorenz Hart, book by Herbert Fields, from the novel by Mark Twain. Martin is hit on the head by a bottle at his bachelor party and dreams that he brings about the industrial revolution at King Arthur's court.

Jumbo (1935). Music by Rodgers, lyrics by Lorenz Hart, book by Charles MacArthur and Ben Hecht. Produced by Billy Rose, with the Paul Whiteman orchestra. This was actually a circus performance, with a number of vaudeville acts, staged at the Hippodrome Theatre in New York City. The plot line was minimal, but the "show biz" was spectacular.

On Your Toes (1936). Music by Rodgers, lyrics by Lorenz Hart, book by Rodgers, Hart, and George Abbott. This was the first musical to make use of serious, artistic dance in the American theatre; and famed ballet creator George Balanchine did the choreography, most notably the "Slaughter on Tenth Avenue" ballet. Phil Dolan, son of two vaudeville hoofers, spurns his girl, Frankie, and yearns for a ballet career and the hand of Russian ballerina Vera. Phil saves the Russian company when a friend of his brings in the "Slaughter" ballet, and Phil finally returns to Frankie.

Babes in Arms (1937). Music by Rodgers, lyrics by Lorenz Hart, book by George Oppenheimer. The teenage children of touring vaudevillians produce a show. Many musicals in the 1920's and 1930's used show business for their settings—usually a heavily romanticized view.

The Boys from Syracuse (1938). Music by Rodgers, lyrics by Lorenz Hart, book by George Abbott. This romp was based on

Shakespeare's *The Comedy of Errors,* which in turn was based upon Plautus' Roman comedy *The Twin Menaechmi.* It is a farce about mistaken identities using many of the oldest devices in the history of comedy. A great many of the aspects of farce are almost two thousand years old.

Pal Joey (1940). Music by Rodgers, lyrics by Lorenz Hart, book by John O'Hara, from the novel by O'Hara. This was the first anti-hero musical, about a small-time male singer who never makes it big. The show won the New York Drama Critics Circle Award for best musical in 1951–52, when it was a hit revival. The critics were so impressed that they ignored their own constitution, which forbade them to vote for a revival. As the American musical continued to evolve, gradually an occasional more serious and believable story line evolved.

Oklahoma! (1943). This musical is important for several reasons. For one, after the long and fruitful collaboration between Rodgers and Hart, the new and even more creative collaboration between Rodgers (music) and Oscar Hammerstein II (book and lyrics) began here. The Theatre Guild brought the two artists together, and the partnership produced some of the greatest musicals in world theatre history. This show is also important because, by critical consensus, it is the first fully mature musical on our stage, integrating music more believably into the plot, using dance very creatively, and telling a story that is not all syrup. Curley's problems in winning Laurey include the stabbing of Jud Fry. The musical remains extremely faithful to Lynn Riggs' original script for *Green Grow the Lilacs,* and many of the songs stemmed from phrases and lines in the original dialogue.

Carousel (1945). Music by Rodgers, book and lyrics by Oscar Hammerstein II, from Ferenc Molnar's European play *Liliom.* The story is transplanted from central Europe to the coast of Maine. Ne'er-do-well carnival barker Billy Bigelow is killed and watches his family's loyalty from his vantage point in heaven. Although heavily sentimental, this show is another good example of the serious

Oscar Hammerstein II

musical that was not afraid to move away from the constant gaiety of the earlier musical comedies; it won the New York Drama Critics Circle Award for best musical of 1945–46.

Allegro (1947). Music by Rodgers, book and lyrics by Oscar Hammerstein II. Another serious musical in which Joe Taylor, son of a country doctor, marries his sweetheart, who wheedles him into a big-city practice. Joe discovers that she is having an affair, and he refuses to head up a big-name hospital in order to return to his father's country practice. His loyal young nurse follows him.

South Pacific (1949). Music by Rodgers, book and lyrics by Oscar Hammerstein II, some help on the book by Joshua Logan, from James Michener's *Tales of the South Pacific*. Nurse Nellie Forbush learns to overcome prejudice, and French expatriate Emile de Becque overcomes his isolationism as the tide of fortune changes in World War II. A great many of the newer musicals have been adapted from books or earlier plays. This highly popular show won the New York Drama Critics Circle Award for best musical of 1948–49.

The King and I (1951). Music by Rodgers, book and lyrics by Oscar Hammerstein II, adapted from the book *Anna and the King of Siam* by Margaret Landon. An English tutor goes to Siam to teach the king's children but falls in love with him. They match wits but do not marry. This was also made into a popular film, as have been most of the postwar hit musicals.

Flower Drum Song (1959). Music by Rodgers, book and lyrics by Oscar Hammerstein II. Joseph Fields also helped with the book. A story about generation gap and Oriental-American culture gap in San Francisco's Chinatown. From the novel by C. Y. Lee.

The Sound of Music (1959). Music by Rodgers, lyrics by Oscar Hammerstein II, book by Howard Lindsay and Russel Crouse. The true story of the Trapp family, with a few romantic embellishments, as they become a singing group and escape from the Nazis. Maria the governess wins the stern Captain Trapp away

from his fiancée and his old ways. This musical, which perhaps shares with *My Fair Lady, Oklahoma!,* and *Show Boat* the honor of having the most all-time hit songs in its score, ran for four years on Broadway before the film version became a then-all-time money-maker.

No Strings (1962). Music by Rodgers, book by Samuel Taylor. An experimental musical, with only brass, woodwinds, and percussion in an orchestra that was hidden behind the stage and had its music piped out to the spectators through a sound system. The plot is about a love affair that must end in order for the leading man to remain creative in his work. Richard Rodgers has remained active long after the death of Oscar Hammerstein II, and he gradually has evolved somewhat nostalgically into the grand old man of musical theatre; but his most important works were done with Lorenz Hart and Hammerstein.

OSCAR HAMMERSTEIN II (1895–1960)
(Shows done with composers other than Richard Rodgers)

Rose Marie (1924). Music by Rudolph Friml, lyrics by Hammerstein, book by Otto Harbach and Herbert Stothart. This was Hammerstein's first major Broadway collaboration. Canadian Rose-Marie LaFlamme has to promise to marry the villain in order to save her loved one, Jim Kenyon, accused of murdering an Indian. All ends happily. Hammerstein worked successfully with a number of composers, but his greatest successes came with Richard Rodgers (*see* above entry). Hammerstein's first New York show was *Always You* in 1920.

Sunny (1925). Music by Jerome Kern, lyrics by Hammerstein, book by Otto Harbach. A tuneful musical in which an English girl circus rider stows away on a ship to follow an American she met in Paris. She becomes a successful singer and dancer. Among the hit songs in the show is "Who Stole My Heart Away?"

The Desert Song (1926). Music by Jerome Kern, lyrics by Hammerstein, book by Otto Harbach and Frank Mandel. Pierre, defending the Riff Tribe in north Africa from cruelties of his own commanding officer, has to contend with his own father; he also kidnaps and wins his love, Margot.

Show Boat (1927). Music by Jerome Kern, book and lyrics by Hammerstein, from the novel by Edna Ferber (1887–1968). This was the first almost-serious musical on the American stage, and it is a landmark in the genre. Verging toward opera, this musical tells of Cap'n Andy and his wife, on the Cotton Blossom Showboat, and their troubles in bringing up their daughter, Magnolia, who marries actor Gaylord Ravenal. All ends well after strong threats of disaster. The play has one of the most memorable scores in American theatre, including such longtime favorites as "Ole Man River," "Only Make Believe," and many others.

The New Moon (1928). Music by Sigmund Romberg, lyrics by Hammerstein, book by Frank Mandel and Laurence Schwab. Robert, a bondman in New Orleans in 1788, loves the daughter of his owner. On a ship heading back to Paris to be tried on an old charge, Robert leads a revolt of bondmen who form their own republic. Robert finally wins Marianne.

Music in the Air (1932). Music by Jerome Kern, book and lyrics by Hammerstein. Three people from the little village of Edendorf go to Munich to get a song, "I've Told Every Little Star," published; before all the complications are unraveled, they are happy to return to the simple village. Hammerstein was the third generation of successful New York theatre people. His grandfather, Oscar Hammerstein I, emigrated from Germany and ran the Manhattan Opera House; his father, Arthur, was a producer whose most notable successes included *The Firefly* and *Rose Marie*. Oscar Hammerstein II was born in New York City, educated at Columbia University, and spent his entire career as a librettist for Broadway musicals. His reputation is secure as one of the outstanding creative minds in American musical theatre.

PAUL GREEN (1894–   )

In Abraham's Bosom (1926). Abraham McCranie, the mulatto son of Colonel McCranie, tries to rise above being a field hand, educates

himself, and struggles for decades to educate fellow blacks. Poor whites beat him, and he kills his jeering half-brother. A powerful Pulitzer Prize-winning drama of the plight of black people in the Southeast. Paul Green said years later that the genesis of this play was an incident he saw as a young boy: a white railroad engineer slashed open the face of a polite black man who dared to ask him a question. Green said, "The school teacher of that spring morning . . . still lives . . . a bad scar still shows on his face . . . and there must be a scar in his heart, too. There is in mine, and always will be."

The Field God (1927). A rural tragedy somewhat in the O'Neill vein. Farmer Hardy Gilchrist and Rhoda, his second wife, have to make their peace with God for their earlier love affair, which led to the death of the first wife, before their farm will prosper again. Paul Green grew up on a farm in eastern North Carolina, won a playwriting contest with his first effort, became disillusioned with war while serving as an enlisted man in France, then returned to the University of North Carolina to study under Professor Frederick Koch, recently arrived from North Dakota. Koch fostered an entire school of regional playwriting at North Carolina, and Green is the biggest name to come from that program.

White Dresses (1928). A powerful one-act play about continuing sex-love tragedies between blacks and whites in the South, with old Granny, a black, convincing her granddaughter Mary that she can't marry the son of their white landlord because he is Mary's half-brother. Mary must remain trapped in her sharecropper-servant poverty existence.

The House of Connelly (1931). A powerful drama of decadent Southern culture. The Connelly family wants to marry spineless Will to a wealthy aristocrat to save the family fortunes; but he marries Patsy Tate, a poor white tenant-farm girl, and together they struggle to attain inner and outer success. Paul Green is one of the nation's greatest regional playwrights, and he did get a good hearing on Broadway despite New York's usual aversion to regional plays. This was one of the Group Theatre's earliest productions.

Roll, Sweet Chariot (1934). This was Green's first play to use music, as he began moving gradually toward his later specialty, symphonic drama. The play puzzled audiences and closed quickly. A black shantytown is destroyed in order for a road to go through, and several of the inhabitants either end up on the chain gang making the road or are killed. At a time when black writers were not turning out plays because their works were not welcomed on Broadway, Paul Green was one of the only honest spokesmen among the white race to tell the plight of blacks in the United States.

Shroud My Body Down (1935). A fascinating theatrical account of the control that religious superstition and fanaticism can have on poorly educated whites in the Deep South.

Hymn to the Rising Sun (1936). A one-act tragedy of life on a Southern chain gang: Runt, a convict locked in the sweat box, a tiny torture chamber, dies as the other prisoners awake to the morning of July 4. This is a powerful combination of social protest, characterization, and poetic power; many call it the finest one-act play in American history. Premiered by the "Let Freedom Ring" Actors Troupe of the Civic Repertory Theatre, New York City.

Johnny Johnson (1936). This is a tragicomic history of a homespun American idealist who enlists in World War I at his girl's urging and who attempts to stop the war. Johnny, the only sane person in the play, is put into an asylum; later, at home, he sells trinkets on street corners and is considered a freak. The staging was partly expressionistic, and Kurt Weill supplied a considerable amount of music, as Green sought to fuse drama and music in serious theatre.

The Lost Colony (1937). With this work, Green moved into the form he has called symphonic drama: outdoor pageants, reflecting the history of a particular region, with music and dance. This work is produced every sum-

mer on Roanoke Island, North Carolina, and tells of Sir Walter Raleigh's ill-fated colony and how Governor White found it abandoned when he returned from England.

Native Son (1941). Written with black novelist Richard Wright, this is a problem drama of blacks trying to exist in the big-city slums. A young man in Chicago is frightened into killing a white woman and is later executed.

The Common Glory (1947). Thomas Jefferson struggles to establish a democracy in this historical pageant produced annually at Jamestown. Green may well have had more viewers than any other 20th-century playwright, with the large number of his symphonic dramas being produced every summer in various parts of the nation.

Texas (1966). One of the more recent of Green's symphonic dramas, this pageant is produced annually in Palo Duro Canyon, just outside of Amarillo, Texas, and is directed by Professor William Moore of West Texas State University, who helped get the pageant started. Young farmer Calvin Armstrong wins out over the arid land of the Panhandle and the stubborn old cattle baron, Uncle Henry, who finally sees the need for progress. Green has written several other outdoor pageant-dramas for other historic parts of the nation. Green's niche is secure as the originator of the historical pageant-drama, and even more, as one of the most honest portrayers of the difficult life facing both blacks and poor whites in the South.

DUBOSE (1885–1940) and DOROTHY HEYWARD (1890–1961)

Porgy (1927). Crippled Porgy, living on Catfish Row in the black section of Charleston, kills the bully Crown, but Bess runs away, leaving Porgy alone and lonely. The Heywards, both white, specialized in writing about black life in the Carolinas and had a keen ear for regional dialects. This was an important folk play and the greatest achievement for the Heywards. DuBose wrote it first as a novel.

Porgy and Bess (1935). Music by George

Gershwin, lyrics by Ira Gershwin, from the Heywards' play, above. This was the pinnacle for the Gershwin brothers; many critics call it more an opera than a musical, and it has remained immensely popular, with a spectacular New York revival as recently as 1976.

Mamba's Daughters (1939). The tragic story of Hagar, a black woman from Charleston, and her vain efforts to escape calamities in life. The production starred Ethel Waters. DuBose also wrote this as a novel first, and Dorothy adapted it for the stage. DuBose grew up in Charleston, but Dorothy was an Ohioan who studied playwriting at Harvard. DuBose actually worked as a laborer on the Charleston docks and mastered the Gullah dialect. He was a well-known poet as well as novelist and playwright.

Set My People Free (1948). This was by Dorothy Heyward and is a historical drama of a slave rebellion in 1822 led by Denmark Vesey, first an African prince and then a slave from age fourteen in Charleston.

S. N. BEHRMAN (1893–1973)

The Second Man (1927). A sophisticated high comedy. Clark Storey is a dilettante writer whose "second man" is his comfort-loving, idealless alter ego. His finally persuades his wealthy mistress to marry him, despite his limitations. Behrman, from Massachusetts, studied playwriting under Professor George Pierce Baker at Harvard, and from his earliest years he aspired to a career in the theatre. From the late 1920's until just before World War II, Behrman wrote a series of sophisticated comedies that almost always contained rich thematic content.

Meteor (1929). Egotistical genius Rafael Lord marries and becomes a millionaire in five years; but when his wife leaves him and failure threatens, he decides he has depended too much on his genius and not enough on his mind.

Biography (1932). Richard Kurt, an intense young journalist, comes to painter Marian Froude to do her biography. When a former lover of hers threatens Richard if he publishes

the information, Richard and Marian realize they love each other. Marian, however, finally destroys the manuscript, and they conclude that they are not destined to be happy together. Behrman contrasts too much tolerance in Marian and too much intense righteousness in Richard. The play, which has some echoes of Molière's *The Misanthrope,* has often been called Behrman's greatest achievement.

Rain from Heaven (1934). Five diverse guests from different countries and backgrounds express their opinions on many social and political evils, including Naziism and race prejudice, at a house party. With the Depression at hand and World War II on the horizon, Behrman almost always showed some sort of humanitarian concerns in his comedies.

End of Summer (1936). A high comedy with serious overtones, this play shows the futility and distress of an idle rich woman, Leonie, and her daughter's search for a purposeful life. Paula, the daughter, breaks up her mother's hoped-for affair with a callous doctor and leaves home to marry a poor young writer.

Amphitryon 38 (1937). Adapted from an earlier comedy by the French playwright Jean Giraudoux and based originally on Plautus' Roman farce *Amphitryon.* A comedy of mistaken identities. As Behrman's career moved along, he began turning increasingly to adaptations that were well done and often successful on Broadway.

Wine of Choice (1938). A proletarian writer finds his sense of humanity warped by hatred; the traditional values must win out, he discovers, in this drawing-room comedy in which Behrman once again definitely states his humanitarian concerns.

No Time for Comedy (1939). Comic playwright Gaylord Easterbook, fretting because his works do not have enough relevance in an increasingly war-torn world, undergoes a marital crisis because of his inner turmoil; he is finally convinced that a comedy about what he has just gone through will, indeed, have something to offer thinking people. This was presumably extremely autobiographical in spirit; Behrman was exceedingly facile as a writer of comedy and often worried that his plays were not serious enough.

Jacobowsky and the Colonel (1944). Adapted from a European play by Franz Werfel, whose own postwar version was more serious than Behrman's version. Jacobowsky, a Polish Jew, and an anti-Semitic Polish soldier make their way through terrorizing and farcical adventures in escaping from the Nazis. The soldier becomes a larger human being from the close contact with Jacobowsky, who knows what it is to endure endless privation and suffering.

Jane (1947). Another high comedy, from a Somerset Maugham story, this opened first in London, then came to New York in 1952. It is the account of an eccentric but lovable woman who loses her dowdiness in a short marriage to a young architect and finally wins an elderly publisher who has long professed to dislike her.

I Know My Love (1949). Adapted from the French play, *Auprès de Ma Blonde* by Marcel Achard. A polished bittersweet comedy written for the 25th anniversary of Alfred Lunt and Lynne Fontanne as an acting team. We see the enduring richness of the love between Thomas and Emily Chanler, beginning with their 50th anniversary in 1939, then flashing back to 1888, 1902, 1918 and 1920. Thomas has always wanted adventure, and this causes several familial crises, but he finds the greatest adventure at home with Emily. The generations before and after them are shown as much less sympathetic people.

Fanny (1954). Music and lyrics by Harold Rome, book by Joshua Logan and Behrman, from plays by Marcel Pagnol. A sentimental musical set in Marseilles, bringing the romantic call of the sea in conflict with the call of love.

The Cold Wind and the Warm (1958). An autobiographical play adapted from a series of sketches he wrote for *The New Yorker* magazine about his boyhood in Massachusetts.

Lord Pengo (1962). Behrman used his own prose work *The Days of Duveen* as the basis for this play about an eccentric but charming art dealer.

But for Whom, Charlie (1964). A cynical comedy about writers and philanthropic foundations, this unsuccessful play was part of the first season at the Lincoln Center for the Performing Arts in New York City.

The Burning Glass (1968). Behrman's final play. In all, he wrote more than thirty plays, a number of film scripts, and also a biography of Max Beerbohm. His major decade was the 1930's, when his polished comedies delighted audiences but at the same time caused them to think.

ROBERT EMMETT SHERWOOD (1896–1955)

The Road to Rome (1927). An antiwar comedy, with a Roman woman stopping the invasion of the empire by arousing Hannibal sexually. Sherwood, a New Yorker and graduate of Harvard, was denied enlistment in the American military forces because of his height (6'7"), joined the Canadian Black Watch, and was wounded on the Western Front. This experience helped color his views for many years. He became one of the nation's first film reviewers for *Life* magazine, but resigned his associate editorship when he felt his work with the Democratic Party precluded objectivity on his part as an editor. He then turned to playwriting and became an immense success on Broadway. His plays were almost always highly entertaining yet contained important social theses.

Reunion in Vienna (1931). A play about breaking with the past, using old Vienna society as the background. Rudolph, the exiled Hapsburg prince, finally sees his past for what it is, thanks to the efforts of a young psychiatrist, who convinces Rudolph that he cannot regain the love of the psychiatrist's wife who was once Rudolph's mistress. Sherwood traveled widely in Europe, and his foreign-based plays are authentically set.

The Petrified Forest (1935). Duke Mantee, a gangster, and Mr. Squire, an itinerant romanticist, both meet death at an isolated gas station in the Arizona desert. Although realistic in staging, this play symbolically shows the suicidal impulse in civilization with the conflict between the "apes" (bullies of the world) and the humans. Sherwood was seriously concerned about the growth of totalitarianism in the world in the 1930's.

Idiot's Delight (1936). A group of people are trapped in a run-down inn on the Italian-Austrian border as war breaks out. Hoofer and vaudeville troupe leader Harry Van recognizes Irene, posing as a Russian princess, as a carnival woman he once spent a night with in a cheap hotel in the American Midwest. Most of the other visitors escape, but Harry and Irene remain together as the bombs begin to fall. Sherwood once said of his own writing, "The trouble with me is that I start out with a big message and end up with nothing but good entertainment." The entertainment is there, true; but this play, winner of a Pulitzer Prize, is one of the most powerful antiwar plays written and was almost uncanny in its assessment of the global situation. Two days after the premiere of the play, Hitler's armies occupied the Rhineland; and one London newspaper said, "The play must have been written over the weekend." The production starred Alfred Lunt and Lynne Fontanne.

Tovarich (1936). An adaptation from a European play by Jacques Deval. A comedy that spoofs class distinctions and the Russian Revolution. Grand Duchess Tatiana and Prince Mikail serve as maid and butler in a French household. This was a tremendous money-maker on both stage and screen; and Sherwood, always interested in the plight of people in trouble, gave most of the royalties as aid to Great Britain when that nation faced the oncoming World War II. Sherwood gave a great deal of his large income to war-related charities. He also wrote several dozen major film scripts.

Abe Lincoln in Illinois (1938). Sherwood's second Pulitzer Prize-winner and the first play to bypass the stranglehold that producers held on Broadway, because Sherwood helped found the Playwrights Company, an organization of writers who produced their own plays. This play shows Lincoln's years before the Presidency and how Lincoln accepts, against his will, a career that brings on more and more responsibility. Entertaining at all times, the play is also an extremely strong statement about political responsibility in times of crisis, and it is one of our top dramas. Sherwood practiced what he preached, because he spent a great deal of his time working for his country. He wrote many of the famous Fireside Chats, the radio speeches that President Franklin D. Roosevelt delivered to the nation as it struggled out of the Depression but slid steadily into the grip of World War II.

There Shall Be No Night (1940). Winner of Sherwood's third Pulitzer Prize for drama. A powerful drama of a peace-loving scientist, Dr. Valkonen, living in Finland, who realizes that much as he hates war, he must stand up and fight for his freedom. Sherwood later did an adaptation set in Greece, to mirror conditions there, too. Sherwood gave much of the royalties from this production to Finnish War Relief. During World War II Sherwood worked as director of the overseas branch of the Office of War Information and was a fine example of a writer-statesman. After the war, Sherwood won a fourth Pulitzer Prize, this time for biography, with his book *Roosevelt and Hopkins: an Intimate Biography*. His many efforts during the war burned him out creatively and increased his difficulties with a painful facial ailment. He wrote several other plays, none of them as great as those listed above. In all, he wrote more than fifteen plays and several dozen films, and he still ranks as one of our most important modern dramatists.

SOPHIE TREADWELL (1890–1970)

Machinal (1928). This is a stylized, partly expressionistic treatment of a woman office worker who, although bored with her boss, marries him, kills him, and is executed. Most of the characters are not named, in order to make the play a more universal damnation of mechanized modern life. Miss Treadwell, of Spanish-American descent, was a Californian who had several other plays produced, none as successful as this. Earlier, she had been the nation's first female war correspondent as part of a successful journalistic career.

BEN HECHT (1896–1964)
and CHARLES MacARTHUR (1895–1956)

The Front Page (1928). Originally intended as an exposé of Chicago newspaper life, the play ends up rather nostalgically. In a combination of wild farce and tense melodrama, hard-boiled veteran reporter Hildy Johnson is about to quit and get married; but when a convict escapes, Hildy saves him from death. Although Hildy goes off with his fiancée, his boss has ordered him arrested on the railroad train, and the audience knows that Hildy will return to his job. Revived successfully in New York in 1969 and superbly at the Old Vic in London in 1972. Hecht and MacArthur both were Chicago journalists early in their careers. Hecht also wrote short stories and novels.

Twentieth Century (1932). Set on a cross-country railroad train, this play shows the duping of a Hollywood star by a lunatic. Both Hecht and MacArthur came to New York; each writer collaborated with others, too. MacArthur became a theatre producer and married actress Helen Hayes.

Jumbo (1935). Music by Richard Rodgers, lyrics by Lorenz Hart, book by Hecht and MacArthur. Produced by Billy Rose, with the Paul Whiteman orchestra. This was actually a circus performance, with a number of vaudeville acts, staged at the Hippodrome Theatre in New York City. The plot line was minimal, but the "show biz" was spectacular. Hecht also wrote a number of popular film scripts, and MacArthur became editor of *Theatre Arts* magazine in 1947.

To Quito and Back (1937). This play, staged by the Theatre Guild, was written by Hecht alone. An American novelist, running away from many things, including himself, finally faces up to himself and is martyred in South America.

COLE PORTER (1891–1964)

Fifty Million Frenchmen (1929). Music and lyrics by Porter, book by Herbert Fields. Porter's first full-scale Broadway triumph, although his work appeared on Broadway as early as 1916 in *See America First*. Born in Indiana, Porter was actually writing musical shows in prep school and as an undergraduate at Yale. In all, he had a hand in twenty-two Broadway musicals between 1916 and 1950. In this production, wealthy Peter Forbes, visiting in Paris, sees lovely LooLoo and wagers with a friend that, without funds, he can win her in a month. He does, of course.

The Gay Divorcee (1932). Music and lyrics by Porter, book by Dwight Taylor, based on an unproduced play by J. Hartley Manners. Mimi goes to a British seaside hotel to arrange a planned assignation in order to get a divorce. Her lover turns up instead of the man hired for the night. Starred Fred Astaire and Clare Luce. Among the memorable songs is the ever-popular "Night and Day."

Anything Goes (1934). Music and lyrics by Porter, book by Guy Bolton, P. G. Wodehouse, Howard Lindsay, and Russel Crouse. Public enemies, romantic stowaways, and floor-show girls all become involved on a steamship bound for London. The hit songs include "Anything Goes," "You're the Top," "I Get a Kick Out of You," and "Blow, Gabriel, Blow."

Jubilee (1935). Music and lyrics by Porter, book by Moss Hart. Among the hit songs: "Just One of Those Things" and "Begin the Beguine." Porter was one of Broadway's greatest composers; he also wrote a number of hit Hollywood musical films.

DuBarry Was a Lady (1939). Music and lyrics by Porter, book by B. G. DeSylva and Herbert Fields. A men's washroom attendant wins the Irish Sweepstakes and woos a floor-show star. In a dream, he thinks he is Louis XIV at Versailles. Porter, at the peak of his career, was thrown by a horse in 1937, became crippled, and composed much of his best music between many painful operations and always in fear of losing his legs.

Panama Hattie (1940). Music and lyrics by Porter, book by B. G. DeSylva and Herbert Fields. The leading lady must win over a young prospective stepdaughter before she can marry into high society.

Kiss Me, Kate (1948). Music and lyrics by

Porter, book by Sam and Bella Spewack. Based on Shakespeare's *The Taming of the Shrew,* this is a play within a play. Actor Fred Graham is reunited with his former wife, Lilli, and Bill is paired off with Lois; but not before all four are emotionally entangled and some gangsters almost destroy the show, which is opening in Baltimore. Top songs include "Wunderbar" and "So in Love."

Can-Can (1953). Music and lyrics by Porter, book by Abe Burrows. Stuffy Parisian judge Aristide Forestier visits the dives of Montmartre to decide whether the can-can dance is immoral; he falls in love with café proprietress La Mome Pistache, ends up in a police scandal, resigns his seat on the bench, and helps La Mome Pistache teach the can-can to others. This show brought Gwen Verdon to fame and is famous for Porter's song "I Love Paris."

Silk Stockings (1955). Music and lyrics by Porter, book by George S. Kaufman, Leueen McGrath, and Abe Burrows, based on the Greta Garbo film *Ninotchka* by Melchior Lengyel. A Russian pianist in Paris for a concert won't return to Russia, nor will the Communist agents who come after him. Cole Porter's final work for theatre was an original television score of *Aladdin* in 1958. He remains one of our greatest popular composers.

MARTIN FLAVIN (1883–1967)

The Criminal Code (1929). A prisoner, Robert Graham, refuses to testify about a murder he witnesses in the warden's office; he later kills an evil guard and will probably be hanged. This powerful indictment of our penal system and of the repressive effects of eye-for-an-eye justice was Flavin's most famous play, although he was represented on Broadway as early as 1923. A Californian, Flavin was perhaps better known as a novelist, winning a Pulitzer Prize in that field.

JOHN WEXLEY (1902–)

The Last Mile (1930). A powerfully realistic melodrama about prison life, this play calls for the abolition of capital punishment. We see the psychology of men on Death Row, their jailbreak, and the death of their leader, Killer Mears.

Steel (1931). Daniel's father dies of a stroke when he learns that his son hates the steel mills and is a radical; more deaths occur when a strike erupts. A powerful play about labor problems and one of several leftist dramas Wexley wrote during the Depression.

They Shall Not Die (1934). Two white girls are bribed by the sheriff to say that two black boys raped them. Their defense attorney exposes the falsehood, but hysterical race prejudice causes the boys to be executed anyway. This play was based on an actual trial in Scottsboro, Alabama, in 1931. Wexley, who was loudly propagandistic in his efforts to bring about social justice, later became a Hollywood screenwriter. There he fell under the infamous blacklist and was one of the "Hollywood Ten" indicted by the House Un-American Activities Committee. While blacklisted, he nevertheless wrote several films under pseudonyms; most of those screenwriters blacklisted did make fools of the producers by continuing to write anonymously.

AGITPROPS

This was not a particular play by a specific author but a series of short improvisational dramas done for political persuasion. The term combines AGITation and PROPaganda. The earliest Agitprops were staged by the Proletbuehne, a German-language workers' laboratory theatre designed to convert onlookers on the spot and enroll them into the Communist Party in New York City in the early 1930's. Agitprops were done on the docks, on the sidewalks, in the parks, and outside factory gates. Gradually the type spread to other political organizations trying to convert Depression-ridden Americans to their various causes. Mostly, they were staged outdoors. They faded as the Depression eased and as the nation edged closer to World War II. None of them were great dramatically because of their shrill tone and one-sided characterizations.

PAUL OSBORN (1901–)

The Vinegar Tree (1930). Middle-aged, married Laura Merrick thinks of possible intrigue with a handsome house guest and is jealous of her daughter who is a competitor; but the guest turns out to be Laura's old flame. Borders on high comedy but ends up conventional in outlook and approach. Osborn was another of the many students of Professor George Pierce Baker and his playwriting workshop at Harvard.

On Borrowed Time (1938). Adapted from a novel by Lawrence Watkin, this play is a fantasy about death. Gramps traps Mr. Brink (Death) in an old apple tree after a family fight in which Gramps wants to keep six-year-old orphaned Pud. Crises erupt in the world, because Death is helpless; but Dr. Evans realizes what is happening. Gramps finally allows Mr. Brink out of the tree when he realizes that he will die at the same time as young Pud, and they will not have to be separated.

Morning's at Seven (1939). One of Osborn's very few totally original plays. An elderly group of sisters, some married, some not, struggle in Chekhovian fashion to understand their lives.

Innocent Voyage (1943). An adaptation of Richard Hughes' novel *High Wind in Jamaica*. A child murders a sea captain, but no one believes her. Osborn's career was far more notable for his adaptations and film scripts. Millions of moviegoers have seen dozens of his films without ever realizing that he was one of the nation's most prolific screenwriters.

A Bell for Adano (1944). Adapted from the novel by John Hersey. An American officer, in the occupation forces in Italy at the end of World War II, obtains a bell for the local townspeople. Many of Osborn's stage adaptations later became hit movies.

The World of Suzie Wong (1958). Adapted from a novel by Richard Mason. The love between a poor American artist and a good-hearted Hong Kong prostitute. To the end of his active career, Osborn continued to adapt others' works for the stage and screen.

LYNN RIGGS (1899–1954)

Roadside (1930). A Paul Bunyan–like play in which the braggart hero, Texas, outtalks the law and wins Hannie away from her timid husband. This was Riggs' first Broadway pro-

duction; and although it only ran for eleven performances, it was done in many other theatres, was anthologized, and was restaged as *Borned in Texas* for another Broadway run in 1950. Many critics have called it one of our best comic folk plays. Riggs was born near Claremore, the Indian Territory (now Oklahoma), and he wrote well of the boisterousness, loneliness, and violent passion of isolated rural life.

Green Grow the Lilacs (1931). An outstanding folk play filled with old ballads. Curley wins Laurey but has to kill rival Jeeter on their wedding night. This play probably would have had an extremely long run, but the Theatre Guild had it booked for a national tour after a nine-week Broadway stay. Lee Strasberg played the peddler, and Franchot Tone made his reputation as Curley. Riggs patterned jovial Aunt Eller after his own aunt who had brought him up as a boy.

The Cherokee Night (1932). Despite praise from critics and theatre people, plus several writing fellowships, Riggs always found it next to impossible to crack Broadway with his folk dramas. This powerful play was premiered at Jasper Deeter's Hedgerow Theatre outside of Philadelphia. Riggs was always welcome at Hedgerow, receiving 102 performances of various plays there, but he received almost no money from them. *The Cherokee Night* was done in New York for only ten days, by a training group for the Federal Theatre. It has received almost no professional production, and yet it remains one of the nation's most powerful folk dramas. In a scrambled time sequence, we see a tragedy of moral disintegration of half-breed Cherokees in Oklahoma. "God is a white man," one of them declares bitterly. Riggs himself was part Cherokee on his mother's side.

Russet Mantle (1936). Idealistic young poet John Galt faces up to responsibilities with Kay, as they try to persuade her mother, uncle, and aunt to live more worthwhile lives. Although a comedy, the play nevertheless had all the idealism that most of the serious plays did during the Depression, with some overstatement about making the world a better place. Set in Santa Fe, New Mexico, where Riggs spent a fair part of his life, and where at one time he built his own adobe house. Riggs received considerable encouragement from members of the Santa Fe art colony, plus several early productions at the community theatre there. This play gave Riggs his longest Broadway exposure: 117 performances.

The Cream in the Well (1941). A powerful tragedy of incest on an isolated farm near Big Lake in the old Indian Territory. The sister drives her own fiancé to alcoholism, her brother's fiancée to death, and herself to a tragic death when she and her brother realize that to live incestuously would not bring happiness, either. Appearing on the Broadway scene about a decade too soon for the public climate to accept the play, it received some of the most shrill and hysterical reviews in the history of modern theatre. Sadly, Broadway's doors were henceforth closed to the nation's top folk dramatist.

Oklahoma! (1943). Music by Richard Rodgers, book and lyrics by Oscar Hammerstein II, based on Riggs' *Green Grow the Lilacs.* Theatre Guild officials had suggested this musical to Rodgers; his partner Lorenz Hart vetoed it, and the Guild brought Rodgers and Hammerstein together, thus starting their long collaboration. Hammerstein remained carefully faithful to Riggs' script, using original dialogue as the basis for many of the hit songs. Riggs, a draftee in the Army at the time, was not part of the project and on opening night was a forgotten man, on duty at Wright Field, Ohio. The show rescued the Theatre Guild from bankruptcy, gave Riggs a $250-a-week fee, and brought him all kinds of recognition nationally and in his own state—but Broadway would not do any of his later plays. For a large part of his adult life, he supported himself by writing film scripts; his reputation as a folk dramatist is secure from *Lilacs* and *Oklahoma!,* but he spent a frustrating lifetime trying to get a hearing in New York.

THORNTON WILDER (1897–1975)

The Pullman Car Hiawatha (1931). A train runs through the night to Chicago, with a stage manager moving chairs about, dead peo-

ple speaking, and finally a cleaning woman scrubbing the stage. This one-act play anticipates *Our Town* by several years. Wilder had plays done off-Broadway, at the American Laboratory Theatre, as early as 1927. In that year, however, he became internationally known with his Pulitzer Prize-winning novel *The Bridge of San Luis Rey.*

Our Town (1938). With this, Wilder won the Pulitzer Prize for drama. A homespun account of life and death in rural Grover's Corners, New Hampshire, around the turn of the century. George Gibbs and Emily Webb grow up, marry, and Emily dies. The stage manager openly controls the play and takes the role of a rural philosopher as he does so. Theatregoers praised Wilder's originality, but he was the first to acknowledge that much of the inventiveness had come from Italian playwright Luigi Pirandello and his play *Six Characters in Search of an Author. Our Town* has been the most frequently produced play in the amateur field for several decades.

The Skin of Our Teeth (1942). Wilder's third Pulitzer Prize-winner. The story of man (the Antrobus family) told allegorically in the New Jersey suburbs and in Atlantic City, as they barely weather the Ice Age, the Flood, and modern war. Wilder enlisted in both World Wars. In his writings he was always interested in the nobility of man, although he was by no means blind to man's pettiness. Always intellectually inclined, Wilder taught in a preparatory school in New Jersey, at the University of Chicago, and at Harvard.

The Matchmaker (1955). A farce, based on his earlier stage failure *The Girl from Yonkers,* done in 1938. Dolly Levi, the matchmaker, ends up getting the merchant from Yonkers as her own mate. Even Wilder never dreamed that this amusing but slight bit of entertainment would turn into:

Hello, Dolly (1964). Music and lyrics by Jerry Herman, book by Michael Stewart, from Wilder's play, above. Staged and choreographed by Gower Champion, it starred Carol Channing and many others in subsequent versions. It won the New York Drama Critics Circle

Award for best musical in 1963–64 and for a time was the longest-running musical in Broadway history, with 2,844 performances.

Plays for Bleecker Street (1962). Three experimental one-act plays: *Infancy, Childhood,* and *Someone from Assisi.* These off-Broadway playlets were part of a proposed cycle designed to show the various ages of man. In almost all of Wilder's dramatic work he was heavily allegorical. Although his output for the theatre was small in quantity, his two major serious plays have given him a solid niche in American drama; further, the professional success of *Dolly* and the amateur enthusiasm for *Our Town* have made him one of the most-produced playwrights in world history.

LANGSTON HUGHES (1902–1967)

Mulatto (1931, 1935). Finished in 1931 and premiered at Jasper Deeter's Hedgerow Theatre outside of Philadelphia, this later became the longest-running play by a black man on Broadway, with 373 performances. A two-act tragedy in which a mulatto son is killed by the mob after he kills his white father, whose power and freedom he envies. This later became a musical, *The Barrier* (1950), with music by Jan Meyerowitz.

Little Ham (1935). A three-act folk comedy about the numbers racket in Harlem in the 1920's. Hughes, our first important black playwright, was also known for his prose and poetry. Born in Missouri of part Cherokee stock, Hughes traveled widely in Europe and Africa before settling permanently in New York's Harlem.

Soul Gone Home (1937). A short one-act play, this is a fantasy about a dead black man who sits up and argues with his mother over race problems.

Don't You Want to Be Free? (1937). A long one-act play done at the Harlem Suitcase Theatre, founded by Hughes, this ran weekends for a combined total of 135 performances and later was published in the October, 1958, issue of *One-Act Play Magazine.* Despite the fact that Hughes had enjoyed one long Broadway run, the midtown theatre doors were not wide open to him or any other black playwright in the 1930's, and his Suitcase Theatre offered several writers a chance to be heard.

Street Scene (1947). Music by Kurt Weill, book and lyrics by Hughes, based on Elmer Rice's 1929 play. A tragically realistic picture of crowded tenement life in New York City and how the lack of privacy destroys people's lives.

Simply Heavenly (1957). A two-act comedy in which we see lovable nonhero Jesse Semple yielding to all temptations. This play was based on a series of short stories by Hughes and featured music by David Martin. After opening in Harlem, it was transferred to Broadway.

Black Nativity (1961). A Christmas musical based on gospel singing, this had successful runs in both New York and Chicago. Although Hughes did excellent work in the drama, he will probably be best remembered as a poet.

Tambourines to Glory (1963). A fablelike and folk ballad–filled two-act comedy written in 1949. Music by Jobe Huntley. A story of good and evil with Faust-like overtones. Hughes was always concerned about racial oppression and wrote steadily about it; one reason he found more of an audience among whites than other black writers of his time is that he clothed much of his outcry against prejudice in comedy.

ALBERT MALTZ (1908–)

Merry-Go-Round (1932). With George Sklar (see below). This play, which officials tried to censor on Broadway, is a critique of New York's Tammany Hall. It depicts a young bellboy, witness to a gangland murder, made the scapegoat for the crime when the mob uses its influence to get off free. The play is also an indictment of corrupt police. One of the great ironies of Maltz's career is that although he was one of the ten Hollywood writers jailed in the 1950's by the House Un-American Activities Committee for his left-wing activities, he was also the author of several motion pictures so patriotic that one even became an Army training film.

Peace on Earth (1933). With George Sklar. This play helped open the leftist Theatre Union in New York. Peter Owen, an economics professor, becomes involved with a strike of longshoremen refusing to load munitions. He is accused of killing and is sentenced to death. He is hanged; but before this occurs, he is converted to Marxism. The Theatre Union staged leftist plays for a workingman audience and received backing from both the Communist and Socialist parties.

Black Pit (1935). A Marxian tragedy written by Maltz alone. A union mine worker, forced to act as a company spy, betrays his fellows and is ostracized; he must join their strike in order to be able to live with himself. The cries of the oppressed workers in this and other works by Maltz or Sklar are strongly influenced by the Agitprop plays.

Private Hicks (1936). A young man in the National Guard throws down his gun and will not fire at strikers but goes to prison instead. First staged by the Communistic New Theatre League at one of their New Theatre Night performances, the play is actually extremely humanitarian and not Communistic. It also foreshadowed to an uncanny degree the turbulence on the Kent State University campus some thirty years later. The play is still powerful and effective. Maltz also wrote a number of short stories and novels, although his career led him primarily to Hollywood. What superpatriots in the 1950's failed to realize is that many a leftist writer in the depths of the Depression was extremely happy to join the American free-enterprise system when Hollywood began rewarding his writing efforts financially.

GEORGE SKLAR (1908–)
Merry-Go-Round (1932). With Albert Maltz (*see* entry above). This play was later made into a film, *Afraid to Talk*. The original play had been done when both Maltz and Sklar were students in Professor George Pierce Baker's playwriting class at Harvard.

Peace on Earth (1933). With Albert Maltz (*see* entry above). After a time spent writing leftist plays during the Depression, Sklar became primarily a novelist.

Stevedore (1934). Written with Paul Peters. A proletarian protest play about a black stevedore who is wrongly accused of rape, is almost lynched, and is shot; but thanks to action by a Communist union, the other workers can look forward to better times. Set in Louisiana.

Parade (1935). A musical revue, written with Paul Peters and Jerome Moross and staged by the Theatre Guild. Satirical in tone.

Life and Death of an American (1939). Jerry, born at midnight, 1900, plugs along as an average young American until the Depression, when his automobile factory goes on strike and he is killed by police. Done by the Federal Theatre. Sklar then turned to Hollywood, where he wrote scores of films, of which the best known was *Laura*.

And People All Around (1966). With this, Sklar's first play in many years, he returned to the social-protest drama. It is a fictionalized treatment of the murder of three civil-rights workers in Mississippi that had shocked the nation two years earlier. Southern white man Don Tindall sees the murders, lives with this, and finally reports them, but he is beaten to death in the local jail by the guilty sheriff and his deputies. The play was produced in more than twenty-five theatres as the second play done by the American Playwrights Theatre, headquartered at Ohio State University. The APT selects one script by a known dramatist and gives it simultaneous production in college and community theatres in order to try to break the stranglehold of Broadway. This play was immensely successful because it was produced during the height of student protest on campus.

ROSE FRANKEN (1898–)
Another Language (1932). Stella, the wife of one of domineering Mother Hallam's sons, finally persuades one of her nephews to rebel in order to pursue an artistic career. A com-

edy, but with a serious theme of parental control. In the process, the disintegrating marriage between Stella and Vickie is repaired.

Claudia (1941). Still attached to her mother's apron strings, Claudia matures, aided by the double discovery of her pregnancy and her mother's impending death. This was an adaptation of one of Rose Franken's extremely popular novels in the *Claudia* series about domestic life.

Outrageous Fortune (1943). The vicissitudes of a Jewish family. Although her several Broadway plays were quite popular, Rose Franken is known best for her fiction.

Soldier's Wife (1944). Kate's letters to her husband, John, fighting in the Pacific, are so good that they bring her a Hollywood offer; but she is satisfied to regain John. The author said of the play's husband and wife: "He is a normal male returning to a wife who, if their marriage is to survive, must find herself equally matured." Most popular plays during World War II were either patriotic, supernatural, or extolled the old-fashioned domestic philosophies; stability was more important for audiences than thought.

ERSKINE CALDWELL (1903–)
Tobacco Road (1933). Written with Jack Kirkland. The disasters that overcome the ignorant poor-white Lester family on a barren farm in the Deep South. Several of them run away, and wife Ada dies, leaving husband Jeeter alone on the rotting porch. There was some social protest in the play, but it was covered over with grotesque comedy. Partly because of the advanced-for-its-time approach to sex on the stage, the production ran for 3,182 performances and remains the third-longest run on Broadway. Caldwell wrote the best-selling novel a year before the dramatization. He has been a popular novelist for many decades, most of his fiction dealing with lower classes in the South.

SIDNEY KINGSLEY (1906–)
Men in White (1933). Young Dr. Ferguson's engagement almost collapses when he must forsake his fiancée in order to perform an operation on a young nurse whom he has impregnated, but the fiancée comes to realize that Ferguson's profession will always come first. This was Kingsley's first professional production, was the first major hit for the Group Theatre after two years of struggle, and won a Pulitzer Prize. Kingsley, a New Yorker, gained fame for writing realistic melodramas of urban life in the 1930's.

Dead End (1935). Drina sees her young brother arrested for a knifing and realizes that young people in New York's poorer sections can have no hopes for the future as long as the deadening slums exist. This is a powerful study of how environment creates criminals. Out of the film version of this play came the group later known as the Dead End Kids.

Ten Million Ghosts (1936). A strong protest against munitions-makers. America's artists, whatever their attitudes toward it, were strongly aware of the oncoming World War. Kingsley's reputation began to fade slightly because he rarely followed his serious themes to grim conclusions, but twisted them to fit contrived endings.

The Patriots (1943). An interesting historical play, featuring George Washington and the conflict between Thomas Jefferson who had faith in democracy and Alexander Hamilton who distrusted it.

Detective Story (1949). A naturalistic study of life in a New York City police precinct. Detective McLeod gains compassion for others only as he is dying from gunshot wounds from an attempted escapee. Previously, McLeod has judged everyone too harshly. The play, which is a plea for tolerance and understanding of the frailties of the human race, is strongly reminiscent of Kingsley's early realistic melodramas of social criticism.

Darkness at Noon (1951). Based on Arthur Koestler's novel, this is a powerful tragedy. Communist leader Rubashov is imprisoned and tortured by the regime he had helped create. He undergoes horrifying treatment, recalls his past, but refuses to sign the confession demanded of him and valiantly goes to his death. An excellent dramatization of an excellent novel, this shows Kingsley's fusion of social realism with his idealistic belief in man's ability to endure.

HOWARD LINDSAY (1899–1968) and RUSSEL CROUSE (1893–1966)

Anything Goes (1934). Music and lyrics by Cole Porter, book by Guy Bolton, P. G. Wodehouse, Lindsay, and Crouse. Public enemies, romantic stowaways, and showgirls become involved in a series of complications on a steamship bound for London. Lindsay, a New Yorker, was a vaudeville performer who turned to directing and writing and had one of his own plays, *Young Uncle Dudley,* succeed on Broadway as early as 1929. He also collaborated with Damon Runyon on *A Slight Case of Murder* in 1935. Crouse, from Ohio, became a highly successful New York City journalist—one of the many who then gravitated toward theatre. The collaboration between Lindsay and Crouse extended over more than a dozen plays and was terminated only by Crouse's death.

Life with Father (1939). One of the most famous period pieces in American theatre, based on Clarence Day's book about his own family. Father, stuffy and angry, is continually outwitted by Mother. Father discovers that he has never been baptized, promises to do so when Mother falls seriously ill, reneges, but is finally cornered by Mother. Lindsay played the father, and his wife, actress Dorothy Stickney, played the mother; for many years the 3,224 performances ranked the show as the longest run in Broadway history. A few years ago the run was surpassed by *Fiddler on the Roof,* which remained on stage in its final months with the avowed purpose of breaking the Lindsay-Crouse record.

Strip for Action (1942). A comedian from the days of burlesque, now in the Army, decides to put on a girlie-show for his soldier-buddies. Much slapstick ensues.

State of the Union (1945). A Pulitzer Prize-winning play, this told of a Midwestern business leader who began a run for the Presidency of the United States; presumably the character was patterned after Wendell Willkie. In order to get the nomination, he must resort to some shabby under-the-table dealing; his integrity will not allow this, and Grant rejects their nomination and repairs his ailing marriage. The most interesting sidelight about this play is that Lindsay and Crouse used real names and real events in the script, altering lines nightly to reflect events in that day's newspapers.

Life with Mother (1948). A sequel to their first big hit, this tells of Mother Day's campaign to get the engagement ring she had never received—it had gone to another girl decades ago; she manages to acquire it on their twenty-second anniversary.

Call Me Madam (1950). Music and lyrics by Irving Berlin, book by Lindsay and Crouse. Based on Washington, D.C., hostess Perle Mesta and played by Ethel Merman. An American woman ambassador to mythical Lichtenburg.

Remains to be Seen (1951). A farce-mystery of a drummer and his girlfriend who manage to solve a murder case.

The Great Sebastians (1956). A man-wife mind-reading act gets caught in Communist intrigue in Czechoslovakia. This was one of several plays that Lindsay and Crouse created for the acting twosome of Alfred Lunt and Lynne Fontanne, husband and wife, who did their first show together (*The Guardsman*) in 1924 and for thirty years maintained their position as the top acting team in New York.

Tall Story (1959). From the novel *The Homecoming Game* by Howard Nemerov, this is a comedy about a basketball scandal. Lindsay and Crouse collaborated not only on scripts but on directing as well; their most famous joint directing venture was Joseph Kesselring's comedy *Arsenic and Old Lace* (1941). Rumor has it that they also did much work on the script.

The Sound of Music (1959). Music by Richard Rodgers, lyrics by Oscar Hammerstein II, book by Lindsay and Crouse. The true story of the Trapp family, with a few romantic embellishments, as they become a singing group and escape from the Nazis. Maria the governess wins the stern Captain Trapp away from his fiancée and his old ways. The musical, which perhaps shares with *My Fair Lady, Oklahoma!,* and *Show Boat* the honor of having the most all-time hit songs in its score, ran for four years on Broadway before the film version became a then-all-time moneymaker.

Mr. President (1962). Music and lyrics by Irving Berlin, book by Lindsay and Crouse. The last few months of a President's term in office and his lonely life afterward. Berlin's last major musical.

LILLIAN HELLMAN (1905–)

The Children's Hour (1934). An extremely powerful study of a neurotic fourteen-year-old, Mary Tilford, who destroys teachers Karen Wright and Martha Dobie with a charge of lesbianism; Mrs. Tilford discovers the truth only after Martha shoots herself. Miss Hellman, daughter of a businessman, alternated between New Orleans and New York in her girlhood, went to New York and Columbia universities, worked for a publisher, and traveled in Europe with her husband, Arthur Kober. When that marriage broke up, Miss Hellman began a friendship with mystery writer Dashiell Hammett, who suggested that as an exercise in playwriting she dramatize the true story of a 19th-century law case in Scotland; the play was quickly produced by Herman Shumlin, for whom Miss Hellman worked. She immediately gained a reputation as a meticulous craftsman who examined the problem of powerful evil in her plays.

The Little Foxes (1939). An analytical study of unscrupulousness in the Deep South in 1900. We see scheming selfishness to try to make a fortune with a cheap-labor cotton mill by the Hubbard family, especially Regina Hubbard Giddens, who lets her husband die of a heart attack she has induced and then tries to use this to further her scheming against her brothers, Oscar and Ben Hubbard, to get more than her fair share. The play is one of Miss Hellman's masterpieces and was given a brilliant revival at Lincoln Center in 1967.

Watch on the Rhine (1941). A powerful anti-Nazi play in which a family vainly tries to stay aloof from World War II. Kurt has come to the United States to see his American wife and child; but he must return to serve in the German underground, even though this decision undoubtedly will mean his eventual death. Winner of the New York Drama Critics Circle Award. Miss Hellman, during the late 1930's, toured extensively in Europe, including Russia and Spain, was extremely upset by the Spanish Civil War, and became a strong moralizer on the side of freedom.

The Searching Wind (1944). A powerful play about escaping from responsibility, as an American diplomat in Italy continually refuses to admit the evils being perpetrated in Europe in the 1930's by Hitler and Mussolini. Miss Hellman was never afraid to take a public stand for what she believed in; neither was her friend Dashiell Hammett, who, despite pulmonary problems, enlisted in World War II as a corporal.

Another Part of the Forest (1946). A look, twenty years earlier, at the Hubbard family of *The Little Foxes,* to show what made Oscar, Ben, and Regina the evil and greedy creatures they became. Here we see father Marcus Hubbard double-dealing, including a revelation of how he had even sold out the Confederate forces earlier in order to increase his personal profits. All of the above plays, Ibsenian in their realism, stern in their portrayals of evil, made Miss Hellman the foremost American playwright for a decade.

The Autumn Garden (1951). After the series of Ibsenian social-thesis plays, Miss Hellman turned to a Chekhovian approach in this play, set at a summer boardinghouse on the Louisiana coast. The group of regular vacationers, growing old and tired, discover things about themselves when artist Nicholas Denery arrives after years abroad and creates turmoil among the group. Constance Tuckerman, who runs the house, and Ned Crossman realize that their old love has gradually faded away. The structure is much less tightly plotted than in Miss Hellman's earlier plays, and the characterizations are rich.

The Lark (1955). A loose adaptation of the contemporary French play, Jean Anouilh's drama *L'Alouette,* this is the account of the fame and martyrdom of Joan of Arc. The production brought Julie Harris to stardom. The mid-1950's were a trying time for Miss Hellman: Dashiell Hammett, brought before the House Un-American Activities Committee, was imprisoned for six months in 1951; she was placed on the Hollywood blacklist as a dangerous leftist, an almost incredible charge after her years of fighting for freedom. When she was haled before the Un-American Activities Committee, she snapped, "I can't cut my conscience to fit this year's fashions." She cared for the ill Hammett with tender care through the last few years of his life. He died in 1959, and Miss Hellman sold the house that they had lived in at Martha's Vineyard.

Candide (1956). Music by Leonard Bernstein, book by Miss Hellman. A retelling of the famous French novel by Voltaire about "the best of all possible worlds," this won the New York Drama Critics Circle Award, not when first done, but after its revival in 1973–74, at which time Hugh Wheeler added material to the book and Stephen Sondheim added music.

Toys in the Attic (1960). A middle-aged maiden sister leads her brother's naive wife unwittingly to wreck his chances of acquiring a fortune in order that the brother remain dependent upon her. A powerful drama of loneliness, incestuous desires, selfishness, and pride —feelings that Miss Hellman handled effectively in many of her plays. Winner of the New York Drama Critics Circle Award. Miss Hellman wrote two excellent volumes of autobiography, *Unfinished Woman* in 1969, and *Pentimento* in 1973. She also edited a collection of Dashiell Hammett's works in 1966. She remains our foremost woman playwright.

CLIFFORD ODETS (1906–1963)

Waiting for Lefty (1935). An expressionistic one-act play set at a taxi drivers' union meeting, with the assortment of Depression-ravaged characters waiting for Lefty to come and provide leadership. When word arrives that Lefty has been shot, the hall rings out with cries of "Strike, strike!" First staged by the Communist

New Theatre League at one of their New Theatre Nights, then soon after staged on Broadway by the Group Theatre, of which Odets was a charter member. Born in Philadelphia, Odets grew up in New York City and while still in his teens was an actor and radio announcer. He was a member of the Theatre Guild when the young members of that organization broke away to form the idealistic Group Theatre, and he acted with the Group until his own plays succeeded.

Till the Day I Die (1935). A one-act anti-Nazi tragedy of a Communist agent, tortured by the Germans, who commits suicide to protect his integrity. Odets wrote this play quickly in order to provide the Group with a full night's bill, to go along with *Waiting for Lefty*.

Awake and Sing (1935). Grandfather Jacob throws himself off a New York tenement roof in order that grandson Moe and granddaughter Hennie can have some money to survive in the Depression. The Berger family is gradually being beaten down economically in their tiny apartment. The play's theme is stated openly by old Jacob: "Life shouldn't be printed on dollar bills." This was probably the single most famous production done by the Group Theatre in its decade of existence. It is a Chekhovian picture of the disintegration of the middle class and the rebellion of the young. Odets gives the play an upbeat finale that is perhaps not in keeping with the rest of the action, which is heavily despairing, but the ending is consistent with the statements of many writers of the 1930's that American society could be improved.

Paradise Lost (1935). An allegorical treatment of middle-class failure in the Gordon family and how people must fight for a better world. Leo Gordon is too humanitarian to succeed in business. One son, Julie, dies of sleeping sickness. The other son, Ben, an Olympic runner, lets himself be killed in a holdup attempt. Daughter Pearl plays the piano constantly and loses her fiancé, who can't support her. Leo's partner, Sam Katz, embezzles money from the business; and the Gordons are about to be evicted from their house, but Leo's final speech is optimistic.

Golden Boy (1937). The ruining force of materialism, as a sensitive young man, Joe Bonaparte, abandons his career in music for the life of a prizefighter. This was made into an extremely popular film and in 1964 was staged as a musical under the same name. Odets, who had actually been a member of the Communist Party for something under a year, resigned when he found membership too stultifying for his creative career. After *Paradise Lost* had not brought in the money he had hoped, Odets moved to Hollywood, where he wrote many films. Feeling some guilt at abandoning the Group Theatre, he wrote *Golden Boy* for them, and its success helped the financially troubled Group stay afloat.

Rocket to the Moon (1938). A middle-class tragedy. Sympathetic Cleo seeks a man who can give her love, but finds none in those around her; the characters grope unsuccessfully for fulfillment. Staged by the Group Theatre.

Clash by Night (1941). Bored Mae Wilensky has an affair with one of their boarders; her husband, Jerry, discovers them and strangles the lover. Not successful at the box office. Odets, with the demise of the Group Theatre, remained primarily in Hollywood and wrote films. Communism held no charm when countered by the large paychecks in the movie capital.

The Big Knife (1949). Charlie Castle, famous actor, tries to resist the many unsavory pressures of Hollywood; his only positive act, however, is his suicide—coming ironically after a possibly blackmailing starlet dies accidentally. This is a powerful exposé of the lengths to which studio heads go to keep their money-producing stars in line. Odets probably felt some guilt throughout his life for taking the easier road to financial security: Hollywood, not Broadway.

The Country Girl (1950). A powerful character study in which wife Georgie helps her alcoholic actor-husband, Frank Elgin, make a spectacular stage comeback, but not before becoming embroiled in an emotional affair with the show's director. One of Odets' few

plays without social commentary. Produced in England, too, and made into a film.

The Flowering Peach (1954). The story of Noah and the Flood. Noah and his family slowly and painfully learn to understand themselves during the long, enforced stay on the Ark and eventually change for the better. Noah and his youngest son struggle stubbornly with each other, as we see old theological rigidities in conflict with newer liberalism. The agony over the death of Noah's wife, just as the Ark reaches land, causes Noah to admit for the first time that he could be wrong about anything.

Two by Two (1970). Music by Richard Rodgers, lyrics by Peter Charnin, book by Peter Stone, from Odets' play *The Flowering Peach*. Starred Danny Kaye as Noah in Kaye's return to the Broadway musical stage. Despite all the commentary during Clifford Odets' career about his being the voice of the proletariat in social-protest plays, the critical consensus now is that Odets' strength lay in depicting loneliness. He refined the Agitprop to its artistic peak in *Waiting for Lefty,* and he accurately depicted the speech of New York's middle class and the struggles of its members as they tried to eke out a living.

SAM (1899–1971) and BELLA (1899–   ) SPEWACK

Boy Meets Girl (1935). A satirical comedy that makes daily life in the Hollywood studios look absolutely insane. Two irrepressible film writers, Law and Benson, become involved in a scheme to make an infant star famous; critics say that the two writers are actually parodies of the real-life Ben Hecht and Charles MacArthur (*see* their entry). The Spewacks emigrated from Europe, married in the United States, worked in journalism, then became an outstanding comic writing team in Hollywood. Their Broadway career actually began as early as 1926.

Two Blind Mice (1949). A comedy of Washington bureaucracy: two old ladies continue to operate a Department of Interior Office of Herbs that has been officially closed; their nephew-in-law conducts a gigantic hoax with the office that fools the press and the military, wins back his former wife, and saves the ladies' jobs.

Kiss Me, Kate (1948). Music and lyrics by Cole Porter, book by the Spewacks. Based on Shakespeare's *The Taming of the Shrew,* this is a play within a play. Actor Fred Graham is reunited with his former wife, Lilli, and Bill is paired off with Lois; but not before all four are emotionally entangled and some gangsters almost destroy the show, which is opening in Baltimore. Top songs include "Wunderbar" and "So in Love."

My Three Angels (1953). Adapted from the French play *La Cuisine des Anges* by Albert Husson. The play has been a comic hit in the amateur field for decades. Three convicts from a penal colony in Guiana in 1910 enter the lives of the Ducotel family in time to thwart a wicked uncle trying to take over papa's business and save the daughter from what would be a miserable marriage. The Spewacks also wrote television scripts and fiction, but they are most widely known and acclaimed for their film and stage comic collaborations.

ARCHIBALD MacLEISH (1892–)

Panic (1935). A radio play about bank failures in the Depression and how fear breeds fear. MacLeish, from Illinois, was graduated from Yale, then from Harvard Law School, and spent some years in Paris. From his early years he was a poet and gained considerable fame. Always interested in theatre, he wrote several plays, all in verse.

The Fall of the City (1937). Another radio play; the armored figure that attacks the city is empty inside, but when overcome with fear the masses invent their own oppressors.

Air Raid (1938). Another radio play that shows a city in the grip of mass terror. MacLeish actually was writing a very sophisticated form of Agitprop in these one-act radio scripts. MacLeish went on to become of the nation's top men of letters.

J.B. (1958). Set in a tattered old circus tent, this is a poetic, symbolic, modern telling of the biblical book of *Job.* Mr. Zuss, who sells balloons, plays God; Mr. Nickles, a popcorn vendor, plays Satan. J.B.'s son is killed in the war, his daughter is raped and murdered, he is burned in an atomic attack, but his wife returns to him at the end with a tiny flower she has found still growing, and they will struggle on. A Pulitzer Prize-winning play. Despite its being written in verse, the play found a large audience and had a long Broadway run followed by productions on many campuses.

SINCLAIR LEWIS (1885–1951)

It Can't Happen Here (1936). Adapted for the stage by John C. Moffitt and Lewis, from Lewis' novel. Doremus Jessup, a Vermont editor, has to flee to Canada in order to battle an American-President-turned-dictator in this powerful statement that a lackadaisical middle class could allow totalitarianism to occur in the United States. This was the first smash hit by the Federal Theatre, an organization funded by Congress in order to provide theatre jobs during the Depression. The play opened simultaneously in twenty-one cities and had 314 performances. Several other novels by Lewis have been brought to the stage by various adapters. See Sidney Howard entry.

CLARE BOOTHE LUCE (1903–)

The Women (1936). A large number of women—38 in all—play their respective roles in modern society, exposing their empty and at times vicious lives as members of the idle rich. Mary, the lead, loses her husband to another woman but at the end is fighting to win him back. There are several divorces in the various plots.

Kiss the Boys Goodbye (1938). A Southern belle, Cindy Lou, comes to a house party in the North, hoping to get a role in a movie titled *Kiss the Boys Goodbye.* She loses her naivete rapidly and triumphs over the others. This is a satire on Hollywood's never-ending search for talent and glamour.

Margin for Error (1939). An anti-Nazi mystery about who kills a German in the United States while he is being guarded by a Jewish policeman. Miss Boothe began as a journalist and magazine editor, became a successful

Irwin Shaw

Broadway playwright, married publisher Henry Luce, and became extremely active in politics, winning a seat in Congress and later becoming the American ambassador to Italy.

IRWIN SHAW (1913–   )

Bury the Dead (1936). A one-act fantasy showing a revolt of the dead in World War I. They refuse to lie down and be buried because they say they have been cheated out of life. Not only their commanding officers argue with them, but so do relatives, friends, politicians, and pastors. This was a strong pacifistic statement by Shaw, with World War II looming on the horizon. Shaw is a New Yorker who was graduated from Brooklyn College, became a radio script writer, and then a Hollywood film writer.

The Gentle People (1939). With the dictators making more and more grabs overseas, Shaw reversed his thesis from his earlier play and in this almost-whimsical script, shows the little people in Brooklyn killing several hoodlums. Shaw was saying that someone must stand up to the militaristic bullies of the world.

Sons and Soldiers (1943). A woman is warned about the dangers of giving birth. She has a vision of the next twenty-five years, with her sons being killed in war; but she decides to take the chance anyway and try to have her first child. Shaw served in the Army during World War II, then became widely known for his novel *The Young Lions* (1948). He continued to write films, novels, and occasional plays; and in the mid-1970's his novel *Rich Man, Poor Man* was performed as a kind of prime-time television serial.

ARTHUR ARENTS (1904–1972) and THE FEDERAL THEATRE

Triple-A Plowed Under (1936). This was the first of the Living Newspapers, which combined many forms of theatricality to state their social theses. This one showed the ultimate defeat of the federal Agricultural Adjustment Administration by the Supreme Court. A team of seventy reporters and writers worked under Morris Watson, Howard Cushman, and head dramatist Arthur Arents. Hallie Flanagan of Vassar College was the general director of The Federal Theatre, which was founded on August 29, 1935, as the Federal Theatre Project of the Works Progress Administration (WPA), designed to reduce unemployment in New York during the Depression.

1935 (1936). A Living Newspaper about the previous year. Most of these plays were never put into print. Music, song, dance, film clips, and pantomime were as important as the text, and they foreshadowed what in the 1960's was called Total Theatre.

Injunction Granted (1936). A Living Newspaper that was a left-wing look at labor problems. The Living Newspapers were one of several Federal Theatre projects that helped keep as many as 1,500 unemployed actors, writers, and stagehands eating during the Depression. The organization also reached audiences that had never seen a live play, and it toured the nation with innovative and timely shows.

Power (1937). Another Living Newspaper, which shows the importance of abundant electricity but also shows rapacious controllers victimizing a helpless public. Congress, after appropriating substantial funds to the Federal Theatre, became increasingly disenchanted with the program because so many of the productions castigated federal policies. In this, however, the writers for the Federal Theatre were little different from the socially conscious writers elsewhere; the 1930's were a decade of strident criticism and reform in all literature.

Pins and Needles (1937). Music and lyrics by Harold J. Rome, book by Arthur Arents, Marc Blitzstein, Emanuel Eisenberg, Charles Friedman, and David Gregory. A revue staged by the International Ladies Garment Workers Union at the Labor Stage Theatre, it began as amateur theatre, turned semiprofessional on weekends, and finally went fully professional and ran for several years. Filled with social criticism.

One-Third of a Nation (1938). With 237 performances, this had the longest run of any of the Living Newspapers. President Franklin D. Roosevelt, in his second inaugural address, had said that ". . . one third of a nation . . ."

was ". . . ill-housed, ill-clad, and ill-nourished." One of the few Living Newspapers to be published, the play features 194 speaking parts in a biting look at profiteering by New York City landlords and the plight of the poor people unable to move out of dangerous and unhealthful tenements. The Living Newspapers used many facts from newspapers, court records, and public documents. In this production a character named Little Man goes back in time and sees the metropolitan housing problem growing over the centuries. The final and almost Agitprop-like message is that only federal construction of urban housing will solve the problem of selfish greed that prevents decent housing everywhere. Ironically, despite the Federal Theatre's support of governmental programs in this script, Congress soon cut off its funds, considering the organization too radical; and it folded soon after this production.

ELLSWORTH PROUTY CONKLE (1899–   )

200 Were Chosen (1936). This was premiered at the University of Iowa before coming to Broadway. Farm families, on relief during the Depression, move to Alaska to stake out new farms and lives. They must conquer bureaucracy and their own stubbornness. A child's death spurs them to action; the farmers tear down their improperly built shacks to construct a sturdy little hospital.

Prologue to Glory (1938). This play shows the early life of Lincoln. Young Abe, through the influence of Ann Rutledge, who dies at the end of the play, gains enough confidence to seek public office. This was also premiered at the University of Iowa, then was a success in New York in a Federal Theatre production. A good play, but not nearly as rich as Sherwood's *Abe Lincoln in Illinois,* which appeared in the same year. Conkle is known best for his long years of influence in drama education, with professorships first at Iowa and later at the University of Texas.

JOHN STEINBECK (1902–1968)

Of Mice and Men (1937). From the novel of the same name by Steinbeck. Slow-witted Lennie cannot live in a world of migrant farm and ranch workers in California; his buddy George mercifully shoots him to save him a mutilation-lynching after Lennie has accidentally killed Curley's wife. A powerful play about the loneliness and entrapment of migrant workers, this is a superb example of a regional folk play that, because of its universality and characterization, rises above mere local color. Steinbeck converted his novel into a play after taking lessons in dramaturgy from George S. Kaufman, who also directed the play brilliantly. It won the New York Drama Critics Circle Award.

The Moon Is Down (1942). This play was also adapted for the stage by Steinbeck from a novel of the same name. In it we see the heroism of the Norwegians as they battle against the Nazi occupation. Steinbeck's controversial thesis is that the Nazis will ultimately be defeated when their men question and finally rebel against their leaders. Steinbeck, of course, is world-famous as a novelist.

MARC BLITZSTEIN (1905–1964)

The Cradle Will Rock (1937). A strident drama of social protest, set in "Steeltown, U.S.A." and using music and much of the approach of the Agitprop plays. A manufacturing boss controls the middle-class puppets, but the downtrodden workers rebel. This play had one of the strangest opening nights in the history of world theatre. Scheduled for production by the Federal Theatre, permission was denied at the last minute. Orson Welles and John Houseman greeted 900 members of the audience in the street in front of the theatre and persuaded them to wait, while musicians played for them, until they could rent a theatre; they did so, rushed back in a taxi, and marched the audience twenty blocks north to 59th Street and the newly rented theatre. Because of union regulations, however, they were not allowed to use costumes or the stage, so they staged the production in the orchestra with Blitzstein playing piano accompaniment and Orson Welles serving as impromptu commentator. When the play moved to Broadway later, as part of Welles' and Houseman's Mercury Theatre project, the stripped-down production approach was maintained.

The Threepenny Opera (1955). An English

adaptation of a musical by Kurt Weill and Bertolt Brecht, based on John Gay's 18th-century British ballad-play *The Beggar's Opera*. Highwayman MacHeath is headed for the gallows until stopped by a deus-ex-machina ending. This held the record for the longest run off-Broadway, with 2,611 performances, until *The Fantasticks* came along to play forever. *Threepenny* is the only Brecht play ever to be a box-office hit in the United States. Blitzstein did several other musical adaptations of lesser importance.

CLIFFORD GOLDSMITH (1900–)

What a Life (1938). Young Henry Aldrich finally gets high-school life untangled. Goldsmith, who had worked with several other people on a couple of earlier comedies, received much assistance on this script from George Abbott and Hollywood writers F. Hugh Herbert and Samuel Taylor. They then used the play as a basis for a series of Henry Aldrich radio series and feature-length films in the years just before and during World War II.

ROBERT ARDREY (1908–)

Thunder Rock (1939). A strong, optimistic social play with Pirandellian overtones. Charleston, a former journalist and now a lighthouse keeper in Lake Michigan, refuses to return to the world he considers hopeless until, in a supernatural sequence, some shipwrecked exiles (whom Charleston has created in his own mind) seeking freedom after Europe's 1848 revolutions, make him realize he must help create a new order out of the current chaos. Produced by the Group Theatre. Ardrey, a Chicagoan, has not only been a dramatist and a novelist, but he has published several major works in anthropology, including *African Genesis* (1961) and *The Territorial Imperative* (1966).

WILLIAM SAROYAN (1908–)

My Heart's in the Highlands (1939). A one-act and the simplest of his plays, this is a hymn to beauty. We see several events in the life of nine-year-old Johnny, we meet old Jasper MacGregor the bugler who has run away from an old folks' home, and see other lovable California eccentrics. The Theatre Guild and the Group joined forces to stage this play. Saroyan, of Armenian heritage, grew up in the San Joaquin Valley in California and had his first writing success with the short story "The Daring Young Man on the Flying Trapeze" in 1934.

The Time of Your Life (1939). A bizarre comedy of good versus evil, set in a San Francisco honkytonk. Blick, a bully of a policeman, is finally shot by Kit Carson, a senile folk-hero of a man. There are many other delightful characterizations. Saroyan's theme is identical with that of many serious plays at the time: the meek little people must kill the dictatorial bullies of the world. Winner of both a Pulitzer Prize and the New York Drama Critics Circle Award, this play has been revived regularly and done constantly in amateur theatre.

Love's Old Sweet Song (1940). A three-act romantic comedy about an old maid and a pitchman. Saroyan was best known, early in his career, for his autobiographical stories and novels, including *My Name is Aram* (1941) and *The Human Comedy* (1943). He says that he got his start in writing by telling a New York magazine that he was going to send them one short story a day until they accepted one. They did.

The Beautiful People (1941). A chaotic poetic fantasy about an oversensitive girl. Saroyan's seemingly unstructured writings have not been part of any "literary pose." He is as delightfully droll as any of his characters. At a 1969 drama conference at New Mexico State University, he came (from Paris) a week early in an old car, wandered about the cotton fields ready for harvest, picked flowers and gave them to students, shopped for knickknacks downtown, and talked readily with everyone. He said at that time that he considers all his writing ". . . a kind of letter to the world."

Hello, Out There (1942). A realistic one-act play about an itinerant tramp called The Young Man, in jail in a Western village, who counsels The Girl, a cleaning woman there, to leave and find happiness. The play ends with a mob coming to lynch him after an immoral woman has accused him of rape. This is a superb play, one of the best short dramas ever written in the United States.

The Cave Dwellers (1957). A group of derelicts, mostly from third-rate show-business careers, share their dreams and crumbs in an abandoned theatre (called The World) in lower New York City, as the demolition crews prepare to move in. As in all his writings, Saroyan's unabashed theme of love comes through with great strength.

JAMES THURBER (1894–1961)

The Male Animal (1940). A college professor's domestic troubles and the stresses upon him as he tries to remain a liberal. This was an immensely popular play in the amateur field for several decades. The play was coauthored with actor-writer Elliott Nugent, who also wrote several light comedies for Broadway in the decade before World War II.

A Thurber Carnival (1960). Many of Thurber's most popular prose selections are blended here into a theatrical revue. Thurber, blind and quite near death, nevertheless played in it for a short time. Since then, the revue has been done widely. Thurber has a major reputation as a member of the editorial staff of *The New Yorker* magazine and as a prose humorist and cartoonist; the theatre, however, has been the richer for the adaptation of some of his better efforts here.

JOSEPH FIELDS (1895–1966) and JEROME CHODOROV (1914–)

My Sister Eileen (1940). Based on Ruth McKenney's comic novel of the same name, this is a light account of two sisters suddenly on their own in a New York City apartment. Fields was a writer, Chodorov a writer and director; they collaborated on a fairly large number of plays, many of them adaptations.

Junior Miss (1941). Another extremely light comedy, quite popular at the time, this is a dramatic adaptation of the Sally Benson stories about an overly romantic thirteen-year-old girl. Fields' brother and sister, Herbert and Dorothy, were another set of collaborators for the theatre; and Chodorov, in collaboration with writers other than Fields, had appeared on Broadway as early as 1931.

Wonderful Town (1953). Music by Leonard Bernstein, lyrics by Betty Comden and Adolph Green, book by Fields and Chodorov. A musical version of *My Sister Eileen,* again we see the two young girls on their own in the Greenwich Village basement apartment. Winner of the New York Drama Critics Circle Award for best musical of the season.

The Ponder Heart (1956). From the novel by Eudora Welty. A charmingly naive Southern gentleman is acquitted of the accidental murder of his child bride. Both Fields and Chodorov collaborated with various other playwrights and novelists in bringing a wide assortment of works to the stage.

JOSEPH KESSELRING (1902–1967)

Arsenic and Old Lace (1941). A farcical melodrama about charming but homicidal old ladies and their eccentric brother who thinks he is Teddy Roosevelt. The play was a New York hit, ran in London for two full years during the middle of the war, and has been staged regularly by amateur troupes everywhere. The play was originally produced and directed on Broadway by Howard Lindsay and Russel Crouse; rumor has it that they contributed much revision to Kesselring's only big hit. Kesselring, a New Yorker and later a professor of music in the Midwest, had several plays on Broadway between 1933 and 1963; none, however, were this successful.

ALBERT HACKETT (1900–) and FRANCES GOODRICH (c.1890–)

The Great Big Doorstep (1942). From a novel by E. P. O'Donnell, this is a tenderly humorous story of a Mississippi shanty family that tries to acquire a home to match a beautiful doorstep that floats down the river to them. Hackett and Goodrich were husband and wife.

The Diary of Anne Frank (1955). From Anne Frank's own wartime diary, published as *The Diary of a Young Girl,* this dramatic adaptation won both a Pulitzer Prize and the New York Drama Critics Circle Award. The account of how Anne, in hiding with her family in an Amsterdam apartment building, tries vainly to escape capture by the Nazis. Ultimately they are all captured and sent to concentration camps. This was a superb dramatization of an intensely moving human document that shows the immense evil and the extreme grandeur of the human race.

F. HUGH HERBERT (1898–1958)

Kiss and Tell (1943). A very light comedy, the first of the many Corliss Archer stories, plays, and films. Corliss is a typical teenage girl with typical crises that of course aren't really crises at all. Herbert was primarily active in Hollywood as an actor and writer, and as a radio writer; he and Samuel Taylor scripted the Henry Aldrich series based on the play *What a Life* (*see* Clifford Goldsmith entry).

For Love or Money (1947). A storm and some car trouble send a young girl into the home of an aging matinee idol, and a romance ensues.

The Moon Is Blue (1951). A high comedy of a whirlwind romance between Patty O'Neill and Don Gresham that begins and ends on the observation deck of the Empire State Building. The play was considered quite daring when first produced but is extremely tame and genial today. Herbert was born in England, began work in a department store in London, and came to the United States to remain in 1920. He turned out a voluminous amount of radio, magazine, film, and stage comedy.

JAMES GOW (1907–52) and ARNAUD D'USSEAU (1916–)

Tomorrow the World (1943). The reeducation of a Nazi-indoctrinated young boy by an American family. Gow and D'Usseau have both been successful Hollywood film writers since the early 1930's, D'Usseau notable for dozens of mystery films.

Deep Are the Roots (1945). A picture of Southern racial prejudice at its extreme. These two plays are the only serious stage efforts made by Gow and D'Usseau, but both are worthy dramas. This play anticipates the tension and militance in the Deep South by a decade, as returning Black war hero Brett finally makes white Alice see his position, as he barely avoids being lynched.

PHILIP YORDAN (1914–)

Anna Lucasta (1944). This play is interesting as an example of how shows appear on Broadway. Yordan, a Hollywood screenwriter, wrote the novel, then adapted it for the stage as an account of a Polish-American family. Before it was produced, he switched the characterizations and settings to blacks in Harlem, where it was produced with an all-black cast. It was then moved, intact, to Broadway. Although title credit is given to Yordan, the actual play was most likely assisted by playdoctors: anonymous writers, sometimes famous playwrights, who rework others' scripts for a flat fee.

LEONARD BERNSTEIN (1918–)

On the Town (1944). Music by Bernstein, book and lyrics by Betty Comden and Adolph Green. Three young Navy trainees, on a pass, hunt up New York City's Miss Subways' Beauty-of-the-Month and take her and her friends out on the town. Bernstein, a versatile musician, composer, and director, was conductor of the New York Philharmonic Orchestra for years.

Wonderful Town (1953). Music by Bernstein, lyrics by Betty Comden and Adolph Green, book by Joseph Fields and Jerome Chodorov. The musical version of Fields' and Chodorov's *My Sister Eileen,* which in turn had come from Ruth McKenney's book. Two sisters from the Midwest are suddenly placed on their own in a Greenwich Village basement apartment. Winner of the New York Drama Critics Circle Award for best musical of 1952–53.

Candide (1956). Music by Bernstein, lyrics by Richard Wilbur, John La Touche, and Dorothy Parker, book by Lillian Hellman. An adaptation of Voltaire's famous prose work in which the lead character believed that this was "the best of all possible worlds." The revival in 1973–74, with additions to the book by Hugh Wheeler and to the music by Stephen Sondheim, won the New York Drama Critics Circle Award for best musical.

West Side Story (1957). Music by Bernstein, lyrics by Stephen Sondheim, book by Arthur

Laurents, original idea and choreography by Jerome Robbins. The *Romeo and Juliet* story set in the ghetto streets of New York City, with the two gangs, the Jets and the Sharks, fighting each other, and the tragic love between Tony and Maria. One of the best musicals in American theatre history, with the music and dance stemming from the plot rather than being grafted on, as was the case with so many early musical comedies.

Mass (1971). Music, lyrics, and book by Bernstein, additional lyrics by Stephen Schwartz. A lengthy modern mass based on the Catholic liturgy but actually a theatrical work for orchestra, chorus, street band, dancers, rock group, and actors, this is a struggle between faith and doubt. It was influenced by the Total Theatre movement and is the most ambitious and serious of the several rock musicals. It inaugurated the John F. Kennedy Center for the Performing Arts in Washington, D.C.

MARY CHASE (1907–)

Harvey (1944). A light fantasy of a man, Elwood Dowd, and his invisible white rabbit, which won a Pulitzer Prize. This was by far the most popular of her three New York plays and has been done widely in amateur and stock theatre. Miss Chase is the first major playwright from the Rocky Mountain area (Denver), and she has also written many plays for both children's and high-school theatre.

NORMAN KRASNA (1909–)

Dear Ruth (1944). A polished comedy about a young girl who carries on a romantic correspondence, in her older sister's name, with a soldier; complications occur when he comes home. Krasna wrote a number of box-office successes, all in comedy; several later became films.

John Loves Mary (1947). Another box-office hit, a comedy about a soldier who marries a woman in order to get her into the United States so that she can marry someone else.

ARTHUR MILLER (1915–)

The Man Who Had All the Luck (1944). Miller's first New York play, a commercial failure. A young garage mechanic who gets everything in life through luck finally becomes terrified as he sees others, better than he, struggling in life. Miller grew up in Brooklyn; interested mostly in sports as a teenager, he dreamed of playing football for Michigan. After working in a warehouse in New York City for more than a year, he saved enough to go to Michigan, where, instead of succeeding in athletics, he won several playwriting awards. After college he returned to New York and wrote for radio until he succeeded on Broadway.

All My Sons (1947). A social drama about war profiteering that won the New York Drama Critics Circle Award and catapulted Miller to fame. Joe Keller's eldest son has killed himself in a plane crash in World War II because he has learned that his father had let other pilots die in defective airplanes. When the younger son, after the War, accuses the father of this, Joe kills himself. This is an extremely well-made play, and critics observed that Miller was a disciple of Ibsenian social realism, although Miller also openly admitted his debt to Clifford Odets, whose plays he had seen while in college.

Death of a Salesman (1949). A powerful family drama with several strong social themes. Miller called it a "middle-class tragedy." The business failure, emotional breakdown, and suicide of salesman Willy Loman, and the struggle by son Biff to understand himself and his family. Biff comes to realize that his father and brother, Happy, have both lived by phony external values. The play won both a Pulitzer Prize and the New York Drama Critics Circle Award and made Miller one of the top half dozen living dramatists at that time. The play has stood up extremely well and remains a modern classic.

The Crucible (1953). John Proctor and many others die in old Salem, Massachusetts, because a group of hysterical girls led by young Abigail, whom John has seduced, accuse others of witchcraft in order to save themselves from embarrassment. Mass hysteria then compounds the original injustice. Miller, always the social dramatist, was appalled at the political hounding of liberals during the Senator

Joseph McCarthy era early in the 1950's and wrote this play as a thinly veiled protest. It did not succeed as well as Miller hoped; but when it was revived off-Broadway several years later, the play received enormous acclaim and ever since has been considered one of our top dramas.

A View from the Bridge (1955). A smashingly powerful tragedy of a Brooklyn longshoreman, Eddie Carbone, who cannot let his niece marry because of his inner incestuous passions. Eddie is killed at the end. Miller wrote this originally as a one-act play, partly in verse; and it was staged as part of a double bill with the following play. He rewrote it into a full-length play, however, for staging in London the following year, and its richness then became apparent. One of the best modern tragedies in its longer form.

A Memory of Two Mondays (1955). Originally the curtain-raiser for the above play, this is set in the shipping room of an automobile-parts warehouse on the west side of Manhattan, much like the one where Miller worked in order to save money for college. People lose their dreams, become alcoholic, and die in the sterile, never-ending world of little jobs in a big city. The Miller-like character manages to escape the stranglehold. Much more Chekhovian than Miller's other plays.

After the Fall (1964). After nearly ten years away from Broadway, Miller helped open Lincoln Center for the Performing Arts with this play, which is now considered one of his weakest. Although it is long and interwoven with many important themes, the complex drama about Quentin is actually a kind of catharsis for Miller. In the ten-year period he was harassed by the House Un-American Activities Committee and almost went to prison, he was divorced from both his first wife and Marilyn Monroe, and he married Inge Morath, an Austrian photographer. The play includes thin disguises of all these events in Miller's life.

Incident at Vichy (1964). His second play at Lincoln Center, this shows the anti-Jewish reign of terror in Nazi-occupied France in

1942. It is a powerful one-hour-and-ten-minute thriller of a group of men rounded up by French police and waiting to be interrogated by Nazi officers. Gradually the diminishing group realizes that all those who are Jewish are to be shipped to concentration camps for cremation. This is a study of submission as well as persecution. A Jewish doctor, who has tried vainly to get the others to help him in an escape effort, finally convinces the one non-Jew, an Austrian prince, of the importance of responsibility; the prince gives the doctor his own pass to freedom and stays to die.

The Price (1968). Two brothers getting on in age, Victor, a policeman, and Walter, a surgeon, meet in the attic of their father's old Manhattan house to discuss the sale of the furniture with an eighty-nine-year-old dealer, Solomon. The serious, realistic drama, written in Ibsenian fashion, uncovers the family's past and shows the lack of love, the deceit, the greed, and the false values that were prevalent. The title, of course, refers to the price both of them have paid throughout life. Many of the themes and patterns are similar to those in *Death of a Salesman,* and they further solidify Miller as a dramatist of middle-class family life who urges people to face up to responsibilities in life.

The Creation of the World and Other Business (1972). Miller's first comedy, which failed after a two-week run. Act I shows Adam and Eve in the Garden of Eden, Act II shows Eve giving birth to Cain, and Act III shows Cain killing Abel. The basic theme is that man's natural innocence is corruptible. Almost all the critics said the humor was weak, but an interesting twist in the play is Lucifer portrayed as frustrated helper of man. Miller revised the play heavily in 1973, adding songs and recorded narration by himself, for a then-successful production at the University of Michigan and other colleges. Whether Miller writes anything further or not, his reputation is secure as one of the top post-World War II dramatists.

JOHN PATRICK (GOGGEN) (1907–)

The Hasty Heart (1945). A heartwarming

war play in a convalescent ward. A proud, wounded Scottish soldier, after falling for his nurse, learns the lesson of loving one's neighbors, too. Patrick's first plays reached Broadway before World War II; he also worked in Hollywood on several dozen films. This play stemmed from his own wartime experience in the Middle East. A Kentuckian, he began his writing career in radio on the West Coast.

The Curious Savage (1950). Greedy stepchildren put father's second wife into a sanatorium to force an inheritance from her; she finds the inmates more humane than the supposedly sane on the outside.

The Teahouse of the August Moon (1953). Based on the novel by Vern Sneider. A stuffy Army colonel sends Captain Fisby to a village in Okinawa after World War II to make it democratic even if they have to shoot everyone to do so. Captain Fisby prefers to adopt native customs rather than force American customs on them, and they build a teahouse instead of a school. The play is narrated by a young Okinawan scamp, Sakini. It won both a Pulitzer Prize and the New York Drama Critics Circle Award, and Patrick turned it into a film; the play has been done in amateur theatre ever since. Patrick never came close to matching this success.

Love Is a Time of Day (1969). Patrick wrote a number of other comedies, several of which, including this one, were premiered by the Albuquerque, New Mexico, Little Theatre. Albuquerque's resident director Bernie Thomas made his directing debut on Broadway with this show.

HOWARD RICHARDSON (1917–) and WILLIAM BERNEY (1924–1964)
Dark of the Moon (1945). A dramatization, set in the Southern mountains, of the old Barbara Allen ballad about witchcraft. The Witch Boy falls in love with a human girl, but their love is doomed in part by the prejudice of the village folk. One of our better regional and folk plays, it is the only one of several collaborations by Richardson and Berney to achieve success professionally.

ARTHUR LAURENTS (1918–)
Home of the Brave (1945). A drama of prejudice and tensions in a wartime hospital, in which a Jewish soldier learns from a one-armed buddy to look prejudice and hurt square in the eye. Laurents grew up in New York City and went to Cornell University. He has directed and written film scripts, but his reputation is primarily as a serious playwright and a collaborator on musicals.

The Time of the Cuckoo (1952). A bittersweet realistic comedy, set in Venice, of a spinster schoolteacher approaching middle age and in search of romance and meaning in life.

A Clearing in the Woods (1957). A psychological drama of a woman's traumatic experiences in life. In this nonrealistic play she meets herself in the form of her childhood, girlhood, and young womanhood; she has to learn to live with herself realistically, with hopes but without dreams. Several of Laurents' plays are interesting psychological studies.

West Side Story (1957). Music by Leonard Bernstein, lyrics by Stephen Sondheim, book by Laurents, original idea and choreography by Jerome Robbins. The *Romeo and Juliet* story set in the ghetto streets of New York City, with the two gangs, the Jets and the Sharks, fighting each other, and the tragic love between Tony and Maria. One of the best musicals in American theatre history, with the music and dance stemming from the plot rather than being grafted on, as was the case with so many early musical comedies.

Gypsy (1959). Music by Jule Styne, lyrics by Stephen Sondheim, book by Laurents. From the memoirs of famous striptease dancer Gypsy Rose Lee, this show tells of her early life in vaudeville and legitimate theatre and of her domineering mother.

Invitation to a March (1960). A comedy set on the beaches of Long Island, about the dangers of conformity in the modern world. Norma dances off into the night with Aaron the plumber, leaving the steady Schuyler behind. Even in his comedies, Laurents has always tried to say something thematically.

Hallelujah, Baby! (1967). Music by Jule Styne, lyrics by Betty Comden and Adolph Green, book by Laurents. This show brought Leslie Uggams to stardom as she and others showed the black people's efforts to gain a place in American society. For more on Betty Comden and Adolph Green, see next entry.

Enclave (1973). When a forty-year-old homosexual wants to live openly with a young man, the rest of a communal living group has its equilibrium jolted. A brittle, sophisticated comedy.

BETTY COMDEN (1919–) and ADOLPH GREEN (1915–)

On the Town (1944). Music by Leonard Bernstein, book and lyrics by Comden and Green. Three young Navy trainees, on a pass, hunt up New York City's Miss Subways' Beauty-of-the-Month and take her and her friends out on the town. Comden and Green collaborated on a number of Broadway musicals.

Wonderful Town (1953). Music by Leonard Bernstein, lyrics by Comden and Green, book by Joseph Fields and Jerome Chodorov. The musical version of Fields' and Chodorov's *My Sister Eileen,* which in turn had come from Ruth McKenney's book. Two sisters from the Midwest are suddenly placed on their own in a Greenwich Village basement apartment. Winner of a New York Drama Critics Circle Award for best musical of 1952–53.

Hallelujah, Baby! (1967). *See* Arthur Laurents entry, above.

Applause (1970). Music by Charles Strouse, lyrics by Lee Adams, book by Comden and Green, based on the film *All About Eve,* which came from a story by Mary Orr. This starred Lauren Bacall in both New York and London productions and basically parallels her lifelong struggle to maintain her integrity in a show-business career. We see the young starlet ever ready to supplant the established star. Comden and Green wrote the play for their longtime friend Miss Bacall. Comden and Green (not related to each other) have worked together for decades, beginning as nightclub performers in an act with Judy Holliday, reaching Broadway in a two-person revue in which they acted and sang, and going on to collaborate on a number of hit Hollywood films as well as their Broadway musicals.

(THOMAS LANIER) TENNESSEE WILLIAMS (1911–)

You Touched Me! (1945). Coauthored with Donald Windham, this was a comedy based on a D. H. Lawrence short story. Williams, born in Mississippi, grew up in St. Louis although he spent much time with his maternal grandparents, the Reverend and Mrs. Dakin. He contracted diphtheria as a boy and was crippled for a time; bookish as a youth, he was taunted by his father, who was a shoe salesman. He was extremely close to his older sister, Rose. He attended the University of Missouri but dropped out after he failed ROTC, and was sent to work in his father's shoe factory. Later he worked his way to a degree at the University of Iowa, where he studied playwriting, won several contests, and began writing plays for amateur troupes. After traveling in the South and on the West Coast, he wrote a group of plays called *American Blues,* which won a prize from the Group Theatre and won the interest of agent Audrey Wood.

The Glass Menagerie (1945). Mother Amanda desires a gentleman caller for her daughter Rose and remembers her own days of popularity in the Deep South; son Tom rebels at his job at the shoe factory and runs away; and daughter Laura, shy and crippled, retreats forever to the world of her glass animal collection when the gentleman caller turns out to be engaged. A tender, poetic, autobiographical play about his family, particularly Williams' sister, Rose, who suffered a mental breakdown and had a prefrontal lobotomy performed upon her when she was in her twenties. The play opened in Chicago and was on the verge of closing for lack of business when critic Claudia Cassidy wrote a series of columns urging attendance. It caught on, came to New York, won the New York Drama Critics Circle Award, and established Williams as one of the top two or three American dramatists since World War II.

A Streetcar Named Desire (1947). Blanche DuBois, alcoholic and fired from her teaching job for immorality, comes to visit her sister, Stella, who is married to rough-and-tough Stanley Kowalski. A passion-hate relationship erupts between Blanche and Stanley; he rapes her, and she is taken away to an asylum. Williams' theme is that modern violence conquers genteel decadence in today's South. The New York production brought Marlon Brando to fame and won both a Pulitzer Prize and the New York Drama Critics Circle Award. The play remains as effective now as when it was first produced.

Summer and Smoke (1948). Miss Alma, a sensitive, puritanical young woman, has long loved Johnny, the young physician who lives next door. Their destiny almost works out, stutters, and collapses; Johnny marries vivacious young Nellie, and Alma sits at the town fountain in Glorious Hill, Mississippi, and picks up a traveling salesman. The Broadway production received mixed reviews, but the off-Broadway revival and subsequent film, both starring Geraldine Page, were outstanding. Williams, who often revises his plays, re-did this in 1967 under the title *Eccentricities of a Nightingale.* Lanford Wilson wrote the libretto when the play was staged as an opera by the New York City Opera Company in 1972. As *Eccentricities of a Nightingale,* the revised play was brought to New York by Williams in 1976. The newest version takes out Johnny's father, Johnny's temporary mistress Rosa, and the shooting by Rosa's father of Johnny's father. Again, the reviews were mixed.

The Rose Tattoo (1951). We see Latin violence and passion and a celebration of life as widowed Serafina finds a new stud male to make her life complete. Williams spent a great deal of time in Italy over the years and often wrote about Italian characters or settings.

Camino Real (1953). Williams' only totally nonrealistic play, this is a murky symbolic account of mankind's final meeting place and lists among the characters Casanova, Don Quixote, Sancho Panza, and the mythical American soldier, Kilroy. The play was not a commercial success, although there were revivals in 1960 and 1970. For the most part, in his other plays, Williams' symbolism has been quite understandable and usually gives a poetic softening to his works.

Cat on a Hot Tin Roof (1955). A powerful study of impotence and greed, based on Williams' earlier short story "Three Players of a Summer Game." Big Daddy is dying of cancer and his son Brick is so tangled up emotionally that he cannot have sex with his hot-blooded wife, Maggie-the-Cat. Elia Kazan, who directed several of Williams' major successes, insisted that the death of Big Daddy before the third act began would weaken the production. Williams revised to suit Kazan; but later, after the production closed, he published the play with his original ending minus Big Daddy. Readers and viewers now have their choice of the two endings. The play was given a brilliant filming for American television in 1976, with Laurence Olivier playing Big Daddy.

Orpheus Descending (1957). With this production Williams began to get increasingly negative reviews. Ironically, this is a revision of Williams' first full-length play to get professional production, *Battle of Angels,* which not only closed out of town before New York, but suffered a smoky fire backstage. Williams later reworked the play again and titled it *The Fugitive Kind.* It is based loosely on the Greek legend of Orpheus and Eurydice, and we see Lady shot by her husband, who is upstairs dying of cancer in their store, and Lady's lover, Val, torn apart by sheriff's dogs.

Garden District (1958). A bill of two one-act plays: *Suddenly Last Summer* and *Something Unspoken.* The sensationalism, which included references to cannibalism in the first play (which was also filmed), turned many critics and audience members against Williams. His reputation dipped in these years, although he remained productive.

Sweet Bird of Youth (1959). A pathetic account of Princess, an aging movie star on drugs and liquor, and her young stud, Chance Wayne. Princess makes one final effort to regain her fading status, but Chance gives up and lets himself be castrated by a local mob. The play is a picture of degeneracy in the old and the young. The production starred Geraldine Page and Paul Newman.

Period of Adjustment (1960). Williams' only true comedy, this play opens on Christmas Eve in a suburban home in the South; the wife has just left the husband. Arriving is the husband's old war buddy and his bride of one night, having their troubles. Both marriages are put back together and the play ends happily.

The Night of the Iguana (1961). The Reverend T. Lawrence Shannon, fired from his seedy tour-guide job after earlier being defrocked because of immorality, finds empathy from recently widowed Maxine at her run-down resort on the west coast of Mexico. Shannon also finds kindness from spinster-painter Hannah, who goes determinedly on her way in the morning after her grandfather, Nonno, dies. This is one of Williams' best plays and had a superb film version. It shows the importance of human compassion, especially to the exiles and outcasts of the world. Nonno was obviously patterned after his maternal grandfather.

The Milk Train Doesn't Stop Here Any More. (1963). Done for the Spoleto Festival in Italy. An old woman dies of cancer in Italy. Williams, obsessed with death, repeated the business of a character dying of cancer in several plays. This play was filmed by Elizabeth Taylor and Richard Burton under the title *Boom*. With this play, Williams began to fall upon difficult times, professionally and personally. His longtime friend Frank Merlo died, he had a series of critical and box-office failures; and in his later autobiography, *Memoirs* (1975), he said that he became increasingly dependent upon barbiturates until a hospitalization in 1969.

Slapstick Tragedy (1966). Two one-act plays: *The Mutilated,* about sailors and prostitutes in New Orleans; and *Gnadige Fraulein,* about bizarre people in the Florida Keys. Williams also has lived extensively in the Florida Keys. This double bill was Williams' first total flop after he attained fame; the plays closed in seven days.

The Seven Descents of Myrtle (1968). Another failure, with critics saying that Williams had begun to parody himself. A triangle: Myrtle, who got her husband through a television quiz program; Lot, her impotent husband; and Chicken, his mulatto and oversexed brother.

In the Bar of a Tokyo Hotel (1969). A long two-scene one-act play about a middle-aged couple, Miriam, who chases young men and is afraid of her waning sexuality, and Mark, a painter, who is afraid of his failing creativity. Mark has a breakdown and dies. Not successful.

Out Cry (1971). Premiered at the Ivanhoe Dinner Theatre in Chicago, to poor reviews, then done after revisions in 1973 on Broadway. Williams returned to theatre with this play, after a hospitalization and regaining of his health. It is a two-character play within a play about a brother and a sister, both actors, performing before an unidentified audience and finding themselves trapped in a cold, empty theatre at the end. The play is probably fairly autobiographical, about Williams' increasing feeling of entrapment and loss in his middle years.

Small Craft Warnings (1972). Done off-Broadway in New York. A major success in London, transferring from a small theatre club to a large West End theatre for a good run. A group of little people, failures in life, in Monk's California coastal-village bar, struggling through another night. The play is a series of soliloquies, without any powerful dramatic climax, but it is a compassionate study of suffering victims: alcoholics, studs, homosexuals, nymphomaniacs, all trying to escape loneliness for a few hours. Williams is still writing, but he probably will be best known for the early half of his professional career when he turned out some of the richest modern plays. At his best, Williams, in a poetic style, shows the victims in life and portrays loneliness with great intensity.

Vieux Carré (1977). Produced on Broadway. The title refers to the Old Square in the French quarter of New Orleans, a favorite haunt of Williams in his earlier years; and the play is set in an old hotel there in the late 1930's. Virtually two one-acts, the first part shows lonely homosexual Painter, dying of tuberculosis, and a character called Writer who is trying to become known; the second half shows Jane, dying of a blood disease, and her stud, Tye. Helping to cement the two acts is the bizarre landlady, Mrs. Wire. The play received mixed reviews and the consensus that Williams was reworking old characters and motifs.

GARSON KANIN (1912–)

Born Yesterday (1946). A farcical comedy of postwar readjustments. Ignorant junk dealer Harry Brock goes to Washington with an uneducated chorus girl, Billie, to buy up government junk. Billie, played on Broadway and in the subsequent film by Judy Holliday, gradually wises up, with help from a sharp young reporter.

A Gift of Time (1962). Adapted from the novel *Death of a Man* by Lael Tucker Wertenbaker, the dramatization was done by Garson and Faye Kanin, brother and sister. Kanin is married to actress Ruth Gordon. The Kanins have a number of other adaptations for both stage and screen, and Garson has also been both actor and director. In this play, a writer is dying of cancer and must face up to and accept death.

JEAN KERR (1923–)

Our Hearts Were Young and Gay (1947). Mrs. Kerr, wife of New York drama critic Walter Kerr, was once his student at Catholic University. She began her professional writing career for the theatre by helping to adapt the book by Cornelia Otis Skinner and Emily Kimbrough that told of their adventures in Europe. Walter Kerr has also been represented on Broadway with several plays; but more important, has written several excellent books about the theatre. After Brooks Atkin-

son retired, Kerr became the dean of New York critics.

Jenny Kissed Me (1948). A warm comedy about a priest who plays matchmaker, this has been a popular play in amateur theatre.

King of Hearts (1954). Coauthored with Eleanor Brooke, this play shows the comic deflation of an egotistical cartoonist.

Mary Mary (1961). A brittle comedy of marriage, with Mary preparing to leave her husband, Bob McKellaway, and run off with fading matinee idol Dirk Winston. Mary and Bob are, of course, reconciled at the comic conclusion. This play was a phenomenal commercial success and came at the same time that Mrs. Kerr hit the best-seller list with several books of comic prose, including *Please Don't Eat the Daisies* and *The Snake Has All the Lines*. For several years she was one of the most widely read and seen writers in the nation.

Poor Richard (1964). A sentimental, girl-gets-man comedy of a British poet who finally admits the several truths about his late wife and himself.

Finishing Touches (1973). The tribulations of family life, and revelations between the sexes. A professor has a crush on a student, a son brings home an older woman, and the wife has to cope with all of this during a weekend. All ends well for the husband and the wife in this witty comedy.

WILLIAM WISTER HAINES (1908–)

Command Decision (1947). An excellent war play, perhaps one of the best ever written, about an officer in the United States Army Air Corps in Britain in World War II who must sacrifice his men on a raid deep into Germany in order to achieve ultimate victory for the Allies. Haines was a combat officer. The play was made into a film and a book.

ALAN JAY LERNER (1918–) and FREDERICK LOEWE (1901–)

Brigadoon (1947). Music by Loewe, book and lyrics by Lerner. A musical fantasy of the Scottish Highlands, contrasting cynical urban life with charming rural ways. Two New Yorkers, Tommy and Jeff, discover a village that comes to life only one day every hundred years. Tommy falls for Fiona, but reluctantly leaves for the reality of the city. Miserable there, he returns to look for Brigadoon at the finale. This production established Lerner and Loewe as the best musical collaboration team of the postwar period. Their first show together had been *What's Up?* in 1943. Loewe was a child-prodigy pianist-composer who was writing songs at the age of nine and soloing with major symphonies in his early teens. Lerner was a Harvard graduate in 1940. He is also a Hollywood Oscar winner for his screenplay of the film *An American in Paris.* *Brigadoon* won the New York Drama Critics Circle Award for best musical of 1946–47 and solidified their reputation.

Paint Your Wagon (1951). Music by Loewe, book and lyrics by Lerner. The tuneful tale of a wandering dreamer, Ben Rumson, who is a prospector in the Mountain West. The boom town becomes a ghost town but will be saved by irrigation and farming, and Old Ben goes on dreaming and following his wandering star.

My Fair Lady (1956). Music by Loewe, book and lyrics by Lerner, from George Bernard Shaw's play *Pygmalion*. Directed by Moss Hart. Linguist and irascible bachelor Henry Higgins (played by Rex Harrison), on a bet with his friend Colonel Pickering, transforms cockney flower girl Liza Doolittle (played by Julie Andrews) into a lady, and they fall in love. Comedy comes from Liza's ne'er-do-well chimney-sweep father, Alfred Doolittle; and Freddy Eynsford-Hill provides the romantic triangle. Liza returns to Henry at the finale, which is more upbeat than in Shaw's original play. The production brought Miss Andrews to stardom, won the New York Drama Critics Circle Award for best musical for 1955–56, and had a Broadway run of 2,717 performances. It has been produced, by professionals and amateurs, all over the world ever since; and in 1976 it reopened on Broadway with Ian Richardson playing Henry Higgins. Of the 1976 production, *The New Yorker* said, "A flawless revival of a flawless musical. How did the world get along without it for fifteen thou-

sand years?" The score includes such favorites as "I Could Have Danced All Night," "On the Street Where You Live," "The Rain in Spain," "With a Little Bit of Luck," and "Get Me to the Church on Time." Lerner and Loewe have earned a reputation that will always rank near the top just from this one musical masterpiece.

Camelot (1960). Music by Loewe, book and lyrics by Lerner, based on T. H. White's *The Once and Future King*. This is a poignant musical about the breakup of King Arthur's court. He welcomes Guenevere, they marry, he creates the Round Table, Lancelot arrives and his love with Guenevere begins, Arthur's evil son Mordred plots against his father, and Arthur and Lancelot go to war against each other; the age of chivalry is dead. A young boy comes to join the court, and Arthur asks him to tell the world about how things were, once, in Camelot.

ROBINSON JEFFERS (1887–1962)

Medea (1947). A poetic retelling of the Greek play by Euripides. Judith Anderson starred in this powerful tragedy, in which Medea takes her revenge on husband Jason by killing their children. Jeffers, a Californian, was one of our major poets.

The Tower Beyond Tragedy (1950). Another poetic version of a Greek play, this is the first two parts of Aeschylus' *Oresteian Trilogy*. Clytemnestra kills her husband Agamemnon when he returns from the Trojan War, and their children Orestes and Electra take their revenge on her. Jeffers' play adds emphasis to the part of the doomed seer, Cassandra.

The Cretan Women (1954). A loose adaptation of Euripides' Greek play *Hippolytus,* with Queen Phaedra falling in love with her priggish stepson, Hippolytus, who dies after his father curses him.

FRANK LOESSER (1910–1969)

Where's Charley? (1948). Music and lyrics by Loesser, book by George Abbott, from the old British farce by Brandon Thomas, *Charlie's Aunt.* A romping musical farce with some college boys disguising a man as a visiting aunt in order to be able to invite some girls to their party. From the time the play was first produced in 1892 until the present, the play and then the musical have been revived virtually everywhere. Loesser was a top Hollywood songwriter.

Guys and Dolls (1950). Music and lyrics by Loesser, book by Abe Burrows and Jo Swerling, based on Damon Runyon's short stories about New York gamblers. Directed by George S. Kaufman. Won the New York Drama Critics Circle Award for best musical of 1950–51. The main plot is the love between gambler Sky Masterson and Salvation Army girl Sarah Brown; the subplot is the endless love affair between gambler Nathan Detroit and cabaret singer Adelaide, who finally marry. Possessor of an extremely tuneful score, the show has had numerous revivals, one of the more recent being an all-black-cast version on Broadway in 1976.

The Most Happy Fella (1956). Music, lyrics, and book by Loesser, from Sidney Howard's play *They Knew What They Wanted*. Elderly Tony, who owns a vineyard in California, accepts a child that is not his from his mail-order bride Amy, in order that he can have a son and she can have a home. Winner of the New York Drama Critics Circle Award for best musical of 1956–57.

How to Succeed in Business Without Really Trying (1961). Music and lyrics by Loesser, book by Abe Burrows, Jack Weinstock, and Willie Gilbert. A window washer becomes chairman of the board of a big corporation in this spoof of big-city life. Won the New York Drama Critics Circle Award for best musical for 1961–62 and the Pulitzer Prize for drama the same year, and many critics are still trying to figure out why; it is a much weaker show than Loesser's earlier efforts.

JAN DE HARTOG (1914–)

Skipper Next to God (1948). An idealistic Dutch sea captain whose passengers, Jewish refugees, are denied admission to the United States, wrecks his own ship so that the passengers can be taken ashore. De Hartog was born in the Netherlands.

The Fourposter (1951). An engaging two-character play about a lifetime of marriage. All the action takes place in the same bedroom as the couple marry, endure the various crises of life, and grow old.

I Do! I Do! (1966). A musical version of the above play, adapted by Tom Jones and Harvey Schmidt.

ROBERT McENROE (1918–)

The Silver Whistle (1948). Oliver Erwenter, a wandering charlatan, moves in with a group of elderly residents at their church-home run by a stuffy minister. In this sentimental, heartwarming comedy, he makes the old people happier with their lives and reduces the pomposity of the minister. Starred Jose Ferrer on Broadway and has been a popular amateur hit ever since.

JOSHUA LOGAN (1908–)

Mister Roberts (1948). Dramatization with Thomas Heggen, who wrote the novel, of a World War II account of both comic and tragic life aboard ship in the Navy in the South Pacific. Lt. Roberts is killed at the end. Heggen was a combat officer in the Navy in the Pacific; Logan gained recognition on Broadway as a director in the 1930's, and went on to become a well-known film director and producer.

South Pacific (1949). Music by Richard Rodgers, book and lyrics by Oscar Hammerstein II, some help on the book by Logan, from James Michener's *Tales of the South Pacific*. Nurse Nellie Forbush learns to overcome prejudice and French expatriate Emile de Becque overcomes his isolation as the tide of fortune changes in World War II. Winner of the New York Drama Critics Circle Award for best musical of 1948–49.

The Wisteria Trees (1950). Logan's adaptation of Anton Chekhov's *The Cherry Orchard*. A Louisiana lady returns home from Paris, her inheritance gone and unwilling to face the future. The play follows Chekhov closely except that the businessman proposes to the lady, Lucy; when she refuses him, he angrily orders the wisteria vines chopped down.

Fanny (1954). Music by Logan, book by S. N. Behrman, from three French plays by Marcel Pagnol. A sentimental musical set in Marseilles, bringing the romantic call of the sea in conflict with the call of love. Produced and directed by Logan.

WILLIAM CARLOS WILLIAMS (1883–1963)

A Dream of Love (1949). Produced at an experimental theatre off-Broadway, this is a poetic and penetrating story of marriage and infidelity. Dr. Williams, a physician in New Jersey, was one of our top 20th-century poets. He always loved the stage, did some acting with the original Provincetown Players in Greenwich Village, and wrote some half dozen plays during his lifetime.

Many Loves (1959). A hit that was performed for a year in repertory by the off-Broadway Living Theatre of Julian Beck and Judith Malina. This is another poetic domestic play, with the action taking place in a theatre where three one-act plays are supposedly in rehearsal. The one-acts are *Serafina, The Funnies,* and *Talk.* One of Dr. Williams' unproduced plays shows how creative minds are often attuned; three years before Arthur Miller staged *The Crucible,* Dr. Williams had written a play about Salem witchcraft and the modern McCarthy era of political witch-hunting, *Tituba's Children.* Dr. Williams is best known for his long poem *Paterson.*

SAMUEL TAYLOR (1912–   )

The Happy Time (1950). From a novel by Robert L. Fontaine. A comedy about a whimsical Canadian family, the Bonnards. Despite many threats of disaster, adolescent Bibi becomes a ladies man like his grandfather, father, and uncle.

Sabrina Fair (1953). The daughter of the family chauffeur comes home from Paris to see if she is still in love with the son of her father's wealthy employer. She is, of course, and all ends well in this romantic high comedy set on Long Island. Taylor is at his best in this polished comedy.

The Pleasure of His Company (1958). Written with Cornelia Otis Skinner. A comedy about an estranged father returning home to visit his marriageable daughter.

No Strings (1962). Music by Richard Rodgers, book by Taylor. An experimental musical, with only brass, woodwinds, and percussion in the orchestra, which was hidden behind the stage and had its music piped out to the spectators. The plot is about a love affair that must end in order for the leading man to remain creative in his work.

The Happy Time (1968). Music by John Kander, lyrics by Fred Ebb, book by N. Richard Nash, from the play by Taylor, from the novel by Robert L. Fontaine. A musical version of Taylor's play (*see* above). Taylor originally came East from California when Sidney Howard got him a job as a playreader. Taylor rewrote *What a Life* for Broadway, then succeeded with his own plays, in between radio and T.V. writing.

CARSON SMITH McCULLERS (1917–1967)

The Member of the Wedding (1950). A dramatization, encouraged by Tennessee Williams, of her own novel published in 1946. A sensitive story of adolescence and loneliness, with twelve-year-old Frankie deciding that she is going to accompany her older soldier-brother on his honeymoon. Berenice, the middle-aged black cook, survives the ups and downs of Frankie's crises, but more important, the death of a relative who hangs himself in jail after being caught by a white mob. The play won the New York Drama Critics Circle Award, is somewhat autobiographical, and is one of our richest modern plays about adolescence and family life. Carson Smith went to New York as a teenager from Columbus, Georgia, to study music, lost her money on the subway on her first day there, studied creative writing at Washington Square College, and began publishing very early. She twice married Reeves McCullers, who committed suicide in 1953.

The Square Root of Wonderful (1957). A twice-married woman tries to work out a third marriage. This play is probably based somewhat upon her marital ups and downs with Reeves McCullers. Mrs. McCullers suffered from poor health: rheumatic fever, arthritis, and strokes. In her final years her hands were so crippled that she could only manage one page of manuscript a day. Although her output was small in quantity, the quality was high enough to list her as one of the major writers after World War II. Everything she wrote was highly sensitive, including a novel, *The Heart Is a Lonely Hunter* (1940), and a novella, *The Ballad of the Sad Cafe* (1951), which Edward Albee dramatized in 1963 (*see* Albee entry).

ABE BURROWS (1910–)

Guys and Dolls (1950). Music and lyrics by Frank Loesser, book by Burrows and Jo Swerling, based on Damon Runyon's stories about New York gamblers. Won the New York Drama Critics Circle Award for best musical of 1950–51. The main plot is the love between gambler Sky Masterson and Salvation Army girl Sarah Brown; the subplot is the endless love between gambler Nathan Detroit and cabaret singer Adelaide, who finally marry. The show was revived successfully with an all-black cast on Broadway in 1976. Burrows, a New Yorker, worked in various businesses for some years, gradually switching over to work as an entertainer at Catskill Mountain resorts. From there he moved to radio writing and then to the stage, where he has been a successful writer, adapter, director, and play-doctor.

Can-Can (1953). Music and lyrics by Cole Porter, book by Burrows. A stuffy Parisian judge, Aristide Forestier, visits the dives of Montmartre to decide whether the can-can dance is immoral; he falls in love with café proprietress La Mome Pistache, ends up in a police scandal, resigns his seat on the bench, and helps La Mome Pistache teach the can-can to others. This show brought Gwen Verdon to fame.

Silk Stockings (1955). Music and lyrics by Cole Porter, book by George S. Kaufman, Leueen McGrath, and Burrows, based on the Greta Garbo film *Ninotchka* by Melchior Lengyel. A Russian pianist in Paris for a con-

cert won't return to Russia, nor will the Communist agents who come after him.

Cactus Flower (1965). A long-running comedy about a romance between a dentist and his receptionist, based on an earlier French play. The dentist, having an affair with a young free spirit, uses his prim receptionist as a pseudo-wife as part of his scheming; he ends up falling for the receptionist.

WILLIAM INGE (1913–1973)

Come Back, Little Sheba (1950). The empty middle-aged marriage between an alcoholic chiropractor, Doc, and his wife, Lola. Bit by bit, the last of their dreams are eroded. This was the first of Inge's realistic domestic dramas of everyday Midwesterners and their frustrations. Inge, from Kansas, went to Peabody Teachers College in Tennessee, was a high-school and college teacher in Missouri and a drama critic in St. Louis. He met Tennessee Williams when *The Glass Menagerie* was going into rehearsal and received a great boost from Williams, who encouraged his writing. *Little Sheba* had a good New York run and established Inge as a success.

Picnic (1953). A braggart vagrant comes to a Kansas town on Labor Day and changes the lives of two families of women in this study of feminine passion. The play won a Pulitzer Prize and the New York Drama Critics Circle Award. It has long been considered Inge's best play and was revived under the title *Summer Brave* shortly before he died in 1973.

Bus Stop (1955). Crosscurrents of the lives of a number of people including an ignorant singer, a cowboy, a drunken professor, a waitress, the bus driver, and the sheriff, who are all marooned overnight in a small Kansas café in a blizzard. It was Inge's third consecutive Broadway hit and subsequently an even more popular motion picture.

The Dark at the Top of the Stairs (1957). This was actually Inge's first full-length play to be produced, as *Farther Off from Heaven*, staged with the help and encouragement of Tennessee Williams in 1947 at the Margo Jones theatre-in-the-round in Dallas. It is the story of a prim mother, an Oedipal son who is afraid of the dark, a father who resents being dominated, and a niece whose cruelty to a Jewish boy at a dance causes him to commit suicide. Inge's fourth consecutive smash on Broadway, followed by an extremely popular film. At this point in his career he was considered one of our top playwrights.

A Loss of Roses (1959). The mother-son relationship between Mrs. Helen Baird, a run-down actress, her twenty-one-year-old son, Kenny, and Lila, a small-time tent-show actress. This play was criticized for its sensationalism and was Inge's first failure.

Natural Affection (1963). Into the lives of a thirty-year-old woman (who is a buyer for a Chicago department store) and her lover comes the woman's teenage son, released from reform school. The play becomes a triangle of sexual tensions. Inge's second straight Broadway failure.

Where's Daddy? (1966). A blend of realism and the absurd, this is the story of an emancipated woman. Inge's third consecutive failure sent his career into eclipse. Earlier, he had done several films including *Splendor in the Grass,* which won him an Academy Award, but his major successes came early in his professional career, and he committed suicide in 1973.

JOSEPH KRAMM (1907–)
The Shrike (1952). Jim Downs, in love with another woman, must renounce her and give the "right" answers if he is to be released from a mental hospital and returned to the wife he does not love. An extremely powerful play about how individuals can be crushed by institutions, this won a Pulitzer Prize. Kramm, a Philadelphian, was first a journalist, then an actor; after this, his only major play, he turned to directing in the United States and England.

GEORGE AXELROD (1924–)
The Seven Year Itch (1952). A long-running sex comedy. Richard Sherman's wife goes away for the summer, and he falls for the girl in the apartment upstairs. Publisher of paper-back books and possessor of a vivid imagination, Richard is boxed between his desires and his terrors about being caught. Axelrod was a top writer of Broadway comedy in the 1950's.

Will Success Spoil Rock Hunter? (1955). A satire on Hollywood, with a Marilyn Monroe–like temptress, an illiterate producer, a playwright whose first script was a hit but who can't write another, and a young fan-magazine writer who becomes a big shot.

Goodbye, Charlie (1959). Charlie, a lecherous young man who has been murdered by a cuckolded husband, returns to earth in a female body and proceeds to fall for his/her best friend, George. The play is quite funny early, but tends to fade later after the cleverness of the original situation wears off.

ROBERT ANDERSON (1917–)
Tea and Sympathy (1953). A tender drama of empathy between schoolboy Tom Lee and the wife of his too-gruff teacher. Tom is considered a sissy by everybody except Laura, who allows him a sexual experience at the end out of kindness, to allay Tom's fears that he might not be a normal male. Anderson, a New Yorker, has an M.A. in English from Harvard, completed all but his dissertation for his doctorate, taught there for a time, then served in the Navy, where he won a playwriting contest. After the War, he received several fellowships for writing. Anderson is one of the most modest and well-liked members of the New York theatre community.

All Summer Long (1954). Anderson's one adaptation, from Donald Wetzel's novel *A Wreath and a Curse,* this was staged in Washington and later came to Broadway. Anderson has also written a number of highly regarded film scripts.

Silent Night, Lonely Night (1959). John, his wife in a nearby asylum, and Katherine, separated from her husband in London, spend Christmas Eve together in an old New England inn, then go their separate ways, the richer for the tender experience. All of Anderson's works are sensitive; the poignancy of this play stems, most likely, from the grief

Anderson felt over the death of his first wife, Phyllis, who had been an extremely well-liked Broadway agent. She was several years older than Anderson. He later remarried and has had a long and happy union with actress Teresa Wright.

The Days Between (1965). David Ives, a creative-writing professor in a small New England college, has to face middle age and the erosion of his dreams of becoming a great writer. David wants only days of glory and finds it difficult living the days between, but his wife, Barbara, reassures him about life and human relationships. This was the first script staged by the American Playwrights Theatre, based at Ohio State University, which has as its purpose the breaking of the Broadway stranglehold by offering production to twenty-five or more regional and college theatres. Anderson has often said that it should be possible to make a living as a playwright, but the Broadway system makes only millionaires or paupers.

You Know I Can't Hear You When the Water's Running (1967). Four one-act comedies: *The Shock of Recognition,* in which a playwright wants to use a male nude on stage; *Footsteps of Doves,* a wife wanting twin beds but the husband still preferring the double bed; *I'll Be Home for Christmas,* about communication difficulty within a family; and *I'm Herbert,* which shows two senile people, married, unable to remember who they are. Anderson intended the title to be *Plays for Saturday Night* because he felt he was merely writing sex comedy; but as always, many perceptive comments on human relationships emerge.

I Never Sang for My Father (1968). A tragedy of old age; we see the lack of communication between middle-aged Gene and his eighty-year-old father, Tom Garrison. Gene's mother dies, and Gene tries to love his father but is prevented by Tom's nature. Anderson closes the play by saying, "Death ends a life but not a relationship." Anderson's most somber play, but an excellent drama.

Solitaire/Double Solitaire (1971). The curtain-raiser in these two one-acts shows computerized, depersonalized life thirty years into the future. *Double Solitaire* shows the insoluble problems of marriage. At a golden wedding anniversary where several people are asked to reaffirm their wedding vows, they all find huge holes in their relationships, with many questions and few answers. This is a penetrating study of marriage. Anderson is one of our top writers of domestic drama.

HOWARD TEICHMAN (1916–)

The Solid Gold Cadillac (1953). Written with George S. Kaufman. A comedy about a little old lady, Laura Partridge, seemingly ignorant and naive about business, who takes over a large corporation. Teichman, a Midwesterner, became Orson Welles' stage manager at the Mercury Theatre in the late 1930's, did information work during World War II, then wrote for television. He has been an English professor at Barnard College for twenty-five years, and he wrote the definitive biography of Kaufman.

Miss Lonelyhearts (1957). An adaptation of the novel by Nathanael West, about a male journalist who writes a female lovelorn column.

The Girls in 509 (1958). A comedy about an elderly lady and her niece who go into hibernation in their apartment when Herbert Hoover loses the Presidential election to Franklin D. Roosevelt; the play shows the farcical events that occur when the building is scheduled to be demolished several decades later.

A Rainy Day in Newark (1963). A comedy about a labor leader who inherits a clock factory and must suddenly turn manager.

JEROME LAWRENCE (1915–) and ROBERT E. LEE (1918–)

The Gang's All Here (1953). This play shows the career of President Warren G. Harding (called Griffith B. Hastings in the script), from the deadlocked convention through his election to his victimization by his cronies who put him in office. Lawrence and Lee see Harding as an amiable man with no aptitude for governing, plus a fatal flaw of trusting thieves and grafters. Both Lawrence and Lee are

Ohioans; Lawrence a Phi Beta Kappa and playwriting-prize winner at Ohio State; and Lee a graduate of Ohio Wesleyan. They became collaborators on radio dramas before World War II and helped to found the Armed Forces Radio Services. Lawrence has written one of the best textbooks on radio writing, and Lee is the author of the first textbook on television writing. Their first effort to hit Broadway was a musical, *Look, Ma, I'm Dancing* (1948); but with this play, on which they received some help from Morrie Ryskind, they became widely known, particularly for their dramas of social concern.

Inherit the Wind (1955). A powerful and effective thesis-play based on the famous Scopes "Monkey Trial" of 1925 and showing the impassioned debate between characters purporting to be William Jennings Bryan and Clarence Darrow to see if a school teacher would be imprisoned for teaching about evolution. The drama is a strong plea for intellectual freedom and was produced during the era of political witch-hunting in the United States.

Auntie Mame (1956). From the novel by Patrick Dennis. Auntie Mame Dennis brings up her orphaned nephew, Pat, in bizarre but very human fashion.

Only in America (1959). Based on the book by Harry Golden, editor of the *California Israelite* newspaper, and in essence the story of Golden's life, from New York con man to founder of a national newspaper in Carolina, where he became loved by the nation.

Mame (1966). Music and lyrics by Jerry Herman, book by Lawrence and Lee. The smash-hit musical version of their play, above. The show raised Angela Lansbury to star status.

The Night Thoreau Spent in Jail (1970). Premiered at more than one hundred theatres—primarily on campuses—around the nation by the American Playwrights Theatre, which Lawrence and Lee helped to found in order to break the Broadway stranglehold on new scripts. Thoreau is jailed for refusing to pay a tax because he opposes the undeclared Mexican War. The authors said the play pointed up the immorality of all wars, but its tie-in to the Vietnam War was obvious, and college audiences responded strongly to it.

The Incomparable Max (1971). Two one-act plays featuring the writings and personality of Sir Max Beerbohm, the Edwardian theatre critic in London. A witty and polished play, but thinner than most of their other works.

(SIDNEY) PADDY CHAYEFSKY (1923–)

Marty (1953). Often called the first great original drama on television. A realistic portrayal of drab lower-middle-class New York life; Marty, a short, fat, homely butcher, finally meets a homely girl who likes him. Expanded in 1956 into a motion picture that won the Academy Award. Chayefsky, a New Yorker, went to the College of the City of New York, was a combat soldier in World War II, and got his writing start in the then-new medium of television. After *Marty,* he turned to the stage and film.

The Middle of the Night (1956). The first major adaptation, by any writer, to come from television to the stage. An agonizing account of a love between a fifty-three-year-old manufacturer and a young woman of twenty-four.

The Tenth Man (1959). Modern Jewish folklore, set on Long Island. An evil spirit is exorcised in a run-down synagogue.

Gideon (1961). A delightful retelling of the biblical legend of Gideon, the little man who has leadership thrust upon him by God. Interesting philosophically for its concepts of a God too great to understand and love, and of aspiring man.

The Passion of Josef D. (1964). A historical account of Russia, from the last Czar down to the struggle between Lenin and Stalin. A failure on Broadway.

The Latent Heterosexual (1968). Premiered at Paul Baker's Dallas Theatre Center, one of the nation's most important regional theatre troupes. Directed by Burgess Meredith and starred Zero Mostel. A homosexual poet is turned into a corporation in order for him to escape enormous taxes. This is a black comedy and fable about how love of money and worship of sex have distorted American values. Chayefsky has written many films in recent years.

N. RICHARD NASH (NUSBAUM) (1913–)

The Rainmaker (1954). Starbuck, a charlatan who calls himself a rainmaker, comes to the parched Curry farm, bilks them of a hundred dollars, and makes fools of them as they do outlandish things to bring on the rain. But he makes Lizzie Curry feel that she is not plain any more; and although Lizzie won't run off with him, she has gained confidence. As the sheriff is about to chase after the fleeing Starbuck, rain suddenly comes—for the first time in Starbuck's years as a con man. Nash reached Broadway shortly after World War II, but this was his first and only success. It has survived well over the years. Nash writes primarily for television.

110 in the Shade (1963). Music by Harvey Schmidt, book and lyrics by Tom Jones, from Nash's *The Rainmaker,* above.

The Happy Time (1968). Music by John Kander, lyrics by Fred Ebb, book by N. Richard Nash, from the play of the same name by Samuel Taylor, from a novel by Robert L. Fontaine. A whimsical comedy about a French-Canadian family, the Bonnards. Despite many threats of disaster, adolescent Bibi becomes a ladies man like his grandfather, father, and uncle.

IRA LEVIN (1929–)

No Time for Sergeants (1955). From the novel by Mac Hyman. A very funny spoof of military bureaucracy, this is a farce about a young hillbilly who wants to be transferred *to* the infantry. Levin has also written a number of novels.

Critic's Choice (1960). A polished comedy about a critic who pans his own wife's play. Levin, a New Yorker, has written several other light comedies for Broadway.

Veronica's Room (1973). One of several popular thrillers Levin has written. College student Susan Kerner is persuaded to impersonate the long-dead girl whom she resembles. Dressed as Veronica, in the Massachusetts room untouched since Veronica's death in the 1930's Susan finds herself trapped in Veronica's identity as the original killer tries to re-enact the crime. Levin is also the author of *Rosemary's Baby,* an extremely popular terror film.

MICHAEL GAZZO (1923–)

A Hatful of Rain (1955). A powerful, naturalistic study of drug addiction that may have been about a decade ahead of its time. Johnny Pope, a young veteran, agonizes with his conscience on whether to use his money for more drugs or for his pregnant wife.

The Night Circus (1958). A complex study of a varied group of "night people." It centers around a young woman walking out of a new marriage to run off with a sailor; she drags everyone around her down in this somber play.

GORE VIDAL (1925–)

Visit to a Small Planet (1957). A supernatural comedy about a visitor from outer space who thinks he is here to witness the Civil War. The human beings have to struggle to make him feel any emotions at all, and to call off his own war.

The Best Man (1960). A political play in which a former President of the United States is determined that he will select the next candidate, with some powerful behind-the-scenes infighting. Vidal is more widely known as a novelist and nonfiction writer, with several books on political subjects.

An Evening with Richard Nixon (1972). A political satire, with George Washington, Dwight Eisenhower, John F. Kennedy, and Richard Nixon all telling Nixon's life story, with many of Nixon's own words. The play is a strong indictment of our political leaders in general.

STEPHEN SONDHEIM (1930–)

West Side Story (1957). Music by Leonard

Stephen Sondheim

Bernstein, lyrics by Sondheim, book by Arthur Laurents, original idea and choreography by Jerome Robbins. The *Romeo and Juliet* story set in the ghetto streets of New York City, with the two gangs, the Jets and the Sharks, fighting each other, and the tragic love between Tony and Maria. One of the best musicals in American theatre history, with the music and dance stemming from the plot rather than being grafted on, as was the case with so many early musical comedies. A New Yorker and a serious student of music, Sondheim has composed many songs and scores for numerous shows. One interesting sidelight is that the crossword puzzle you did this morning may have been Sondheim's; he has syndicated several crossword puzzle series.

Gypsy (1959). Music by Jule Styne, lyrics by Sondheim, book by Arthur Laurents. From the memoirs of famous striptease dancer Gypsy Rose Lee, this show tells of her early life in vaudeville and legitimate theatre and of her domineering mother.

A Funny Thing Happened on the Way to the Forum (1962). Music and lyrics by Sondheim, book by Bert Shevelove and Larry Gelbart, from the Roman comedies of Plautus. This is a farcical romp featuring all the stock devices and characters from classic comedy: trickster slave, mistaken identities, husbands trying to dupe their wives, and young people winning out over their elders.

Company (1970). Music and lyrics by Sondheim, book by George Furth. Robert, thirty-five and single, is constantly entertained by the five couples he knows in his apartment building; he sees all the troubles in their lives and remains single, though lonely. The theme is that people marry mainly to have company. Winner of the New York Drama Critics Circle Award for best musical for 1969–70.

Follies (1971). Music and lyrics by Sondheim, book by James Goldman. All the old cast members from Dimitri Weismann's "Follies," which played from 1919 to 1942, are on stage for a party before the theatre is torn down to become a parking lot. We see the empty marriages of Sally and Buddy, Phyllis and Ben, and see both the tinsellike pleasure and the dreary emptiness of show business in this serious musical, which won the New York Drama Critics Circle Award for best musical of 1970–71.

A Little Night Music (1973). Music and lyrics by Sondheim, book by Hugh Wheeler, from Ingmar Bergman's film *Smiles of a Summer Night*. Hugh Wheeler is an Englishman who has become an American citizen and who has written several plays for Broadway; he has also written dozens of popular mystery novels under the pen name of Patrick Quentin. The show is a maze of intrigues in upper-class Swedish circles one weekend at a château; Frederick Egerman loses his young virgin wife Anne to his son, thus allowing him to reunite permanently with his old mistress, Desirée. Winner of the New York Drama Critics Circle Award for best musical of 1972–73. Sondheim thus won three Drama Critics Circle Awards in four years, a noteworthy achievement.

Pacific Overtures (1976). Music and lyrics by Sondheim, book by John Weidman, the son of Jerome Weidman; additional book material by Hugh Wheeler. A fable about the changes in Japan after its "discovery" by the Western world in the 19th century. There are definite influences of Japanese Kabuki Theatre in this production, and the music is a blend of Oriental and Occidental.

Side by Side by Sondheim (1977). A two-piano, three-singer entertainment featuring the best of his songs, with music and lyrics by Sondheim and Leonard Bernstein, Mary Rodgers, and Jule Styne, this opened in London in 1976 and proved as big a hit in New York. Although most of the songs are from *Company* and *Follies,* all his major works are represented, and a few are from extremely out-of-the-way sources such as *The Mad Show* (off-Broadway revue in 1966), which had one song, "The Boy From," billed in its original program as by Esteban Ria Nido (Spanish for Stephen Sondheim). His list of major musical triumphs over two decades certainly entitled Sondheim to a kind of nostalgic tribute.

KETTI FRINGS (c.1915–)

Look Homeward, Angel (1957). From Thomas Wolfe's famous novel. The painful adolescence of young Gant, the death of his brother, and his growth of awareness about his parents. Won both a Pulitzer Prize and the New York Drama Critics Circle Award; in an era of many mediocre adaptations on Broadway, this one rose to true theatrical greatness.

MEREDITH WILLSON (1906–)

The Music Man (1957). Music, lyrics, and book by Willson, from a story by Willson and Franklin Lacey. The idea grew originally out of old hometown anecdotes about Iowa that Willson told to Frank Loesser. A charming, foot-tapping musical of a romantic charlatan in an Iowa town at the turn of the century: Professor Harold Hill, salesman de luxe, promises to give the town a band composed of their children, falls in love with Marian the librarian, and is saved from tarring and feathering by the starry-eyed kids. Among the many tuneful numbers is "Seventy-Six Trombones." Winner of the New York Drama Critics Circle Award for best musical of 1957–58.

The Unsinkable Molly Brown (1960). Music and lyrics by Willson, book by Richard Morris. Willson, interested in Americana, joined forces with Morris, who had heard Molly Brown legends in the Colorado mining towns. Molly, a tomboy from Missouri, marries a poor miner in Leadville and becomes one of the richest women in Denver, where she is several times snubbed by high society. Molly and Johnny travel to Europe, where they are accepted. They bring back a crowd of European royalty, but their homecoming party in Denver is disrupted by a brawling group of old mining friends. Molly flees again to Europe, her marriage shaky, but returns on the *Titanic* and escapes drowning to reunite with Johnny. Starred Tammy Grimes on Broadway and Debbie Reynolds in the 1964 hit film.

Here's Love (1963). Music and lyrics by Willson, based on the film *A Miracle on Thirty-Fourth Street* by Valentine Davies and George Seaton. This is a Santa Claus sentimental fantasy.

DORE SCHARY (1905–)

Sunrise at Campobello (1958). The young Franklin Delano Roosevelt contracts polio and despairs for the future; in this play, at the family summer home, F.D.R. recovers his spirit, will, and determination. Dore Schary was first a Hollywood producer before turning to playwriting. Of several scripts to appear on Broadway, this is his only lasting success. He has also written a number of books.

WILLIAM GIBSON (1914–)

Two for the Seesaw (1958). A two-character comedy that succeeded well. New Yorker Gittel Mosca and Midwestern lawyer Jerry Ryan have a brief but meaningful affair before he returns home to try again with his wife. Gibson, who began his writing career as a novelist, followed up this play with a book, *The Seesaw Log,* which exposed and indicted many of the practices of the Broadway theatre: frenzied revisions made from fear, the temperament of people in show business, the wildfire feelings of panic before an opening, and the immense emphasis on making the big money.

Dinny and the Witches (1959). A comic-supernatural tale, staged off-Broadway.

The Miracle Worker (1959). A gripping and heartwarming drama of the years in which Annie Sullivan trained the child Helen Keller and opened the horizons for this to-be-famous handicapped woman. Gibson's biggest hit and still done regularly by amateur troupes.

A Cry of Players (1968). An imaginative re-creation of the young Shakespeare living at Stratford-on-Avon, who finally has to leave home, wife, and family to see if he can make it in the world of professional theatre in London. It is a thought-provoking play about the restrictive pressures that threaten any creative artist, and about the theatre as a way of life.

Seesaw (1972). Music by Cy Coleman, lyrics by Dorothy Fields, book by Michael Bennett. Musical of Gibson's first play (*see* Michael Bennett entry).

Jerry Bock and Sheldon Harnick

JERRY BOCK (1928–)
and SHELDON HARNICK (1924–)

Fiorello! (1959). Music by Bock, lyrics by Harnick, book by George Abbott and Jerome Weidman. A musical biography of Fiorello H. La Guardia, the famous mayor of New York City from 1934 to 1945. In the prologue, Mayor La Guardia reads the comics over the radio to children during a newspaper strike; the show then flashes back to his early career as a lawyer interested in the plight of the poor, his election as the first Republican in Congress from New York's 14th District, his loss in the mayoralty race against Jimmy Walker, and finally his victory and personal ups and downs. The show won a Pulitzer Prize, the New York Drama Critics Circle Award, and the Tony Award and ran for 795 performances.

Tenderloin (1960). Music by Bock, lyrics by Harnick, book by George Abbott and Jerome Weidman, based on a novel by Samuel Hopkins Adams. A musical about a clergyman crusading against sin in New York City around the turn of the century.

Fiddler on the Roof (1964). Music by Bock, lyrics by Harnick, book by Joseph Stein. A musical adaptation of Shalom Aleichem's story "Tevya and his Daughters." The longest run of any kind in Broadway history, with 3,242 performances. An excellent serious musical drama of the persecution of the Jews in Russia and the breakup of a traditional old family, caused in part by the pogroms. Winner of the New York Drama Critics Circle Award for best musical of 1964–65, it starred Zero Mostel as the first of many Tevyas. Bock and Harnick will find their reputation secure forever with this one great musical play. Revived again, with Mostel, in 1976, for another long run.

The Apple Tree (1966). Music by Bock, lyrics by Harnick, book by Jerome Coopersmith. Three one-act plays set to music: Mark Twain's *The Diary of Adam and Eve;* Frank Stockton's old favorite, *The Lady or the Tiger?* and Jules Feiffer's *Passionella.* Prepared as a starring vehicle for Barbara Harris.

LORRAINE HANSBERRY (1930–1965)

A Raisin in the Sun (1959). A superb first play and the first by a black woman on Broadway. Mama Younger plans to use the insurance money from her husband's death to buy a house and move out of the ghetto in Chicago. Son Walter, however, loses the money in a get-rich-quick scheme that backfires. A group of whites offer them a profit not to move into their neighborhood, but Mama helps Walter regain his spirit, and they plan to move. Won the New York Drama Critics Circle Award. Miss Hansberry, born in a well-to-do Chicago family, began as a painter, but switched to writing after she moved to New York.

The Sign in Sidney Brustein's Window (1964). Sidney, a Jewish liberal in New York, almost loses his wife as he struggles for various causes. Miss Hansberry, a cancer victim as this play went into production, attended rehearsals in a wheelchair and went blind shortly after opening night. Her former husband, Robert Nemiroff, mounted a campaign to keep the play on the boards; it limped along to mixed reviews for two months, at which time Miss Hansberry died and the play closed. It was revived in the same theatre in 1972, with some songs added, but only played five performances. The play is rich in its human moments but weak in its political oratory. Miss Hansberry was on much more solid ground in her first play, where characterization was more important than thesis.

To Be Young, Gifted and Black (1969). A posthumous off-Broadway compilation of Miss Hansberry's letters and mementos, plus excerpts from her plays, compiled by Robert Nemiroff, which showed what it was like to be a black artist in a white world. This play also toured nationally.

Les Blancs (1970). A powerful posthumous drama, with the script completed by Robert Nemiroff and Charlotte Zaltzberg, about racial violence in an emerging African nation. Tshembe, a black who would like to return to his European wife in London, instead kills his Catholic-priest brother and sides with the revolution that he has been trying to sidestep.

78

Raisin (1973). Music by Judd Woldin, lyrics by Robert Brittan, book by Robert Nemiroff and Charlotte Zaltzberg. The musical version of Miss Hansberry's first play, praised by critics for its sharpening of the original story. Won the Tony Award for best Broadway musical of 1973–74. Miss Hansberry's position seems secure despite her short career; she brought serious concern about race relations to Broadway but wrote rich character drama rather than shrill Agitprop.

JACK GELBER (1932–)

The Connection (1959). An avant-garde play about dope addiction, with the action of the junkies set to jazz played by the addicts themselves. The big moment of the play, which has the characters waiting endlessly for their fix, is an overdose of heroin administered on stage to raucous jazz accompaniment. The actors beg in the lobby at intermission for money for their habit. This was the first critical success for the off-Broadway Living Theatre, directed by Julian Beck and Judith Malina, which eventually moved to Europe to escape harassment for its social-protest plays. Jack Gelber, a Chicagoan, was a journalism student at the University of Illinois.

The Apple (1961). Another highly experimental play done by the Living Theatre, but more turgid and less successful than Gelber's first work. This is a play about actors and the theatre.

Square in the Eye (1965). A satirical look at modern life that shows the problems facing a pop artist.

The Cuban Thing (1968). The effects on a decadent, middle-class Cuban family of the last days of Batista and the first five years of the Castro regime. This was Gelber's first Broadway production.

TOM JONES (1928–)
and HARVEY SCHMIDT (1929–)

The Fantasticks (1960). Music by Schmidt, book and lyrics by Jones. From Edmond Rostand's first play, *Les Romanesques* (1894). Schmidt and Jones collaborated for a number of years, with several versions of *The Fantasticks,* including one staged at Columbia University, before, after much effort, it arrived at the Sullivan Street Playhouse off-Broadway. Since then it has made theatre history as the longest-running production in the United States. As this book went to press, the show was still very much alive and was nearing 7,000 performances. It has also been staged all over the world, and the Sullivan Street Playhouse has virtually become a museum devoted to the history of various productions. It is a simple story about a boy, a girl, their fathers who build a wall to separate the young couple, and how the boy and the girl come to realize that without the bitter moments of life, there can be no savoring of the sweeter times. The most famous song is "Try to Remember." The stage is tiny and only two musical instruments are used.

110 in the Shade (1963). Music by Schmidt, book and lyrics by Jones, from N. Richard Nash's *The Rainmaker.* Starbuck, a charlatan who calls himself a rainmaker, comes to the parched Curry farm, bilks them of a hundred dollars, and makes fools of them as they do outlandish things to bring on the rain. But he makes Lizzie Curry feel that she is not plain anymore; and although Lizzie won't run off with him, she has gained confidence. As the sheriff is about to chase the fleeing Starbuck, rain suddenly comes.

I Do! I Do! (1966). Music by Schmidt, book and lyrics by Jones, from Jan De Hartog's play *The Fourposter.* Written as a starring vehicle for Mary Martin and Robert Preston, this is a musical account of a lifetime of marriage, set in a bedroom, as the couple marries, survives the tribulations of life, and grows old.

Celebration (1969). Music by Schmidt, book and lyrics by Jones. A morality play set on New Year's Eve, this makes use of the ancient religious origins of theatre, stresses Sir James Gould Frazer's myth-lore of the new year conquering the old, and features a young boy and a decadent old man struggling for a young actress. The show also has a master of ceremonies dressed as a tramp. A failure on Broadway. Jones and Schmidt had met while students at the University of Texas, collaborated as undergraduates and in the Army, and eventually came to New York to write nightclub acts. Their many years of honing *The Fantasticks* paid off, and it is for that long-running masterpiece that they are famous.

RICK BESOYAN (1924–1970)

Little Mary Sunshine (1960). Music, lyrics, and book by Besoyan. This was a long-run, highly praised off-Broadway spoof of the sentimental operettas of the 1920's. The show features lovely ladies, cowboys and Indians, and a finale complete with dozens of American flags. Besoyan, a Californian, studied music in London and toured with an English light-opera company before writing this, his first show.

The Student Gypsy, or the Prince of Liederkranz (1963). Music, lyrics, and book by Besoyan. More satire on the early operettas but not as successful as his first script. Besoyan also was an off-Broadway director in his relatively short career.

EDWARD ALBEE (1928–)

The Zoo Story (1960). A powerful one-act play about the lack of communication in the world. Peter, insulated from the world as he reads on a New York park bench, is confronted by Jerry who has tried desperately, with dogs, alcoholic landladies, playing cards, and zoo animals to have a relationship. The brief interlude is concluded by Jerry's impaling himself on his own knife, held by a horrified Peter. First produced in Germany, after Albee was unable to get a hearing in the United States, the play was quickly moved to New York and placed on a double bill with Samuel Beckett's *Krapp's Last Tape;* the production, one of the greatest in off-Broadway history, established Albee.

The Death of Bessie Smith (1961). An angry social-protest play in one act that shows black singer Bessie Smith's companion trying to get her admitted to a segregated hospital in Tennessee while she lies bleeding to death outside. We also see a liberal young interne trapped by the system and the girl he loves. This play, too, was premiered in Berlin two years before its New York opening.

The Sandbox (1960). Albee's third play, although it was produced in New York before *Bessie Smith,* above. A short avant-garde work that sharply satirizes many of the conventional values in American society. A muscular lifeguard does calisthenics to show off his body while Grandma is left to die in a nearby sandbox. Mommy and Daddy are also castigated. Albee, adopted in infancy by Reid Albee of the famous family of vaudeville theatre owners, grew up in a wealthy New York suburb and rebelled constantly against his domineering stepmother and retiring stepfather. He also rebelled against prep school, and after a year at Trinity University in Connecticut he moved to Greenwich Village, where he lived with composer William Flanagan, who encouraged Albee to write plays. He had been writing fiction and poetry from his childhood.

The American Dream (1961). Another satire on American culture, with most of the same characters that appeared in the previous play. We see a rapacious Mommy, an inept Daddy, and a sensible Grandma who again is cast aside. Grandma is presumably being sent away in a van to a nursing home. The young man —the American dream—is an emasculated creature. At this point in his career, Albee had a solid reputation as a creator of short avant-garde plays, in the Theatre of the Absurd tradition, that attacked middle-class America.

Who's Afraid of Virginia Woolf? (1962). Albee's first full-length play and almost immediately reputed one of the greatest works in our dramatic history. A savage marital love-hate battle between George, a professor not going any place academically, and Martha, the daughter of the college president. In a long drunken night spent with another faculty couple, newcomers Nick and Honey, the titanic struggle between George and Martha culminates in the "killing" of their imaginary child by George. The central theme, seen in the conflicts within both couples, is that reality is healthier than illusion. Later made into a superb film with Richard Burton and Elizabeth Taylor. Albee wrote some of the most crackling, rhythmic dialogue ever heard on the New York stage.

The Ballad of the Sad Cafe (1963). Adapted for the stage from the novella by Carson McCullers. A sex triangle of a physically powerful woman with aversions toward normal men, a violent man whose love turns to hate, and a malicious dwarf.

Tiny Alice (1965). An obscure study of modern religion that had a short New York run, this play has been a battleground for critics ever since it opened. A rich woman living in a large house, which is reproduced in a tiny model, has a former lover and present lover under the same roof and forces a cardinal into strange acts in order to seek a large bequest.

Malcolm (1966). Another religious allegory, this time adapted from a novel by James Purdy. A boy, Malcolm, sitting on a bench waiting for his father, is taken up by an elderly astrologer who sends him out into the world to observe a December–May couple, a middle-aged couple, a hip couple, and finally a pop singer who kills Malcolm with too much liquor and sex. A commercial failure.

A Delicate Balance (1966). A tense, terror-filled analysis of friendship, fear, and marriage. Middle-aged neighbors Edna and Harry suddenly arrive at the home of Agnes and Tobias and want to stay forever because of the nameless terror that has invaded their own home. The nature of this play and *Virginia Woolf* are quite similar: realism except for one unexplained aspect (the imaginary child in the first play, the unexplained terror in this); and the combination works well upon the stage. Albee deservedly received a Pulitzer Prize for this play, but many theatre people believed that it was also the Pulitzer Committee's way of rewarding Albee belatedly for *Virginia Woolf;* the earlier Pulitzer Committee had been "shocked" by Albee's masterpiece. *A Delicate Balance* was made into an excellent motion picture in 1973 by the American Film Theatre.

Everything in the Garden (1967). An adaptation of a play by British author Giles Cooper (1918–1966), this is a domestic drama of housewives who must keep up with the Joneses in their fancy suburbs and who turn to high-priced prostitution to maintain family affluence. When a friendly alcoholic neighbor discovers the secret, the several husbands, who know about their wives, smother the man and bury him in the garden. Richard, one of the husbands, is at first horrified at his wife, but gives in, just as the others have done before him. A powerful realistic drama that has been extremely timely in our postwar age of affluence.

Box-Mao-Box (1968). The world premiere of these two one-act plays was held at the Studio Theatre in Buffalo, New York. There are no actors on stage at all in *Box,* an offstage monologue by a woman; and in *Quotations from Chairman Mao Tse-tung* there is juxtaposition of several monologues including party-line statements by Mao and autobiographical accounts from an old lady who has jumped off an ocean liner. A failure on Broadway.

All Over (1971). Reactions about living and dying from a stern wife, a warm mistress, an ineffective son, a shrill daughter, a well-meaning best friend, an elderly doctor, and a lonely nurse, to a famous man's death. The dying man never appears and is behind a curtain on stage. Many critics praised the play, but it had a fairly short run. It is extremely powerful because of the continuing tension about the impending death and the extremely rich characterizations. We see the influence the dying man has had on each of the characters and how each one is trying to cope with life.

Seascape (1975). A powerful, upbeat play that won a Pulitzer Prize. Albee makes the thematic point—that life should never stagnate but must move ever onward, ever upward—through two couples: Nancy and Charlie, in late middle age; and Leslie and Sarah, two lizards who crawl out of the sea. The females are the seekers and strivers, the males more ready to drift along comfortably. Very theatrically, Albee makes several other statements about prejudice, reactions to strangers, and marital relationships. A look at Albee's work to this point indicates that he is at his best when he writes a primarily realistic play that contains some aspect of the Theatre of the Absurd within it. Albee also forces audiences to examine mid-20th-century values and mores. He has a superb ear for rhythmic dialogue.

Counting the Ways (1976). Premiered by the National Theatre of Great Britain, this is a one-hour, two-character series of rapid blackouts in which a husband and wife try to decide how much, if at all, they love each other. Late in the play the two actors step forward, drop their characterizations, and talk about their own lives to the audience. London critics called it the best part of this playlet, which seems much thinner than Albee's earlier domestic plays. First produced in the U.S.A. in 1977 by the Hartford Stage Company as part of a double bill with *Listening,* a short chamber play by Albee.

IMAMU AMIRI BARAKA (LE ROI JONES) (1934–)

Dante (1961). His first one-act play staged off-Broadway. Jones, who graduated at nineteen from Howard University in Washington, D.C., and who received a number of fellowships while in his twenties, has become one of the nation's most polemic black writers in drama, prose, and poetry. After attaining success as a writer, he changed his name.

Dutchman (1964). A long one-act play staged off-Broadway and subsequently made into a film, this is his best play. Lula, a while girl, antagonizes Clay, an earnest young black man, on a subway train. With the passengers ignoring the increasing conflict, Lula kills Clay, and the audience gets the impression that Lula will go on killing black men after seducing them. This is an extremely theatrical play, somewhat Pinter-like, and rich because its theme of the oppression of the black race is handled almost mythically.

The Baptism (1964). A biting satire on church

services, the play also satirizes sexual and social hypocrisies.

The Slave (1964). A violent racial play, also done off-Broadway, in two acts. Black militant Walker Vessels comes to a professor's house in the midst of a race riot and kills the professor, whose white wife, Grace, had once been Walker's wife. Grace is killed by the explosions from the riot.

The Toilet (1965). Deliberately shocking and filled with violent language and action, this is a one-act drama of a race fight in a high-school lavatory. The adolescent code of violence crushes any efforts at tenderness.

Slaveship (1969). A short full-length play set in the hold of a ship and aimed at the conscience of a nation, this is an expressionistic capsule-history of the black man's oppression and subsequent rebellion and is a bitterly militant play. In recent years Jones has turned away from writing and into active politics in the Newark, New Jersey, area; he has said that the black man must enter into the mainstream of American politics and win his way by victories at the ballot box. Jones is a highly talented writer, speaker, and politician who is totally dedicated to the cause of improving the status of blacks in the world.

OSSIE DAVIS (1917–)

Purlie Victorious (1961). One of the first Broadway successes by a black playwright. Ossie Davis, an actor as well as writer, also played the lead. Purlie is a fast-talking black Georgia minister who succeeds in getting the deed for his church despite the conniving of a prejudiced white land owner, old Cap'n Cotchipee. The play contains many of the old Southern stereotypes, but Davis approaches the theme of racial injustice through humor—almost the exact opposite of the strident approach of Le Roi Jones, above. (The first black theatre in the New York area was the African Grove Company, in Greenwich Village in 1821, but it was soon closed down by the city. The first black playwright was William Wells Brown, who wrote *The Escape, or, A Leap to Freedom* in 1858.)

Purlie (1970). Music by Gary Geld, lyrics by Peter Udell, book by Davis, Philip Rose, and Peter Udell, based on Davis' earlier play. A well-received musical version that ran for seven months, then was staged in other cities.

ROBERT LOWELL (1917–)

Phedre (1961). Lowell is one of the nation's leading contemporary poets and has also done some interesting work in the theatre. This, his first important play, is a retelling in verse of the Greek Phaedra-Hippolytus legend in which Phaedra falls tragically in love with her priggish stepson, who refuses her, thus bringing on the deaths of both of them.

The Old Glory (1964). Three one-act plays held together by the unifying symbol of the American flag, these were produced off-Broadway at the American Place Theatre, a creative and active production group in the 1960's. The plays were *Endecott and the Red Cross,* from Nathaniel Hawthorne; *My Kinsman, Major Molineaux,* from Thomas Morton and Hawthorne; and *Benito Cereno,* from Herman Melville. The plays won five Obie Awards for best work done off-Broadway, and *Benito Cereno* has been staged often around the nation.

Prometheus Bound (1967). A loose adaptation of Aeschylus' Greek drama about Prometheus, who defies the rigid order of the old gods and prefers to suffer and feel inwardly free rather than be comfortable under someone else's power. This production was premiered at the Yale School of Drama with a fine professional cast. Robert Lowell has also done some of the best translations of the plays of Molière. In verse, they are literate and play superbly.

(MARVIN) NEIL SIMON (1927–)

Come Blow Your Horn (1961). A domestic comedy about the Baker family, which runs an artificial-fruit company. Young Buddy joins playboy older brother Alan in rebelling against parental domination, leaving his folks a note announcing that he is moving out. The father's reaction foreshadows all of Simon's plays in the clever lines: the father says, "My sister Gussie has two grandchildren; I have a bum and a letter." Another aspect of Simon's work also appears early, though: his creation of

comedy that stems out of character. Simon, like George M. Cohan a New Yorker born on the Fourth of July, served in the Army (also in New York City), and prepped for his playwriting career by writing a number of comic television series, including the *Sergeant Bilko* program. By his own admission, Simon is a "watcher of people," and he has concentrated on the lives of harried, middle-class urban folk.

Little Me (1962). Music by Cy Coleman, lyrics by Carolyn Leigh, book by Neil Simon, from a book by Patrick Dennis. A tour de force for performer Sid Caesar, who played a number of parts including a rich boy, an old miser, a music-hall singer, a stupid farmer, a German teacher in Hollywood, and a Slavic prince. The plot is about a young girl in search of wealth, culture, and social position. Much of Simon's writing here is still strongly related to his television script work.

Barefoot in the Park (1963). This long-running comedy established Simon as Mr. Box Office in New York. Kookie Corie Bratter and stuffy young lawyer Paul Bratter, newlyweds, move into a walkup apartment on the fifth floor; their marriage survives the stairs, the suave neighbor Victor Velasco, and the inevitable mother-in-law. Paul learns that spontaneity is important in human relationships. Ran on Broadway for 1,532 performances. This, along with many other of Simon's top plays, has become a staple of dinner theatre fare in the U.S.A.

The Odd Couple (1965). Slovenly sportswriter Oscar Madison and fussy Felix Unger, separated from their wives, share an apartment and experience the identical problems that they had undergone in their marriages. The plot is based very loosely on some experiences of Simon's brother, Danny. Many people consider this Simon's greatest comedy; not only is it very funny, but like the world's comic masterpieces, it also says something about human relationships.

Sweet Charity (1966). Music by Cy Coleman, lyrics by Dorothy Fields (1904–1975), book by Simon. A bittersweet musical about a warm-hearted taxi dancer, Charity, who never gets her man. Starred Gwen Verdon. Based loosely on Federico Fellini's screenplay *The Nights of Cabiria.*

The Star-Spangled Girl (1966). A boy-meets-girl triangle in a San Francisco apartment. Andy runs an underground protest magazine, Norman does all the writing under many names, and Olympic swimmer and superpatriot Sophie Rauschmeyer moves in next door and overturns their equilibrium. A very light, gag-filled comedy.

Plaza Suite (1968). Three one-act plays in which Simon returned to his blend of witty comedy and domestic problems. *Visitor from Mamaroneck* has a wife trying to preserve a marriage with a husband who is having an affair with a younger woman; *Visitor from Hollywood* shows a clod of a producer seducing a star-struck married woman who was once his high-school date; and *Visitor from Forest Hills,* the most farcical of the three, is about two hysterical parents trying to get their daughter out of the bathroom, where she has locked herself, in order to get her married downstairs. All three plays take place in the same suite in the Plaza Hotel in New York City.

Promises, Promises (1968). Music by Bert Bacharach, lyrics by Hal David, book by Simon, from the previous film *The Apartment* by Billy Wilder and I. A. L. Diamond. Chuck Baxter, a meek clerk, lends his apartment to executives of his company in order to carry on extramarital flings.

Last of the Red Hot Lovers (1969). Another very funny comedy that in places comes very close to tears. Barney Cashman, forty-seven years old and afraid that the sexual revolution has passed him by, tries for three acts to seduce somebody in his fussy mother's apartment. In Act I, married Elaine Navazio wants a fling, but Barney is too scared; in Act II, hippie Bobbi Michele blows Barney's mind; and finally his wife's best friend, Jeannette Fisher, goes to pieces emotionally after Barney has at last gotten up his courage. A rich comedy, but Simon has made successful production

a bit difficult by taking the plot around in the same circle for three straight times.

The Gingerbread Lady (1970). After being the nation's most successful playwright in history during the 1960's, Simon finally wrote a serious play, although it does have many laugh lines. This is the story of Evy Meara, a middle-aged singer on the skids from too much liquor, who is helped by her idealistic daughter. Neither the public nor the critics supported this play too strongly, evidently expecting constant comedy; what they had not noticed, however, was that Simon in comedy after comedy *had* been saying something serious about life.

The Prisoner of Second Avenue (1971). Although filled with the usual Simon one-liner laughs, this play is about a serious subject: forty-seven-year old Mel Edison loses his job and has a nervous breakdown; his wife, Edna, loses her job, too. The play is set against a background of mechanical conveniences continually breaking down in their apartment, plus the ongoing rage and violence of New York life. Although a comedy, it is a damning exposé of contemporary urban life.

The Sunshine Boys (1972). Another rich comedy of character. Willie Clark, a seventy-one-year-old former vaudevillian, fights with his old partner, Al Lewis, as they try to do a television special; and Willie has a heart attack. At the end both Willie and Al are headed, separately, for the same home for aged actors. They have never been able to work together happily, yet they have absolutely nothing left in life but each other. Simon at his best.

The Good Doctor (1973). Simon's adaptation of some early short stories by Anton Chekhov. Music in the production by Peter Link. Some of the stories are farcical; others are bitter-sweet. The doctor, who is a good listener in the tales, serves as a linking character and is probably a cross between Chekhov, who was a physician, and Simon the watcher-of-people, who has long answered to the nickname "Doc."

God's Favorite (1974). Joseph Benjamin is a modern Job who lives in Oyster Bay, New York. An assortment of horrifying troubles befall him, but when his wastrel son finally thanks God for not killing his father, the play ends on an upbeat note. Simon leavens the horrifying story with his usual array of polished one-liners. Critics and public again were uneasy at Simon's turning away from pure comedy. As the New York City portion of his career drew to a close, Simon had been so successful with his plays that he had actually bought his own theatre: The Eugene O'Neill, a famous Broadway house.

California Suite (1976). Four one-act plays, each set in the same suite in the Beverly Hills Hotel this time. One: a New York magazine editor (female) and a screenwriter (male) fight over custody of their teenage daughter. Two: an Eastern businessman, out for a family bar mitzvah, wakes up with a prostitute in his bed. Three: a British actress is in California in hopes of winning the Academy Award. Four: two couples who have vacationed together end up in a fight. Three of the four sketches show Simon's increasing seriousness of vision underneath the finely honed comedy. Shortly before this play, Simon moved to Los Angeles in order to change several patterns in his life. He announced that henceforth he would concentrate on films and immediately turned out the comic-mystery *Murder by Death*. Earlier, Simon had found time in his busy schedule to write several other film scripts. At this point in his career, which presumably is far from over, Simon ranks as our top comic writer, both in quantity and quality.

ARTHUR KOPIT (1937–)
Oh Dad, Poor Dad, Momma's Hung You in the Closet and I'm Feelin' So Sad (1962). An avant-garde spoof of Mom-ism. Momma carries Father's corpse around with her and keeps her son a prisoner. The play was wildly popular for a time but has dated considerably. Kopit, a New Yorker, won two playwriting contests and had nine plays produced while he was at Harvard; he was still an undergraduate when he wrote this, which brought Barbara Harris to stardom.

Indians (1969). After seven years of trying to fulfill the promise shown in his first New York production (except for a few one-acts), Kopit finally succeeded with this full-length play that was premiered by the Royal Shakespeare Company in England and then done first in the United States at Washington's Arena Stage before moving to Broadway. (Arena Stage, run by Zelda Fichandler, has been a creative and courageous enterprise for several decades and has given hearings to many important writers.) This play is a ritualistic Wild-West extravaganza featuring Buffalo Bill and showing the white man's persecution of the Indians and their way of life, the government's total callousness to the Indian, and Bill Cody's senseless slaughtering of so many buffalo and his sellout to the entertainment industry.

FRANK GILROY (1926–)
Who'll Save the Plowboy? (1962). Off-Broadway success that won an Obie Award as best new play of the year, this is the story of a failure of a husband who continues to try to live by pipe dreams; but his wife and an old Army buddy, who once saved his life, have their illusions stripped away. Gilroy grew up in New York City, was a soldier in World War II, and went to both Dartmouth and the Yale School of Drama. He began his writing career in television.

The Subject Was Roses (1964). Timmy Cleary, returning home from World War II, causes his ever-wrangling parents, John and Nettie, to make their first moves toward understanding. Won both a Pulitzer Prize and the New York Drama Critics Circle Award. Gilroy served as his own shoestring-producer to force this play onto Broadway; his book, *About Those Roses*, details how the play almost closed, limped along financially, and finally became a double award winner.

That Summer, That Fall (1967). The Phaedra-Hippolytus story of Euripides set in present-day New York. A powerful play about Angelina Capuano's passion for her stepson, Steve Flynn, but it was extremely short and laconic and closed in two weeks.

The Only Game in Town (1968). A comedy about a liaison between a compulsive gambler and a Las Vegas chorus girl he picks up; they embark on a no-strings affair, only to find themselves caught in "the only game in town": love and marriage. The play closed in two weeks, but was made into a popular film. Gilroy has been widely praised for his talent but has had a difficult time gaining substantial runs for his plays.

HERB GARDNER (1934–)

A Thousand Clowns (1962). A popular comedy that satirizes bureaucracy and stuffiness. The welfare department tries to take Murray Burns' young nephew away from him; Murray wins not only the case but the girl from the welfare department, too. Gardner is well known for his cartoons and greeting cards featuring the Nebbishes, plus other comedies.

SIDNEY MICHAELS (1927–)

Tchin-Tchin (1962). Based on a French play by François Billetdoux, this is a fragile and charming sex comedy. An Italian-American contractor's wife and a surgeon are having an affair; the play is primarily about the other halves of the couples: Pamela Pew-Pickett, the doctor's wife, and Caesario Grimaldi, the blue-collar boss, who meet and have a tender, bittersweet affair of their own. Michaels, a New Yorker, has written extensively for film and television.

Dylan (1964). The story of Welsh poet Dylan Thomas' visits to the United States and his death, this a vivid picture of a flamboyant yet tormented artist closely surrounded by a wide variety of people. Many of Thomas' own lyrics are used in this rich play.

Ben Franklin in Paris (1964). Music by Mark Sandrich, book and lyrics by Michaels. Franklin is shown as a lecherous old patriot as he alternates between seductions and statesmanship designed to acquire help for the colonies from Louis XVI.

DALE WASSERMAN (1917–)

One Flew over the Cuckoo's Nest (1963). Adapted from the novel by Ken Kesey. Randle P. McMurphy, sent to a mental hospital because of his violence on a prison farm, engages in a fierce power struggle with Nurse Ratched and forces his wardmates to reassess their lives. He helps several of them, but he is finally given a prefrontal lobotomy by the hospital and then is smothered by his companions, who know he wouldn't have wanted to live like a vegetable. A powerful play about leaders and followers, bureaucracy, and the nature of sanity. Wasserman had written more than fifty films and television scripts before turning to the stage.

Man of La Mancha (1965). Music by Mitch Leigh, lyrics by Joe Darion, book by Wasserman. A musical adaptation of Cervantes' *Don Quixote*. Set in the form of a play-within-a-play, this begins with Cervantes and his servant being locked in a prison dungeon. When the prisoners begin to attack him, he gets them to reenact the manuscript they have threatened to destroy. We see the most famous episodes from the book as the musical makes the thematic statement that man must have his dream. A frightening interlude in which soldiers from the Inquisition break into the story serves instead of an act break in this serious musical, which played for 2,328 performances and won the New York Drama Critics Circle Award for best musical of 1965–66.

MURRAY SCHISGAL (1926–)

The Typists and *The Tiger* (1963). Two one-act plays done off-Broadway. In the first, people age by decades in a few minutes as we see a romance of two clerks; the second shows a bashful clerk trying to rape a too-grateful woman. Schisgal left high school in New York City to serve in the Navy in World War II, worked as a musician, graduated from Brooklyn Law School, quit law to become a junior high-school teacher in Harlem, and finally had these two plays premiered in London in 1960.

Luv (1964). His first Broadway hit, which became a top movie after failing, ironically, in London where it was premiered. This is a superb three-character lampoon of the banal idiocies of conventional love and conventional modern life. The show takes place on a walkway atop the Brooklyn Bridge where the characters keep trying to jump off. Schisgal said "Luv" is a perversion of love.

Jimmy Shine (1968). A loosely plotted comedy of an ineffectual nonconformist and a wretched painter whose defense mechanisms against society include beating the system by never accepting it. Jimmy is a would-be lover who suffers diarrhea whenever his romantic love draws near.

The Chinese and *Dr. Fish* (1970). Two one-act plays; the first, set in a Chinese laundry, is a comic search for identity by the main character; the second is a spoof of modern America's quest for sexual enlightenment. Dr. Fish is a history professor who writes a book on sex.

An American Millionaire (1974). A plotless, grotesque comedy done off-Broadway. A wealthy young man, unable to consummate his third marriage because of fainting spells, seeks to avoid being murdered. Very short run, after being panned by the critics.

All Over Town (1974). A Feydeau-like farce, directed by Dustin Hoffman and called Schisgal's funniest play since *Luv.* Madcap humor in a Manhattan duplex owned by an eccentric psychiatrist, Dr. Morris, who decides to treat an incredible seducer of many women but who confuses a black delivery boy with the white seducer and sets off a chain of wildly farcical shenanigans inside his house.

MARTIN DUBERMAN (1930–)

In White America (1963). Historical documents, tailored into a play, which give an account of the black people's history in the United States. Duberman is a professor of history at Princeton. He has also had several avant-garde one-act plays staged in the New York area.

The Memory Bank (1970). Two one-act plays: *The Recorder,* about a young historian interviewing an eminent man; and *The Electronic Map,* which explores the natures of two young men and their relationship to their dead mother.

KEN BROWN (1936–)

The Brig (1963). His first play, done off-Broadway at the Living Theatre, this is an hour-long, ultrarealistic recreation of tortures

in a contemporary United States Marine prison in the Far East. Several actors suffered severe injuries including fractures in this production, which is one of the least preachy, most powerful indictments of violence ever seen on our stage.

JOSEPH STEIN (1912–)

Fiddler on the Roof (1964). Music by Jerry Bock, lyrics by Sheldon Harnick, book by Stein. A musical adaptation of Shalom Aleichem's story "Tevya and his Daughters." The longest run of any kind in Broadway history, with 3,242 performances. An excellent serious musical-drama of the persecution of the Jews in Russia, and the breakup of a traditional old family, caused in part by the pogroms. Winner of the New York Drama Critics Circle Award for best musical of 1964–65. Starred Zero Mostel as the first of many Tevyas. Bock, Harnick, and Stein will find their reputation secure forever with this one great musical play. Revived with Mostel, in 1976, for another long run.

Zorba (1968). Music by John Kander, lyrics by Fred Ebb, book by Stein. A musical version of the film *Zorba the Greek* by Nikos Kazantzakis. A young man, Nikos, comes into an inheritance; but his primary inheritance is the knowledge to live for today, which comes from the strange man, Zorba, whom he meets.

Irene (1973). James Montgomery wrote the play *Irene O'Dare,* which he, Joseph McCarthy, and Harry Tierney adapted into the 1919 smash-hit musical comedy *Irene,* which ran for 670 performances. It was revived several times on Broadway and was made into two films. Stein and British writer Hugh Wheeler modernized the show, which again tells the story of Irene O'Dare, a piano tuner from Ninth Avenue who makes a success of Long Island millionaire Donald Marshall's business effort with a phony Paris dressmaker and finally makes the millionaire realize he loves her. This was, and still is, innocuous entertainment filled with every cliché in the history of show business. The modern version toured the nation and also had a long run in London. Top songs include "Irene" and "Alice Blue Gown."

WILLIAM HANLEY (1931–)

Slow Dance on the Killing Ground (1964). A powerful, tense three-character drama of an old German, Glas, trying to live down the fact that he did not go to a concentration camp; Randall, a young black who has just killed his mother; and Rosie, who is seeking an abortion. They meet one night in the old man's candy store in Brooklyn, and Randall terrorizes the other two before going out to his death. The play makes a strong statement about the need to face up to responsibility in life. Hanley, an Ohioan, is now a New Yorker.

Mrs. Dally (1965). Domestic problems involving an older woman and a young boy, based on two earlier off-Broadway one-act plays that actually preceded *Slow Dance* to the stage: *Whisper into My Good Ear* and *Mrs. Dally Has a Lover.*

Flesh and Blood (1968). Interesting because this is one of the few plays in recent years to be premiered on national television. A family is disintegrating just as their neighborhood is being torn down for new construction. Two brothers, Harry and John, who have been workers on skyscrapers, face their fears, their consciences, and their soon-ending futures.

ADRIENNE KENNEDY (1931–)

Funnyhouse of a Negro (1964). One-act play done off-Broadway by Edward Albee's playwrights' workshop and winner of an Obie Award, this is a searing expressionistic examination of black people in America and their efforts to come to terms with being black. A black woman awakens in a New York City rooming house and is visited by the Duchess of Hapsburg, Queen Victoria, Patrice Lumumba, and Jesus. Miss Kennedy is one of the most experimental of the black playwrights. She grew up in Cleveland, dropped out of Ohio State University when she felt ostracized there, joined Albee's workshop, and eventually moved permanently to London, where her work has been produced by the National Theatre.

The Owl Answers (1965). A highly avant-garde one-act play, dedicated to Albee, this is about the bastard daughter of a black cook and a rich white man. The daughter leaves her teaching job to visit London in search of the father's ancestors. This is a nightmarish play about a woman who wants to feel a sense of roots and family and love, but who seeks it vainly in cheap hotel rooms.

A Beast's Story (1969). Part of a bill of one-act plays done at the New York Shakespeare Festival Theatre, an organization created by Joseph Papp that has given many a new playwright a hearing. A young woman is raped, has a stillborn child, and murders the rapist—who may or may not be her father. The themes are of sexual repression and awakening in life. Several actresses play the part of the young woman in this cryptic play. Miss Kennedy has had several other one-act plays produced in the New York area.

LANFORD WILSON (1937–)

Home Free (1964). A poignant one-act play about a brother and his incestuously pregnant sister. Wilson got his first hearing with the production of ten short plays by the late Joe Cino at Caffé Cino in Greenwich Village, a home in the mid-1960's for experimental playwrights who received inexpensive public mountings of their efforts. Cino did much to further the cause of modern drama with his café-theatre. Lanford Wilson was born in Lebanon, Missouri, grew up in the Ozarks, and started writing at the University of Chicago. He is the first of the off-off Broadway writers to make a name in drama. Off-off Broadway is a movement designed to give writers and actors a chance after the off-Broadway theatre began to grow almost as prohibitive, financially, as Broadway. Many off-off Broadway shows do not pay royalties to the writers or salaries to the actors, as they seek larger recognition and a stepping-stone to higher-paying theatre.

The Madness of Lady Bright (1964). Done at Caffé Cino. "Lady" Bright is forty-year-old Leslie Bright, an aging homosexual. One act.

This is the Rill Speaking (1965). A one-act play that received fine critical notice, this is a counterpointing of six voices in a slice of life in the Ozarks. It premiered at Caffé Cino, then toured Europe with the Café LaMaMa group, another early off-off Broadway troupe.

Ludlow Fair (1965). Two women, one attractive, one homely, but both terribly lonely, share an apartment. Another one-act play premiered at Caffé Cino. The off-off Broadway movement arose in the mid-1960's.

Balm in Gilead (1965). A two-act look at thirty-two hustlers, junkies, prostitutes, and derelicts who wander in and out of an all-night café. Premiered at Café LaMaMa, which was founded and directed by Ellen Stewart, a dynamic black woman devoted to furthering serious theatre in New York.

The Rimers of Eldritch (1966). Premiered at Café LaMaMa but quickly moved to the Cherry Lane Theatre off-Broadway for a long run, it was voted best off-Broadway play of 1966–67. Later, in the 1970's, a fine film was made from the script. It depicts the drives, fears, and hypocrisies of small-town life, similar to *Winesburg, Ohio* in some ways. Skelly, the local hermit, is shot by a middle-aged woman, Nelly, who is acquitted of the murder; the townspeople assume he had raped a fourteen-year-old crippled girl, Eva. In reality, the girl had led on her boyfriend, and the tramp had tried to stop the boy, Robert. This play reveals an interesting use of a jumbled time sequence to heighten both the poetic quality and the suspense.

The Gingham Dog (1969). Wilson's first Broadway production, this starred Diana Sands and George Grizzard. The breakup of the three-year marriage between Vincent, white, and Gloria, black. From a once-good relationship, Vincent has sold himself out to a drafting company building cheap housing, and Gloria has joined all the many causes, splitting them apart. They fight, then part.

Lemon Sky (1970). A highly praised off-Broadway full-length drama and a biting satire on California life, although basically the story is about a father-son conflict. Seventeen-year-old Alan leaves his mother in Nebraska, joins his remarried, lecherous father, and serves as catalyst to bring the family into crisis and expose the father's total lack of human goodness.

Summer and Smoke (1972). Lanford Wilson wrote the libretto for an opera version of Tennessee Williams' play for the New York City Opera Company (*see* the Williams entry for details on the story).

The Hot L Baltimore (1973). A Gorki-like character-drama set in the sleazy Hotel Baltimore (one letter has burned out of its neon sign), which has become a home for prostitutes and derelicts. The characters, going nowhere, match the faded old building, which is scheduled for demolition. Winner of the New York Drama Critics Circle Award, this play had an extremely long off-Broadway run and was redone for television.

The Mound Builders (1975). Strong in dramatic metaphor, this play tells about a group of archeologists who have spent their summers digging into old Indian mounds in southern Illinois. Using a scrambled time sequence again, Wilson writes an epic drama asking many questions about mankind's understanding of his own past, what the future will say about man today, and what it takes in order for us to understand life. Wilson counterpoints his characters and does his own digging into a number of thematic areas. Presumably, he has many good plays still ahead of him.

JAMES BALDWIN (1924–)

Blues for Mister Charlie (1964). A powerful study of racial violence in the South, this is an outstanding example of what has been called the "lynch play." Baldwin's idea came from the murder of a fourteen-year-old black boy in Mississippi in 1955; the accused white man was acquitted. In this play Richard, a black singer in New York, returns South to his parents, Meridian Henry, a minister, and Mother Henry. Richard is shot by a white man, who is acquitted when racial tensions flare up in the small town. Baldwin dedicated the play to his friend Medgar Evers, who had recently been killed for his civil-rights activities. Baldwin grew up in Harlem, the son of a minister, and worked at odd jobs to help support his eight brothers and sisters. He lived in Paris for almost a decade and received numerous awards and grants for his writing promise. He became a leading man of letters in the 1950's and 1960's with his prose works such as the novels

Go Tell It on the Mountain, Giovanni's Room, and *Another Country,* and his collections of essays, *Notes of a Native Son, Nobody Knows My Name,* and *The Fire Next Time.*

The Amen Corner (1965). A sensitively written character study of a woman preacher in a Harlem storefront church. Sister Margaret, with her young son, David, left her husband, Lukey, years ago after their second baby died. Margaret has turned to the church as an escape from the hurts of life and has tried to keep her son "safe" in that life. But when her husband comes home to die, eighteen-year-old David leaves home in order to live his own life, and the congregation pushes Margaret out as preacher. Margaret finally realizes the many wrong choices she has made in life. Baldwin actually wrote the play a decade earlier, and it was staged at Howard University, a black school. Not until he had made a substantial name in letters did the professional theatre take a chance on this rich play.

SAM SHEPARD (1943–)

Cowboys (1965). His first off-off-Broadway production, at Theatre Genesis. Shepard was born in Illinois, grew up near Los Angeles, and has been active in New York's experimental theatre circles, including Caffé Cino.

Chicago (1966). Done by the Café LaMaMa troupe on a European tour. An avant-garde one-act play in which Joy leaves Stu; Stu spends the play in a bathtub, in his clothes. Shepard likes to use a stark theatrical metaphor, such as the tub in the middle of an empty stage.

La Turista (1967). Done by the American Place Theatre, this is a nonrealistic play in two acts. Salem (a woman) and Kent are visiting Mexico in Act I, and Kent dies of diarrhea (called La Turista) while witch doctors chant over him in a hotel room. In Act II, set earlier in time, Kent has sleeping sickness. The play is symbolic of modern man's schizophrenia and weaknesses.

Red Cross (1968). A one-act play staged first at Judson Church Theatre, in Greenwich Village, another hospitable place for off-off-Broad-

way writers. Carol, at a ski-resort cabin, complains that one day her head will explode. She goes shopping; and when the maid, in to change the linen, takes Jim's games even more seriously than Jim does, Carol returns to find Jim's head exploded. The set and costumes are all stark white, making the blood imagery more powerful.

Operation Sidewinder (1970). Done at Lincoln Center, this is a comic-strip-like cartoon of a play set at a Southwestern airbase that is studying UFO's. The plot centers around the search for a missing computer, which is a giant sidewinder snake loose on the desert. Satirizes both military life and Western films.

The Tooth of Crime (1971). Premiered at Princeton, then done at the Open Stage, a famous avant-garde theatre in London. A bizarre, surrealistic play about the rivalry between two rock music stars; one became famous in the 1950's, the other in the 1970's. The older is involved with a crime syndicate, and in the second act he is challenged to a private rock contest by the younger singer and finally kills himself. Much rock music in the play, but there is satire of it, too. An extremely jargon-filled play.

LEONARD MELFI (1935–)

Birdbath (1965). A one-act play premiered at Theatre Genesis, St. Mark's Church-in-the-Bowery, New York; done off-Broadway in 1966 at the Martinique Theatre; and given a fine television production in the early 1970's. A poignant account of Frankie Basta, who does not know if he is a good poet and who wants companionship; and Velma Sparrow, a homely woman afraid of everything, who has just killed her domineering mother. They share an evening of bewilderment, tension, and kindness.

Night (1968). Part of a bill called *Morning, Noon, and Night,* done by the Circle in the Square troupe on Broadway. The first play is by Israel Horovitz, the second by Terrence McNally, and the third by Melfi. This is a one-act avant-garde play about a funeral late at night and the loneliness of several empty lives. Melfi grew up in Binghamton, New York, went to St. Bonaventure College, studied to be an actor, returned from Army service to try his hand as a writer, and received encouragement from Ellen Stewart at Café LaMaMa. Melfi has also done some film work.

TERRENCE McNALLY (1939–)

And Things That Go Bump in the Night (1965). A bizarre three-act play about supernatural creatures proclaiming man's decadence and despair. First done at the Tyrone Guthrie Theatre in Minneapolis, one of the best of the new regional theatres in recent years, the play then came to Broadway. McNally grew up in Corpus Christi, Texas, went to Columbia University where he wrote the Varsity Show, then received several fellowships. His first professional work was an adaptation of Dumas' *The Lady of the Camellias,* which appeared briefly on Broadway in 1963.

Noon (1968). Part of a bill called *Morning, Noon, and Night,* done by the Circle in the Square troupe on Broadway. The first play is by Israel Horovitz, the second by McNally, and the third by Leonard Melfi. This is a comedy about a number of assorted sexual perverts who can't get along with each other after answering an enticing ad placed in an underground newspaper by a practical joker.

Sweet Eros and *Witness* (1968). Two one-act plays. In the first, a quiet rapist ties and strips a woman, then lectures her. The second has a somewhat similar situation: an assassin ties up a man and threatens to kill him. Done off-Broadway.

Next (1969). Off-Broadway, the second part of a bill that opened with performer Elaine May's one-act play *Adaptation.* A flabby forty-year-old is called up for a draft physical and is subjected to many indignities, nude, in front of a woman sergeant. What is really exposed, however, is the emptiness of his life. Begins comically and ends poignantly, and has been called McNally's best play.

Where Has Tommy Flowers Gone? (1971). A full-length, off-Broadway critical success. Tommy, in rebellion against everything, ends up with no one, and blows himself up.

Bad Habits (1974). A bill of one-act plays, premiered off-Broadway at the Astor Place Theatre. Each play is named after the sanatorium in which it is set: *Ravenswood* has a doctor who allows his patients to do anything; *Dunelawn* has its patients given a knockout shot by Doctor Toynbee whenever they come to life. Both, through black comedy, show people unable to cope.

The Ritz (1975). A Feydeau-like farce loaded with dozens of doors and mistaken identities. Gaetano Proclo, of Cleveland, escaping his gangster brother-in-law who has vowed to kill him, hides in a men's bathhouse that turns out to be a gathering for homosexuals. Proclo triumphs over his relative after two acts of sex comedy, wild farce, and terror. McNally seems to be in mid-career as a writer of extremely bizarre black comedy.

LUIS VALDEZ y EL TEATRO CAMPESINO

When the economic plight of the Mexican-American farm workers in California became acute in 1965, Luis Valdez helped found El Teatro Campesino (rural worker) in order to promote the grape-pickers' strike. Valdez, a graduate of San Jose State University, later became a drama professor at the University of California at Santa Cruz. The group created among themselves a series of fifteen-minute bilingual plays that they called Actos, dealing with the problems of the farm worker. The Actos often use masked characters and use comedy to engage rather than alienate their audiences. Lopez has said, "Slapstick can bring us very close to the underlying tragedy, the fact that human beings have been wasted for generations." The Actos owe much to the Agitprops of the 1930's. The troupe has toured the nation several times and won numerous awards including an Obie in 1968. Two of the most famous plays are *Los Vendidos* (1967), which takes place on Honest Sancho's Used Mexican Lot and shows, with wit and anger, how Chicanos have been, in essence, bought and sold by Anglos. Another is *No Saco Nada de la Escuela* (I Didn't Get Nothing from School) (1969), which shows how the Chicano has been shortchanged educationally. One of the most famous speeches goes: "You call yourself a teacher? I can communicate in two languages. You can only communicate in one. Who's the teacher, Teach?" The play ends in Agitprop fashion with the students shouting, "Who's going to teach us? Our own people!"

WILLIAM ALFRED (1922–)

Hogan's Goat (1965). A lyrical, poetic tragedy of an Irish immigrant in New York City who seeks political success in Brooklyn around 1890. Matthew Stanton loses his nomination and, afraid that his wife will leave him, pushes Kathleen down the stairs and kills her. Premiered at the American Place Theatre and given almost unanimously favorable reviews, the play had a long off-Broadway run. Alfred has been on the faculty at Harvard since 1954 and a professor of English there since 1963; he has also done a number of translations of Greek tragedies.

ROCHELLE OWENS (1936–)

Futz (1965). A highly avant-garde one-act play premiered at the Tyrone Guthrie Theatre in Minneapolis, then brought to Café LaMaMa, off-off Broadway, about a man who loves a pig. The play reveals man's sexual, animalistic drives, plus the cruelty of others in the world to people with strong sex drives. Winner of the Obie Award for best off-Broadway play of 1967. Miss Owens, who grew up in New York City, has won several writing fellowships.

Beclch (1966). Another avant-garde play in which a white woman rules as a ruthless jungle queen but is finally killed by the natives. The title is pronounced Beklek.

DOUGLAS TURNER WARD (1930–)

Happy Ending and *Days of Absence* (1965). A pair of one-act plays criticizing and satirizing the racial situation in the United States. The first play shows how a black domestic sits calmly while her young relatives rage at her for not being part of the rebellious movement; but she has the last laugh when she reveals that she has been stealing from her white employers for years and owns as many valuables as they. The second play shows how a Southern city is paralyzed on a day when all the black people mysteriously disappear; the theme, made comically, is that the blacks do all the real work.

Brotherhood (1970). A powerful one-act play that says whites and blacks are all racists and that hatred is man's central emotion. Ward is also a fine veteran actor who performs under the name of Douglas Turner; he has been a major member of New York's Negro Ensemble Theatre, which he and Robert Hooks founded in 1967, with Ford Foundation help.

MEGAN TERRY (1934–)

Viet Rock (1966). Subtitled *A Folk War Movie*. Music and sound by Marianne de Pury. Premiered off-off Broadway at Café LaMaMa, then done at Yale, then in New York again. Using Total Theatre techniques, the play tries to get at the essence of violence through criticism of American involvement in Vietnam. The play grew out of improvisational exercises by the Open Theatre Troupe.

Approaching Simone (1970). Premiered at Café LaMaMa. A ritualistic, improvisatory dramatization of the life, before her suicide by starvation at thirty-four in 1943, of French philosopher, mystic, and women's-fulfillment advocate Simone Weil. The play combines elements of Greek tragedy, rock opera, and psychological drama. Miss Weil was hospitalized for tuberculosis in England and died when she refused to eat more than the resistance underground fighters in France had available to them. A highly praised drama that shows a woman determined to use the mind fully and to rise above the clichés of the body, which are shown not by sex but by migraine headaches. Miss Weil was a woman ahead of her time in teaching, in wartime life, in philosophy. Megan Terry uses the Total Theatre approach in most of her experimental plays; the device was popularized in the Western world by director Peter Brook with his production in the mid-1960's of Peter Weiss' *Marat/Sade* by the Royal Shakespeare Company in London, New York, and other cities.

JAMES GOLDMAN (1927–)

The Lion in Winter (1966). A historical play about Henry II, a businessman-king, and Eleanor of Aquitaine. Later a major film success with Peter O'Toole and Katharine Hepburn. Henry's sons Richard, Geoffrey, and John struggle for succession, but Henry remains in power. Goldman first appeared on Broadway with the play *Blood, Sweat and Stanley Poole,* which was coauthored with his brother, William Goldman, and had a short run in 1961.

Follies (1971). Music and lyrics by Stephen Sondheim, book by Goldman. All the cast members from Dmitri Weisman's "Follies," which played from 1919 to 1942, are on stage for a party before the theatre is torn down to become a parking lot. We see the empty marriages of Sally and Buddy, Phyllis and Ben, and see both the tinsellike pleasure and the dreary emptiness of show business in this serious musical, which won the New York Drama Critics Circle Award for 1970–71.

JOHN KANDER (1927–)
and FRED EBB (1932–)

Cabaret (1966). Music by Kander, lyrics by Ebb, book by Joe Masteroff, based on John Van Druten's play, *I Am a Camera,* which was based on Christopher Isherwood's *Goodbye to Berlin* stories. An excellent account of the hedonistic life in Germany just as the Nazis are coming to power. Young writer Cliff falls for dancer Sally Bowles, but they go their separate ways. The main plot is set against a series of decadent nightclub scenes that heighten the themes of refusing to care about people and fiddling life away while Rome burns. The catchy score was enriched still more by the masterful acting of Joel Grey as master of ceremonies. It won the New York Drama Critics Circle Award for best musical of 1966–67 and later was made into a popular film.

The Happy Time (1968). Music by Kander, lyrics by Ebb, book by N. Richard Nash, from the play by Samuel Taylor, originally from the short stories by Robert L. Fontaine. A musical about a whimsical French-Canadian family, the Bonnards. Despite many threats of disaster, adolescent Bibi becomes a ladies man like his grandfather, father, and uncle.

Zorba (1968). Music by Kander, lyrics by Ebb, book by Joseph Stein. A musical version of the film *Zorba the Greek* by Nikos Kazantzakis. A young man, Nikos, comes into an inheritance; but his primary inheritance is the knowledge to live for today, which comes from the strange man, Zorba, whom he meets.

JOHN GUARE (1938–)

Something I'll Tell You Tuesday and *The Loveliest Afternoon of the Year* (1966). A double bill premiered at Caffé Cino that helped Guare get his start. In the first play an elderly couple are going to the hospital for major surgery on the wife; they listen to the ugly fighting between their daughter and son-in-law, and the woman laments that they have grown too old even to fight; life holds nothing any more. The second is a bizarre black comedy of two lovers who are shot by the man's wife. Guare grew up in New York City and was graduated from Georgetown University and the Yale School of Drama.

Cop-Out (1969). Premiered at the Eugene O'Neill workshop in Connecticut, then came to Broadway for a very short run that nevertheless tagged Guare as a promising newcomer to the theatre. *Cop-Out,* the title play in the double bill, is a spoof on police and their women; *Home Fires* is a black farce set in a Massachusetts funeral home on World War I Armistice Day, with a German family trying to bury its mother.

The House of Blue Leaves (1971). Done off-Broadway for a run of almost a year and stopped only because the theatre burned down. Winner of the New York Drama Critics Circle Award, this is a combination of tragedy and farce. Artie Shaughnessey, a frustrated middle-aged songwriter who has never made it, loses his mistress to his old friend and now a movie tycoon, Billy; he has his son arrested for trying to blow up the Pope—the son kills three other people instead; and he finally strangles his possibly demented wife, Bananas. In the introduction Guare says that he purposely tried to blend savage, serious drama with farce; he also says that the germ of the play came from his grade-school nuns saying if only they could all see the Pope, but when Guare finally made a trip to Rome, on that very day the Pope was riding in a car back on Queens Boulevard in his old neighborhood. He also admits that the play is autobiographical in spirit.

Two Gentlemen of Verona (1971). Music by Galt MacDermott, lyrics by Guare, book by Guare and Mel Shapiro. First produced at Joseph Papp's New York Shakespeare Festival outdoor theatre in July, then moved to Broadway in December, ran for 613 performances, and transferred to London. A rock and pop version of Shakespeare's play about silly lovers.

Rich and Famous (1974). Premiered at Chicago's Academy Festival. A manic account of a playwright, Bing Ringling, trying to make it in a crass commercial world. Opened off-Broadway, produced by Joseph Papp in March, 1976, to generally devastating reviews, although highly praised for its originality by some of the critics.

Marco Polo Sings a Solo (1977). A science-fiction comedy set in the year 1999 on a Norwegian island, this play bubbles over with Guare's special brand of bizarre humor, although it does imply amid the riotous and at-times confusing goings-on that civilization repeats itself. Staged by Joseph Papp at the Public Theatre and starred Joel Grey.

BARBARA GARSON (1941–)

Macbird (1966). A Shakespearean parody by a young graduate of Berkeley, the play insinuates that Lyndon Johnson engineered the Kennedy assassination. In larger terms, the play is a satire on the public's trust in popular leaders. It reads more seriously than it plays. Done off-Broadway, it brought Stacey Keach to stardom. The play is a good example of the kind of irreverent satire done during the years of protest in the nation, highly popular for a time, but soon dated.

JULES FEIFFER (1929–)

Passionella (1966). Music by Jerry Bock, lyrics by Sheldon Harnick, book by Jerome Coopersmith. This was the third act of the musical *The Apple Tree,* and it came from a short story by Feiffer. A spoof of a temptress who wants to be a movie star but in reality is only a chimney sweep. Feiffer attained national acclaim as a satirical cartoonist; his first stage work was the adaptation of some of his cartoons for a revue at Chicago's famed improvisational theatre nightclub, The Second City, back in 1963. Since then he has continued with his cartoons, plays, films, and novels.

Little Murders (1967). A satire on random noise and violence in our big cities. An impassive man marries a girl who is accidentally shot dead at their wedding in New York. The man gains revenge by shooting people at random through his window. The play failed on Broadway, possibly because the conventional audiences were jolted by the black comedy; but it had a good run in London by the Royal Shakespeare Company, and later off-Broadway at the Circle in the Square. The play does have much to say about modern urban life.

The White House Murder Case (1970). Staged off-Broadway, this is another attack on violence and bureaucratic dehumanization. A President, whose wife has just been murdered, has to calm the public for a bureaucratic error in our war with Brazil in which we have released nerve gas that has blown back and is killing our own men.

Knock Knock (1976). Two middle-aged Jewish recluses, Abe the skeptic, and Cohn the realist, have their twenty-year life of bickering turned topsy-turvy when Joan of Arc appears at the door with a knock-knock joke. In three acts of wild farce and constant punning, Cohn finally comes to realize, after he has made mistake after mistake, that life has much more complexity than the simplifications he has always sought. Filled with what has come to be called the Feiffer humor.

WOODY ALLEN (1935–)

Don't Drink the Water (1966). A thoroughly conventional comedy about a New Jersey family taking refuge in an American embassy behind the iron curtain. A native of New York City, Allen has been a humorist since boyhood, sending jokes to newspaper columnists. Gradually he began supplying comic material to television personalities, then started performing his own material in nightclubs. Soon he was a television personality and wrote and starred in films such as *What's New, Pussycat?*

Play It Again, Sam (1969). Another lightweight comedy in which Allen played the lead role of Allan Felix, a writer for a long-hair film quarterly. His hero is Humphrey Bogart, and he tries to become a Bogart-like ladykiller. Allen's approach to comedy is always to play the loser in life, the little man who is always stepped on. His writings and his performances have honed this type to a fine edge. Like Molière, Allen knows that people like to laugh at other people, not themselves; and he has made a fortune by being the perennial butt of every joke.

JEAN-CLAUDE VAN ITALLIE (1936–)

America, Hurrah! (1966). Three one-act plays: *Interview, TV,* and *Motel.* All strongly satirize American mass culture as sterile and junky and Americans as callous and often vicious. The first shows the inhumanity of job-seeking; the second shows the most sterile side of television and daily life; and the third shows the total destruction of a motel room, wantonly and obscenely, by two huge stuffed dummies while the recorded voice of the little-old-lady proprietress recites chamber of commerce platitudes. A powerful bill that had a long run off-Broadway.

The Serpent (1969). A collaborative, pantomimic work, done with Joseph Chaikin's Open Theatre Troupe, which provided many of the ideas for business. The Book of Genesis is set to improvisational, ritualistic theatre, but preceded by the assassinations of John F. Kennedy and Martin Luther King. Chaikin, a New Yorker, was one of the original actors in Julian Beck's and Judith Malina's Living Theatre Troupe; he broke away to form his own troupe, which has been in the forefront nationally in pantomimic theatre. Van Itallie was born in Brussels but grew up on Long Island, was graduated from Harvard in 1958, and joined the Open Theatre when it opened in 1963. He was a forerunner in improvisational theatre for a decade, but in 1977 said that the use of language in theatre cannot remain down played, if theatre is to thrive.

HAPPENINGS

The Happenings were a type of improvisational theatre that mushroomed in the mid-1960's and began to fade after the era of youthful rebellion calmed. Some of the Happenings were actually a latter-day version of the Agitprops of the 1930's. One of the most talked-about took place on the steps of the Capitol in Washington with a group of people, portraying the poor, asking several people dressed in 19th-century elegance (the Congressmen) for pennies; the Congressmen threw the pennies violently into the faces of the beseechers. Other Happenings were descended from the post-World War I Dada Movement; in one particular instance, patrons paid to enter a theatre in New York and watch the cast live out their daily lives on stage for as long as the spectators cared to stay—for days, if they wished.

BRUCE JAY FRIEDMAN (1930–)

Scuba Duba (1967). A wild black comedy about a thirty-five-year-old New Yorker in a château in France, whose wife has apparently just left him for a black skindiver. His bikini-clad neighbor arrives to discuss sex, and nervous Harold Wonder phones mama back in New York for help. Friedman, who grew up in New York City and was graduated in journalism from the University of Missouri, succeeded first with short stories and then with highly acclaimed novels, *Stern* (1962) and *A Mother's Kisses* (1964).

Steambath (1970). Another black comedy, this is a fantasy set in a bathhouse, with Tandy pleading with God for a second chance in life. God, in this production, is a Puerto Rican steambath attendant, and the bathhouse is Purgatory.

CLARK GESNER (1939–)

You're a Good Man, Charlie Brown (1967). Music, lyrics, and book by Gesner, from material from the *Peanuts* comic strip by Charles Schulz. A charming, low-key musical with only two instruments, it features the baseball team, kite-flying, the Red Baron, Lucy's voracious mouth, and of course the delightful antics of Snoopy, who stops the show by singing for his supper. One of the most whimsically engaging plays in American theatre, this had a long run off-Broadway and then was staged virtually everywhere. Gesner, from New England, is a Princeton graduate, an Army veteran, and for several years was a staff writer for the *Captain Kangaroo* television program.

PAUL FOSTER (1932–)

Tom Paine (1967). A partly improvised, partly musical play, with music by the director Tom O'Horgan, which premiered at Café LaMaMa, then played in expanded form at the Edinburgh Festival, and finally ran for a year on Broadway. Paine is shown as an egotistical libertine, but his ideas are championed. Foster, from New Jersey, was an English major at Rutgers and a law student at New York University who was one of the very early members of Ellen Stewart's LaMaMa Troupe. O'Horgan was directing Foster plays at LaMaMa early in the 1960's, but it was with *Balls* (1965) that Foster first drew notice. The play had no characters on stage, only two swinging Ping Pong balls. Clive Barnes has pointed out that several aspects of staging in *Tom Paine* foreshadowed *Hair*.

ISRAEL HOROVITZ (1940–)

It's Called the Sugar Plum (1967). Premiered by the Eugene O'Neill Foundation in Waterford, Connecticut, an organization that fosters promising writers with its annual playwriting contest and summer workshops for writers, actors, and critics. The play then came to off-Broadway in 1968. A one-act work in which a young woman whose boyfriend has just been run over and killed comes to the driver's house for vengeance but becomes attracted instead.

Line (1967). Premiered at Café LaMaMa, then done off-Broadway. In this one-act play, Fleming is standing facing a white line (a piece of tape) on the floor as the audience enters. Four others appear, and the play is a series of tricks and attacks, with each person trying to attain first position in the never-explained line. It is an interesting visual metaphor for man's sheeplike nature, and also for his competitiveness.

The Indian Wants the Bronx (1968). An extremely powerful one-act play about two New York City teenagers who harass and do violence to a middle-aged man from India who cannot speak English and who is trying to find his son's home in the Bronx. This is a fine theatrical visualization of the random and not-so-random violence in the modern world.

Morning (1968). The first play in the bill of *Morning, Noon, and Night* done on Broadway by the Circle in the Square Troupe. The second play is by Terrence McNally, and the third by Leonard Melfi. Horovitz's play is a powerful, creative account of a black family, Updike and Gertrude and their children Junior and Sissy, who take a pill that turns them white. Tillich, the white landlord, comes with a gun to avenge Junior's getting his daughter pregnant; and after several exciting twists and turns, we learn that Tillich is also part black. Horovitz, who has brought a highly creative mind to contemporary theatre, is from Massachusetts; he studied at London's Royal Academy of Dramatic Art and was a resident playwright for a time with the Royal Shakespeare Company.

JAY PRESSON ALLEN (–)

The Prime of Miss Jean Brodie (1968). Adapted from the novel by Muriel Spark. A powerful story about an unmarried teacher, gifted and dedicated, who gradually narrows —possibly because she never marries—and is finally ruined by an adolescent student. Set in Scotland. A superb film version starred Maggie Smith. Jay Presson Allen grew up in west Texas, moved to New York and wrote dramas for television, gave up writing for a decade to marry and begin raising a family, then was lured back by *Miss Brodie*. Mrs. Allen is married to a film producer, and they live in New York and Connecticut.

Forty Carats (1968). From the French play *Quarante Carats* by Pierre Barillet and Jean-Pierre Gredy. A long-running comedy of loves between a middle-aged woman and a young man, and an elderly man and a teenaged girl. Mrs. Allen is an extremely good adapter; she has also done a number of films and did the film script adaptation of *Cabaret*.

HOWARD SACKLER (1929–)

The Great White Hope (1968). Protagonist Jack Jefferson is based on famous boxer Jack Johnson; this powerful play shows the white world's efforts to dethrone this black man as world heavyweight champion because he is a threat to their collective ego. Made into a superb film starring James Earl Jones. Sackler has written and directed extensively for television and is the winner of a number of literary grants and awards. He has had plays produced in the United States, Europe, and South America.

GEROME RAGNI (1943–)
and JAMES RADO (1940–)

Hair (1968). Music by Galt MacDermot, book and lyrics by Ragni and Rado. Produced first by Joseph Papp at the New York Shakespeare Festival in 1967 and then moved indoors, the show was subsequently revised and with direction by Tom O'Horgan opened for a long run on Broadway—and in many other major cities of the world. Subtitled *The American Tribal Love-Rock Musical,* it ushered in a whole era of rock-music productions. It was influenced by the period of student revolt, by the Total Theatre movement, and by the Happenings (*see* entry). Berger is thrown out of high school, Claude is about to be drafted, and Sheila lives with both. The emphasis is on music and production rather than plot, however; it might better be called a protest-revue. Many conservatives clucked their tongues over the nudity, but by today's standards the show already seems tame—and a bit dated.

JOSEPH HELLER (1923–)

We Bombed in New Haven (1968). An openly theatrical play, set in a theatre, of soldiers in a bizarre war. Ultimately, we don't know whether we are watching stage or real deaths. The play attacks people who do nothing to stop war. Heller, from New York City and a combat bombardier in World War II, attended Oxford, taught at Penn State, and worked as an advertising copywriter before he published his famous novel *Catch-22*. This was his first play.

RON COWEN (1946–)

Summertree (1968). A dying soldier in Vietnam recalls the tree in his backyard at home, his children, and his parents. Structurally reminiscent of *Death of a Salesman,* this play is notable because its author was only twenty-two years old and just out of U.C.L.A. when

he wrote the script; it received its first hearing by the Eugene O'Neill Foundation. The play was extremely popular among college audiences nationally because of its timeliness.

ED BULLINS (1935–)

Goin' a Buffalo (1968). Young Art takes Curt's wife, Pandora, when Curt is arrested in a heroin raid. There is not as much about race relations in this play as there is about the stronger conquering the strong in the dog-eat-dog world of bars, strippers, hustlers, and pushers. Bullins has emerged as perhaps the best contemporary black writer. Born in Philadelphia, he served in the Navy from 1952 to 1955, traveled extensively, attended school in various places, and has settled down as resident playwright and associate director of Harlem's New Lafayette Theatre, which has given many black writers a hearing.

The Electronic Nigger and Others (1968). A bill of three one-act plays done off-Broadway. *The Electronic Nigger* is a satirical comedy about an eccentric, loquacious black man who disrupts a creative-writing class in a California community college. *Clara's Ole Man* has a man coming in to visit Clara while her regular man is out; the regular man turns out to be a woman, Big Girl, who has stayed home from work and is present the entire time. Big Girl has the would-be schemer thrashed by some bullies. *A Son, Come Home* has a poet return home to visit his impoverished, religious mother, but there is no real communication between them.

In the Wine Time (1968). A three-act drama of Cliff, his wife, Lou, and their nephew, Ray, who wants to be a sailor and stud like Cliff, over Cliff's protests. Cliff loves Lou but slaps her around, and when the block erupts into a gang fight Cliff kills another man. Done at the New Lafayette Theatre.

In the New England Winter (1968). A continuation of the life of Cliff Dawson, from the previous play, but most of the emphasis is upon his half-brother, Steve. Steve masterminds a large holdup in Los Angeles, kills another black man he didn't like, and remembers Liz, with whom he had spent a winter in New England. Many of Bullins' plays are extremely rich pictures of contemporary black life.

The Pig Pen (1970). Done at the American Place Theatre. Black and white relationships at a pot-liquor-and-pill party in California, on the night that Malcolm X was assassinated. Bullins often uses a party as a big scene in his plays. He has an excellent ear for dialogue.

The Duplex (1970). Done at the New Lafayette Theatre. Slices of life of a number of blacks in Los Angeles in the 1960's. Much of the action takes place during several card-and-drinking parties. Velma Best, afraid of her bully husband, O. D., has an affair with Steve Benson, a young intellectual who knows he should not get entangled but can't help himself.

The Fabulous Miss Marie (1970). Done at the New Lafayette Theatre. A humorous look at black middle-class existence. Bullins, who can write powerful dramas about blacks being oppressed by whites, can also write extremely rich comedy about black life. Of the several important black playwrights in the past decade, he has the most versatility.

House Party (1973). Music by Pat Patrick, book and lyrics by Bullins. Subtitled *A Soulful Happening,* this was premiered at the American Place Theatre. A revuelike series of vignettes of life in Harlem. Much gentle satire on politicians, drama critics, writers, revolutionaries, and others. Again we see emphasis upon a party motif.

The Taking of Miss Janie (1975). An off-off-Broadway production that moved to Lincoln Center. A highly praised play about an anti-integrationist black college student's encounter with a liberal white girl, who thoughtlessly seeks to have a platonic relationship with him. Set in the 1960's, it captures well the college life of the time. Monty, the black, has just raped Janie, the white, and she protests. We flash back to a party at which a mixed group of black and white students mingle and argue; each character delivers a monologue in which the time sequence is scrambled and we see into black-white rela-

tionships. At the finale Janie allows Monty to seduce her again. Winner of the New York Drama Critics Circle Award.

Jo Anne! (1976). A powerful dramatic version of the story of Joan Little, the black woman in jail who was raped by her prison guard and killed him with a knife, but was acquitted in the subsequent murder trial, which drew extensive media coverage. In the play, done off-off-Broadway, the white guard, named Al Goode, remains on stage and plays several characters, including the ghost of his former self; the production shows the events both from Joan's and the guard's points of view. Bullins undoubtedly has many more plays still to come.

JOSEPH TUOTTI (1935–)

Big Time Buck White (1968). This play began as a twenty-minute exercise in Budd Schulberg's Writers Workshop in Watts, California, was expanded after being staged in Watts, and then was brought to New York. A black militant play (the author, though, is white) in which the audience is supposedly at a protest meeting, with much improvisation in the form of questions from the audience, much threatening of the audience—but also much satire on the foibles of the militants themselves. The device of threatening an audience is part of the Total Theatre technique and was begun in the United States in Peter Brook's production of *Marat/Sade*.

DONALD DRIVER (c.1920–)

Your Own Thing (1968). Music and lyrics by Hal Hester (1933–) and Danny Apolinar who conceived the idea and enlisted Driver's help; book by Driver. An off-Broadway musical, which later toured nationally, it combined Shakespeare's *Twelfth Night* with modern rock music. The mistaken sexual identities bring out the play's primary theme that it is the inner person, not the sexual exterior, that is important in love. It won the New York Drama Critics Circle Award for best musical of 1968–69, the first time an off-Broadway production had received this honor.

MART CROWLEY (1935–)

The Boys in the Band (1968). An extremely

effective and powerful play that has been called a homosexual *Who's Afraid of Virginia Woolf?,* as a group of men tear and slice at each other verbally at Harold's thirty-second birthday party. Although much antagonism erupts, we also see deep caring, too. The play treats homosexuality with extreme honesty. The play was made into an excellent film. For a first play, its success was phenomenal; it ran off-Broadway for exactly one thousand performances, then transferred to London's West End and had several national road shows.

A Breeze from the Gulf (1973). Sensitive young Michael sees his father die of alcoholism and his mother become an institutionalized drug addict, in Mississippi. A powerful and angry play, but it drew mixed reviews and did not fare as well as Crowley's first production. Crowley was born in Vicksburg, Mississippi, attended Catholic University, and did some television writing before his stage success.

LONNE ELDER III (1933–)
Ceremonies in Dark Old Men (1969). An excellent and powerful first play about a father, two sons, and a daughter trapped in the Harlem ghetto. The men think they can find a way out through bootlegging, but the youngest son is shot. In this ritualistic play Elder implies that contemporary blacks must invest their lives with ceremonies to cover up the emptiness of life in a white-racist society. The play is far richer than a "get whitey" document, however; it blends moods effectively and presents rich characterizations. Elder, born in Americus, Georgia, went to school in New Jersey, and worked at a diverse assortment of jobs until he began receiving fellowships for his writing. He admits that black actor and playwright Douglas Turner Ward turned him on to playwriting; the play was one of the first big hits of Ward's Negro Ensemble Company. Elder now works in films and television, and wrote the screenplay for Martin Ritt's novel *Sounder.*

SHELDON EDWARDS (1919–) and PETER STONE (1930–)
1776 (1969). Music and lyrics by Edwards, book by Stone. The original idea came from Edwards, a New Yorker, who had been a high-school history teacher before turning songwriter. Stone is a second-generation Hollywood writer. A musical about the Continental Congress as it discusses, and then passes, the Declaration of Independence. Winner of the New York Drama Critics Circle Award for best musical of 1968–69 and the Tony Award for best musical of the year, the production ran for 1,217 performances. Stone is also the author of the books for two other Broadway musicals, *Kean* and *Skyscraper.* He has written numerous movies, including *Charade* and *Father Goose.*

CHARLES GORDONÉ (1925–)
No Place to Be Somebody (1969). Billed as a black-black comedy, this mostly realistic play with a few surrealistic moments takes place in a New York bar run by a black man with ambitions to be as powerful as the white gangsters, but who is finally killed. A powerful, effective, and violent play. Gordoné has been an actor; the play was produced experimentally, free, for two weekends by Joseph Papp, but then was given regular production at the New York Shakespeare Festival. From there it played in other cities. A Pulitzer Prize-winner.

ROBERT MARASCO (1937–)
Child's Play (1970). A powerful first Broadway drama about tensions and trouble in a Catholic boys' school. A veteran teacher, pal of all the boys for thirty years, is the evil force behind many acts of brutality, including the death of another teacher. Marasco, a New York native and former office boy at *The New Yorker* magazine, taught for nine years at a Catholic prep school.

LEONARD GERSHE (–)
Butterflies Are Free (1970). A young blind man, Don, learns to live alone in a New York City apartment; and his mother, Mrs. Baker, finally learns that her son must stand on his own feet. Jill Tanner, the flighty girl next door, also learns some responsibility in this sentimental drama that contains much comedy. A big popular success, with a long run, a film, a road show, and many amateur productions. Gershe, who is reluctant to give out information about his life, has been a Hollywood film-

writer, doing scripts for *Funny Face,* the Cole Porter musical *Silk Stockings,* and many others. He says the idea for the play occurred to him when he heard over the radio how well a young blind law student was coping with life.

KURT VONNEGUT, JR. (1922–)

Happy Birthday, Wanda June (1970). An off-Broadway success that moved uptown in the middle of its successful run. It satirizes the Hemingway-type killer-man, and also ridicules the simp-like quality of the gentle-hearted man. Hunter Harold Ryan returns after being lost in the jungle for years, to find his wife courted by Dr. Norbert Woodley, a doctor, and Herb Shuttle, a vacuum-cleaner salesman. A black comedy. Vonnegut, of course, is known primarily for his novels, including such best sellers as *Cat's Cradle, Slaughterhouse Five,* and *Player Piano.*

Welcome to the Monkey House (1970). Dramatized for the amateur theatre by Christopher Sergel, from Vonnegut's famous novel. Basically, it is a play within a play, with a community theatre doing three one-act plays: the first in the future about a government that controls all its subjects and equalizes them with one another by loud sounds and heavy weights; the second about a scientist who discovers a sound from outer space that creates euphoria in everyone; and the third about a high-school music teacher who finally reaches the toughest guy in town.

PAUL ZINDEL (1937–)

The Effect of Gamma Rays on Man-in-the-Moon Marigolds (1970). A poignant and powerful drama of a neurotic, desperate mother, Beatrice, with two teenage daughters, Ruth and Tillie. Tillie quietly succeeds in finding herself despite the destructive home environment and the family history of mental illness. Premiered in 1965 at Houston's Alley Theatre, where Zindel was resident playwright for a time. The play won the New York Drama Critics Circle Award and a Pulitzer Prize in 1970–71. Zindel grew up on Staten Island and spent ten years there teaching science in a high school. Before his success in the theatre he published three highly acclaimed books for young people: *The Pigman; My Darling, My*

Hamburger; and *I Never Loved Your Mind.*

And Miss Reardon Drinks a Little (1971). An extremely powerful story of three middle-aged schoolteachers, sisters, and their selfishness and hurts to one another. We see their frustrations and their respective breakdowns as the story of the influence of their dead mother unfolds.

The Secret Affairs of Mildred Wild (1972). Zindel's first venture into comedy, but with serious undertones. Mildred, middle-aged, dreams through movie magazines and the movies, while her diabetic husband is slowly eating himself to death running a New York City candy store. Mildred wins a big contest promising rich prizes and a screen test, but it proves to be a giant ripoff. House wreckers begin to destroy the candy store, and Mildred finally agrees to join her husband as caretakers at a Staten Island convent. Many Walter Mitty–like scenes. Although this play did not have as successful a run as the earlier two, it would appear that Zindel has already made a niche for himself in American theatre, with many years of writing still ahead.

Ladies at the Alamo (1977). Opened on Broadway to fairly hostile criticism, with the reviewers calling all the characters unpleasant. The play is set in the modernistic office of a new theatre complex in Texas called The Alamo, and includes rehearsal excerpts from Chekhov's *The Sea Gull,* being piped in over the sound system, as we watch five women struggle fiercely with each other over control of the theatre troupe.

DAVID RABE (1940–)

The Basic Training of Pavlo Hummel (1971). A powerful Vietnam War play that met with great critical acclaim when staged by Joseph Papp's New York Shakespeare Festival. Pavlo Hummel is killed by a grenade thrown by one of his own men, in a whorehouse. The play shows the bestialization of men in the military. Rabe grew up in Dubuque, Iowa, was drafted into the Army and served in Vietnam. Upon his discharge, he studied playwriting at Villanova University. He helped bring considerable acclaim to Joseph Papp, who had done sum-

100

mer plays in Central Park and then enlarged his operation when he acquired the old Astor Library as an indoor theatre. Papp later took over control of the theatre at Lincoln Center for the Performing Arts; in all his ventures he has helped bring many new playwrights to public attention.

Sticks and Bones (1971). Another extremely powerful Vietnam War play that began off-Broadway, produced by Papp, and then was moved to Broadway for 245 additional performances. Although the play drew critical praise, it operated in the red; and Papp subsidized it with profits from his *Two Gentlemen of Verona* production. A teleplay was made but canceled; the network feared public opinion, because the production was scheduled for the same week that Vietnam War prisoners were being released. In the play, son David comes home to parents Ozzie and Harriet, after he has been blinded in Vietnam. He upsets the comfortable family routine so much that they finally kill him. The play is a sharp attack on prejudice, escapism, human cruelty, and national blindness. It won the New York Drama Critics Circle Award. Premiered in short form at Villanova in the late 1960's.

The Orphan (1973). This is the third in Rabe's trilogy of Vietnam War plays. It is a murky interweaving of the Oresteian Trilogy with the Charles Manson murders, with My Lei, hallucinogenic drugs, and the information explosion tossed in, too. Rabe says that murder has always been rationalized by men and nations. This play fared the poorest with public and critics.

In the Boom-Boom Room (1973). This play opened Joseph Papp's general directorship of Lincoln Center and is about a misfit go-go dancer, Chrissy, who works in a sleazy Philadelphia nightclub and who aspires to "fame" but ends up a topless dancer in a New York dump. We see a not-too-bright woman struggling vainly in a man's world.

Streamers (1976). Another powerful military play, premiered at the Long Wharf Theatre in New Haven, then moved to Lincoln Center and directed by Mike Nichols. Finally moved

to Broadway for a long run. Set in Virginia in a recruits' barracks in 1965, when the Vietnam War is just heating up, the play begins with a recruit's attempted suicide and ends with two murders. The title refers to a parachute that does not open. Life in the training barracks erupts into violence, reflecting the tensions felt by the soldiers as they are pushed inexorably toward further violence in Vietnam. Highly praised, with some critics affirming that this is Rabe's best play. Hopefully, Rabe is still early in his playwriting career.

JASON MILLER (1939–)

That Championship Season (1971). A twenty-year reunion of a coach and four of his players who had won the Pennsylvania high-school basketball championship is the setting of this play, which exposes their hypocritical weaknesses and failures as they fight over an approaching election for mayor. The play, a powerful exposé of middle-class bigotry, won the New York Drama Critics Circle Award, a Pulitzer Prize, and a Tony Award. Miller, from Scranton, Pennsylvania, went to school there and at Catholic University. He has been a well-known actor, performing with several repertory groups and gaining international visibility playing the lead male role of Father Karras in the film *The Exorcist*. Miller has had several plays done off-Broadway, including *Nobody Hears a Broken Drum* and *The Circus Lady*. Joseph Papp produced *That Championship Season* and moved it on to Broadway after its successful beginning with the New York Shakespeare Festival.

MICHAEL WELLER (1942–)

Moonchildren (1971). A comedy about college students living together and inventing ways to protect themselves against their emotions. Bob, despite his shell, proves very vulnerable. After a good opening run, the play had a highly praised off-Broadway revival in 1973 and has been popular on campus theatre nationally. Premiered at London's Royal Court Theatre.

Fishing (1975). This is a drug-filled weekend at a Pacific Northwest cabin. There is rich characterization of some postcollege drifters. Robbie visits old friends and wants to move on but gives his money to his host in order for him to buy a fishing boat. Weller, a New Yorker, was graduated from Brandeis University and has lived and worked in recent years in London.

MELVIN VAN PEEBLES (1932–)

Ain't Supposed to Die a Natural Death (1971). Subtitled *Tunes from Blackness,* the music, lyrics, and book are by Van Peebles. He wrote an album of songs in 1969 and uses them, spoken, not sung, in this musical play. Against the background of a rotting city, we see the New York black world of the early 1970's; and the picture of a society pushed down by whites into the ghettoes is powerful. Done on Broadway. Van Peebles grew up in Chicago on the South Side but began his creative career by making films in France. He has been a writer, a composer and lyricist, and a director of several major American films after working for some years in Paris and Brussels. He has also written several novels.

STEPHEN SCHWARTZ (1948–)

Godspell (1971). Music and lyrics by Schwartz, conceived and directed by John-Michael Tebelak. A musical based upon the Gospel according to St. Matthew. The longest-running of the religious-rock musicals, the off-Broadway production had logged more than 2,000 performances when this book went to press. Each era of theatre has tended to interpret the Bible according to its own cultural background; we have had *The Second Shepherd's Play, The Green Pastures,* and now religious plays staged as rock musicals. Tebelak got the idea for *Godspell* when he came out of Easter Sunday services in a church in Pittsburgh and was searched for drugs; the early form of the play was his master's thesis at Carnegie-Mellon University. Schwartz wrote the title song for Leonard Gershe's *Butterflies Are Free* and collaborated with Leonard Bernstein on some of the music for Bernstein's *Mass* (*see* Bernstein entry).

Pippin (1972). Music and lyrics by Schwartz, book by Roger O. Hirson. A Total Theatre approach to the story of Charlemagne's son, Pepin, in the 8th century as he tries to find fulfillment in life. He never finds it and is coaxed by a group of players to burn himself alive at the finale, to achieve his one perfect moment, but refuses; and as the players dismantle the colorful set and lights and urge Pippin out of the theatre, Pippin realizes that everyday life, "trapped but happy," is the best that most average people can achieve.

JOSEPH A. WALKER (1935–)

The River Niger (1972). A powerful play done by the Negro Ensemble Company, starring Douglas Turner Ward, which moved to Broadway in 1973. A significant number of good black plays have transferred to Broadway in the past decade. The play first won an Obie Award for best off-Broadway play in 1972–73 and then won a Tony Award for best Broadway play in 1973–74. Walker's third play, this probably depicts some aspects of his own family. Johnny Williams, father of Jeff who is just out of the Air Force, has worked as a house painter to give his family a chance. He is a black poet and an unfulfilled revolutionary. When some of Jeff's militant friends try to escape the police, Johnny kills the local stool pigeon but is killed himself; the rest of the family unite to make sure Johnny did not die in vain. Walker is a writer of great and rich talent.

JIM JACOBS (1943?–)
and WARREN CASEY (1935–)

Grease (1972). Music, lyrics, and book by both Jacobs and Casey. A rock musical about the 1950's, both satirizing the early rock 'n roll days in high school and at the same time putting a nostalgic glow on that era of slicked hair and black leather jackets. The plot line is minimal: as long as Sandy Dumbrowski stays virginal and Sandra Dee–like, she is an outsider to the gang; finally, more sophisticated, she wins Danny Zuko's affections. The long-running production is already in the top dozen Broadway hits after opening in Chicago in 1971, then moving to off-Broadway, and finally to Broadway. Warren Casey, from Yonkers, New York, attended Syracuse University and was a high-school teacher in the late 1950's before moving to Chicago and turning to acting, writing, and composing. Jim Jacobs is a Chicagoan, a musician, and a veteran of scores of little-theatre productions in the Midwest. Casey and Jacobs collaborated in Chicago for almost a decade before *Grease* was born.

MICHAEL BENNETT (1943–)

Seesaw (1972). Music by Cy Coleman, lyrics by Dorothy Fields, book by Bennett. A musical version of William Gibson's *Two for the Seesaw*. Kookie New Yorker Gittel Mosca and lawyer Jerry Ryan have a tender, bittersweet affair before he returns to his wife in the Midwest.

A Chorus Line (1975). Music by Marvin Hamlisch, lyrics by Edward Kleban, book by James Kirkwood and Nicholas Dante, produced by Joseph Papp. Bennett, a dancer and choreographer, conceived the idea, choreographed, and directed. The show, which originated in a series of improvisational sessions, consists of tryouts for the chorus of a supposed musical; by the time the tryouts are over, we know all about the lives of the candidates. Each candidate tells and sings about his childhood, adolescence, and early efforts in theatre. The production has had long runs in both New York and London, and won both a Pulitzer Prize and a Tony Award. Bennett wanted to portray the tensions of show business from the point of view of the usually anonymous group of dancers.

BOB RANDALL (1937–)

6 Rms Riv Vu (1972). Anne Miller and Paul Friedman find themselves locked in a New York apartment for rent, return that evening for a picnic there, then spend the night. Next morning their spouses bring them back to inspect the same apartment; and in a short time alone, they decide not to continue their affair. A romantic comedy that had a good run, then a national television production. Randall, a New Yorker, began as a singer and actor, then became a writer in advertising and television.

MARK MEDOFF (1940–)

When You Comin' Back, Red Ryder? (1973). Into a run-down diner in a small Southwestern town comes the mysterious Teddy, who terrorizes the plump counter girl, the big-talking little guy Red Ryder, and several other cus-

tomers. The play is a lament for the death of the American heroic myth; the dialogue crackles and the tension is strong. Medoff, from Miami, is a graduate of the creative-writing program at Stanford and is a professor of English at New Mexico State University. He had stage hearings in Albuquerque, Dallas, Los Angeles, and Miami before this play opened in New York. Medoff played the role of Teddy in the Chicago production and won best actor of the year there. A film version is also scripted by Medoff.

The Wager (1974). Directed by Tony Perkins off-Broadway and given a strong review by the New York *Times*. Leeds, a college student, bets his roommate, Ward, that if he seduces the wife of the professor next door the professor will kill him in forty-eight hours. A comedy of menace with much verbal wit, this was Medoff's first play, revised and expanded for the New York production. Medoff, still young in his career, has done several film and television scripts plus a number of short plays.

MIGUEL PINERO (1946–)

Short Eyes (1974). A powerful drama about a child molester who is killed in prison. Winner of the New York Drama Critics Circle Award. Pinero, who was born in Puerto Rico, grew up in the New York City ghetto and was a drug addict and convict while still in his teens. The play was begun in Sing Sing Prison and was staged by "The Family," a group of former addicts and prisoners seriously interested in the theatre.

RON MILNER (1938–)

What the Wine-Sellers Buy (1974). A black-ghetto play about the opposing pressures on a teenage boy, whether to go straight or to follow the lures of the high life as represented by a money-making pimp.

EDWARD MOORE (1935–)

The Sea Horse (1974). A sentimental, realistic play about two people nearing middle age: a sailor, Harry Bales, who wants to marry Gertrude Blum, the fat proprietor of a run-down West Coast bar. Gertrude, who has seen her father killed years ago and who was hurt by her ex-husband, tries to go on living without needing anybody. Harry spends two acts convincing her otherwise. Moore is an actor from Chicago who spent a hitch in the Navy. He wrote the play first as a one-act, to showcase himself as an actor, and then enlarged the script at Alan Arkin's encouragement. Moore played Harry in the New York production and received praise for his writing and acting.

ANNE BURR (1937–   )

Mert and Phil (1974). Middle-aged Mert is at a crisis point in her life and marriage after a mastectomy that further erodes her feelings of womanliness. Husband Phil is the butt of most of her pent-up pressures in this powerful play about the nature of sexuality. Produced by Joseph Papp at Lincoln Center to some of the most hysterically savage reviews in the history of American theatre. Anne Burr won the Avery Hopwood Award for Playwriting at the University of Michigan in 1965, the Sam Shubert Fellowship in Playwriting, the ANTA Playwriting Contest, the Martin Luther King Playwriting Contest, and two Creative Artists Public Service Program fellowships in playwriting.

LESLIE LEE (1934–   )

The First Breeze of Summer (1975). A highly praised first play done off-Broadway by the Negro Ensemble Company directed by Douglas Turner Ward, and then moved to Broadway, where it got more good reviews. A rich, realistic character study of the Edwards family in a northern city. Milton Edwards and his older son work as plasterers; younger son Lou wants to be a doctor or a scientist. We see the family over a hot weekend in June when Milton's mother, "Gremmar," visits; and in a series of flashbacks we come to learn about her life. Gradually we realize the similarities between Gremmar and young Lou as they try to cope with sexuality, blackness, and life in general.

BERNARD SLADE (NEWBOUND) (1930–   )

Same Time, Next Year (1975). George and Doris meet at an inn and have a one-night affair; they take time out of their marriages to repeat the tryst on the same night for the next twenty-five years, from 1951 to 1975. Their relationship virtually becomes a marriage, and also serves as a capsule-history of American life during that era. A major hit on Broadway and in London, this was Slade's first New York play after several successes in Canada, plus considerable TV writing in Canada, England, and U.S. Slade, a native of Canada, went to school in England and then became an actor in Canada for a decade before gaining success as a writer. He is now a writer-producer in Hollywood.

CHARLIE SMALLS (1943–   )
and WILLIAM F. BROWN (1928–   )

The Wiz (1975). Music and lyrics by Smalls, book by Brown. A black musical version of *The Wizard of Oz* that won seven Tony Awards and has enjoyed a long New York run. The production features a black director, black cast, black backstage workers, and black slang in the script and songs. Audiences black and white have delighted in its spontaneity, and it is one of the most joyous musicals to come along in some years. William F. Brown was actually represented on Broadway earlier with his play *The Girl in the Freudian Slip,* has written for nightclub entertainers, has more than a hundred television script credits, and is the author of five books of comedy plus a nationally syndicated comic strip, *Mixed Singles.* Charlie Smalls, an actor and singer, studied classical music at the Juilliard School, played in an Air Force band, and toured with Harry Belafonte. This is his first New York show.

ROBERT PATRICK (1937–   )

Kennedy's Children (1975). Patrick, a Texan, came to New York early in the 1960's and was part of the off-off-Broadway café theatre movement in Greenwich Village and the East Village. Portions of this play were done in café theatre as early as 1970, but it was the 1974 production in London, which received considerable acclaim, that helped bring the play to Broadway. New York, in recent years, has imported many a British play from London to fill out its Broadway schedule; but occasionally an American play also gets its start in London, which has been a vigorous center of theatrical activity for the past decade. In this play, five people in a New York bar, speaking their thoughts and never addressing one another, show the high hopes and then the extreme disillusionment of American life in the 1960's: the decade of involvement, protest, Vietnam, and corruption.

RONALD RIBMAN (1932–)

The Poison Tree (1975). A grimly realistic study of the brutality, corruption, racial tensions, and dehumanizing effect of prison life on four black inmates and a white guard. The play toured nationally before its New York opening. Ribman, the holder of Rockefeller, Guggenheim, and National Foundation for the Arts fellowships, previously had a number of plays staged off-Broadway, including *The Journey of the Fifth Horse* (an Obie Award winner), *Harry, Noon and Night* (starring Dustin Hoffman), *Ceremony of Innocence* (done on public television in both the United States and Canada), and *Fingernails Blue as Flowers*.

Cold Storage (1977). A highly praised black comedy that opened off-Broadway at the American Place Theatre, this is an extremely moving play about both death and guilt. The script opens with a brief scene in Portugal in 1941, with Jews being deported to Germany. The main part of the play, however, takes place on a rooftop solarium of a New York hospital, where middle-aged Richard Landau is waiting for exploratory surgery and meets elderly Parmigian (played brilliantly in New York by Martin Balsam), a wheelchair-confined Armenian grocer dying of cancer. Landau has repressed his guilt because he was the only member of his family to survive the Nazi purges; but Parmigian's torrential conversation, much of it hilarious, gradually leads Landau's repressions out into the open where they can be faced.

DAVID MAMET (1948–)

Sexual Perversions in Chicago (1975). Written in 1974, done off-off-Broadway in 1975, and then done as part of a double bill with *Duck Variations* off-Broadway at the Cherry Lane in 1976. A brilliantly written comedy about a pair of lovers whose former partners, both homosexuals, cause problems. Mamet

grew up in Chicago and had a number of plays staged there before receiving a hearing in New York. Much is expected of him.

Duck Variations (1975). A comedy about two old Jewish men on a park bench. Mamet has been highly praised, winning the Best New Playwright Award from *The Village Voice* and receiving acclaim from critics for his rapierlike command of language.

American Buffalo (1977). Staged on Broadway under Ulu Grosbard's direction after being premiered off-off-Broadway two years earlier. Donny, owner of a junk shop, sells a buffalo nickel, belatedly realizes its worth, and conspires with retarded junkie Donny and Teacher, a violent, foul-mouthed hackie, to try to steal the nickel back. Mamet makes clever metaphorical use of the buffalo as a symbol of America's past and the overpoweringly realistic junk shop as our present. Gripping, earthy dialogue reflects the violent tensions among the three characters. Although reviews were mixed, some critics called it the most important play of the season.

MILAN STITT (1941–)

The Runner Stumbles (1976). This highly acclaimed first New York play chronicles the trial of middle-aged Father Rivard for the murder of Sister Rita in a small community in Michigan some years ago. Love grows between priest and nun, but Father Rivard refuses to admit his human feelings. At his trial we finally discover that his unlearned, superstitious housekeeper had buried Sister Rita alive, to prevent people from learning about her love. Father Rivard will spend the rest of his life mourning. Stitt, from Detroit, the University of Michigan, and the Yale School of Drama, has won many writing awards; this play progressed over a decade through a series of workshops until it finally reached Broadway.

PRESTON JONES (1936–)

A Texas Trilogy (1976). Three full-length plays, as listed below. Jones, born in Albuquerque, was graduated from the University of New Mexico and has been a member of Paul Baker's Dallas Theatre Center for more than a decade, acting, directing, and working backstage. His wife comes from a small town in west Texas, which Jones rechristened Bradleyville for his trilogy. The plays were premiered in Dallas on New Year's Eve, 1974, from 7 P.M. to 2 A.M., with a dinner break, and have been done with immense success at many regional theatres since. They received great acclaim at the Kennedy Center in Washington in the summer of 1976 and then went to Broadway. The trilogy includes:

The Last Meeting of the Knights of the White Magnolia (1976). The handful of remaining members of a racist society meet in Bradleyville's run-down hotel to initiate Lonnie Boy McNeil, who finally runs away from the bizarre meeting that has been filled with vicious and stupid arguments plus the senile ramblings of old Colonel Kincaid. Jones is strong in capturing small-town dialogue and the flavor of place. He readily admits that the characters in most of his plays live almost totally in the past. Jones has been likened to William Inge in his portrayal of small-town life. This play was also staged in London in 1977.

Lu Ann Hampton Laverty Oberlander (1976). Just as the Knights in the first play showed the stagnancy of life in Bradleyville, so does Lu Ann in this play. In the three acts she moves from empty-headed high-school cheerleader in 1953, to easy-moraled divorcée who has become a hairdresser in 1963, to a widow running a welcome wagon for a neighboring town and watching her daughter turn into a replica of herself in 1973. A powerful study of the waste of human lives, although Jones leavens all his plays with considerable humor.

The Oldest Living Graduate (1976). The third play in the trilogy takes place during the same time span as the first. Colonel Kincaid's middle-aged son, Floyd, trying to plan a big resort development, rigs up a ceremony supposedly to honor the Colonel but actually to get Floyd's business venture off the ground. We get a glimpse into the Colonel's background just before he dies, and we see the emptiness in the lives of Floyd and his wife. The overall effect of the trilogy is quite powerful.

A Place on the Magdalena Flats (1976). Premiered at Paul Baker's Dallas Theatre Center. Based in part on events in Preston Jones' brother's life, at the Jim Kelly Ranch near Magdalena, New Mexico, in the drought of the early 1950's. This play has been called more tragic than those in the trilogy. Jones is one of the several highly talented newer voices who give promise that theatre is alive and well in the United States.

Santa Fe Sunshine (1977). Premiered at the Dallas Theatre Center, where Jones remains an actor and writer, this is a light play based on some earlier experiences in Santa Fe. Jones says of the play, "It's a comedy about a group of artists in Santa Fe . . . a writer, a poet, sculptor, painter, woodcarver, and the characters who run a gallery in town. The central character is a sculptor who has finished a new piece of work. There's a party to unveil it and each character shows up and each has something he wants to do."

MICHAEL CRISTOFER (1946–   )

The Shadow Box (1977). This fine first play is an example of how young writers now reach Broadway. It opened at the Mark Taper Forum in Los Angeles, then was produced at New Haven's Long Wharf Theatre, and finally came to New York—ironically, on the final day it was eligible for the 1976–77 Pulitzer Prize, which it immediately won. Cristofer, an actor-writer, studies death in this gentle and at-times funny play in which eight people cope with the impending death of three of them, at a hospital-cottage area used for terminal patients.

Economic pressures on and off Broadway became so constricting about a decade ago that fewer young writers were willing to attempt careers as dramatists. In more recent years, however, the continuing growth of strong regional and university theatres (often with extremely helpful foundation support), plus the public realization that a serious playwright can achieve critical recognition even before a Broadway production, is helping American theatre toward healthier times.